SECRETS
OF THE
KNIGHTS
TEMPLAR

SECRETS
OF THE
KNIGHTS
TEMPLAR

The hidden history of the
WORLD'S MOST POWERFUL ORDER

CONTENTS

The Origins
of the Order

From the time the Knights Templar formed as an order of military monks early in the 12th century, stories began proliferating about them. Legends and tales varied from positive to negative and from ambiguous to unequivocal.

To most outsiders, they were valiant defenders of Christianity throughout the crusading years, admired for their resolve and bravery. To others, their extraordinary success in banking, building, farming and other secular areas was questionable alongside their religious beliefs and austere lifestyles. The shock felt by almost everyone when they were accused of dubious crimes by Philip IV of France in 1307, however, sent tremors of indignation and horror throughout Europe. What's more, the Pope—who was supposed to protect them—facilitated their demise. To be destroyed in the end not by their Muslim adversaries, but by their fellow Christians, shook society to its foundations, and the story has (erratically) continued to arouse interest for the 700 years that have followed.

This interest has become greater than ever in recent years, with countless sensational claims about the Templars emerging, many of which have captured the collective imagination. What is it about this Brotherhood that arouses such interest? Can any of the theories be substantiated? Why have so many of these ideas only come to light relatively recently, and how many mysteries can be resolved now—with greater methods of authenticating evidence and the benefit of hindsight? This book sets out to discuss many of the theories that have been put forth about the Knights Templar, from such elusive notions as what secrets they possessed or what their alleged secret rituals were, to more concrete areas, such as their buildings, constructed using forgotten knowledge of sacred geometry, or their development of banking that has since become the model for banking practice everywhere.

Fighting brothers

Established in Jerusalem in the 12th century, the Knights Templar were European Christians who chose to live as warrior-monks—a type of brotherhood that had never been seen before. Formed after the First Crusade with just a few men, their aim was to

A 14th-century manuscript showing the unrest and violence between the Seljuk Turks and Christians in Jerusalem just before the First Crusade.

protect Christian pilgrims in the Holy Land and to defend the territory conquered by the Crusaders. Traditionally, knights came from noble families but, like most monks, the Templars were recruited from all echelons of society. Not all joined as knights, and the majority came from ordinary backgrounds—many were craftsmen, farmers, masons, or cooks, for example—and as such were not educated; few left personally written records about their daily lives. Many could read and write in their own languages but, apart from religious material, book-learning was discouraged as the objectives of the Order focused on other things. Official records were kept nonetheless, but after the Templars' dissolution in 1312, these were stored in Cyprus by the Knights Hospitaller in their headquarters. In 1571, during the Ottoman–Venetian war, Cyprus fell to the Ottoman Turks who destroyed many Hospitaller documents, along with the Templar records. With their archives destroyed and no contemporary chronicler mentioning their existence, it fell to later generations to piece together their history.

They are now connected variously with the Holy Grail, the Ark of the Covenant and other sacred artefacts; the practice of strange initiation rites and clandestine treasure.

Mysteries, myths, and realities

It was not until the 18th century, with the formation of a new society called Freemasons, that the Knights Templar were considered earnestly once more. Since then, they have been researched and written about profusely. Sensational books, such as Dan Brown's novel *The Da Vinci Code*, and *The Holy Blood and the Holy Grail* by Michael Baigent, Richard Leigh and Henry Lincoln, plus ensuing films, documentaries and further books advanced their popularity enormously. Speculation about their lives, and enigmas surrounding their existence, have never been so intense, and many of the stories about them have become so tightly interwoven into European history that it is extremely difficult to separate the myths from the realities. The broad range of opinions, theories and suppositions about them have meant that, over time, they have been variously lauded and criticized, romanticized and undermined, elevated and denounced.

They are now connected with a wide range of disparate mysteries, linked variously with the Holy Grail, the Ark of the Covenant and other sacred artefacts; the worship of ancient gods; the practice of strange initiation rites; secret travel; clandestine treasure; and esoteric knowledge about the life of Christ. They have also been linked with the untimely death of a king, a Pope's perfidy, and even with putting a curse on the French royal family. When they started out, they were seen as devout and courageous Christian saviors. Their rigorous, monastic way of life coupled with physical warfare troubled some, but aroused pride and respect in others. They began humbly, rose with incredible alacrity, as financiers, builders, disciplined and efficient fighters—and more. Yet with just two centuries of known existence, their dramatic rise and violent downfall left a fertile base for speculation, generating many misconceptions and intrigues. With such a dearth of documentation, many of the stories can still not be verified, but with evidence continuing to be uncovered by reputable historians, false leads and questionable claims can be assessed, separated from the hype, and pieced together rationally.

▶

This fresco shows the Battle of Lepanto in October 1571. Although the Ottomans destroyed a great deal on the island of Cyprus, including the Templars' and Hospitallers' records, ultimately, the Christians were the victors and it became known as the great victory of the Christians over the Turks. The artist of this work was the Greek Antonio Vassilacchi (1556–1629), who was active mainly in Venice. This was painted nearly 30 years after the event, in 1600.

One massive breakthrough came in 2007, when the Vatican published a copy of a parchment written in August 1308 that shed new light on the Pope's involvement in the Order's downfall, and his belief in their innocence—despite his actions that seemed to prove the contrary. Discovered in the Vatican Secret Archives in September 2001 by Italian paleographer Barbara Frale, the Chinon Parchment was written by three cardinals and proves irrefutably that the Knights Templar were not deemed heretics by the Pope and so should never have been persecuted.

This book tells the Templar story and considers the various enigmas, intrigues and conjecture that surround them, attempting to clarify some assumptions and beliefs and to reassess both the facts and the falsehoods behind the legendary Brotherhood.

CHAPTER 1

Holy War

Although many books have been written about the Knights Templar, scholars and archaeologists are frequently uncovering new evidence about them, calling into question many previously accepted theories. This book, while not a chronological history of the Order, is an up-to-date account of many of the events and mysteries that surrounded the legendary soldiers of Christ.

The Order of the Knights Templar originated after the First Crusade and thrived over the entire crusading period. The Crusades were a series of wars fought between Christian Europe (Christendom) and the Muslim Empire (Islam). They were established because of the political and spiritual issues in society at the time, emerging from the feudal mentality of those Europeans living in the Middle Ages, and of religious fanaticism, and they lasted from the end of the 11th to the late 13th centuries. At the close of the 11th century, the First Crusade was launched by Christians against increasing Muslim incursion into Christian-ruled lands, and also to regain control of the Middle Eastern Holy Land from the Muslims. Over the following 200 years, more crusades were fought and the issues and outcomes became more complex. So complex in fact that there are differing views among historians about exactly how many crusades there were. Some maintain that there were eight, while others claim that there were only four, and still others contend that there were five, or even six. This is partly because many insist that only a pope can call a crusade and so those started by others are not officially crusades, although their purpose was the same.

Since the seventh century, Muslim armies emerging originally from Arabia had frequently attacked traditionally Christian territories, including parts of Europe, North Africa and the Middle East in efforts to take the land. Quickly and violently, the Arabs captured large tracts of land and stopped the lucrative trade that had been thriving around the Mediterranean. The speed of the Arab conquests and the losses suffered by Christians meant that something had to be done to prevent the whole of Christendom being annihilated. Although not used until the 13th century, the word "crusades" described the attempts by Christians to fight back and regain control of the lands they had previously occupied, as well as the holiest sites in the Middle East, locations described in the Bible—in particular, the city of Jerusalem.

◀

Even after the Islamic armies had taken Jerusalem from the Byzantines, it remained the most sacred destination for all Christian pilgrims. This miniature from *Speculum Historiale* by Vincent of Beauvais (1190–1264) depicts a battle between the Byzantine and Islamic armies in the seventh century.

Pilgrimage

Despite the difficulties of travel, since the second half of the fourth century the tradition of pilgrimage had been well established by the Christian Church. Acts of pilgrimage, where the faithful traveled to holy places to receive forgiveness for their sins or cures for ill-health, had become an integral part of Christian life. Popular shrines included the tomb of Thomas Becket at Canterbury Cathedral in England; the site of St. Paul's execution in Rome; the Abbey of Vézelay in Burgundy, which housed the relics of Mary Magdalene; Santiago de Compostela in northwestern Spain, where the apostle and martyr St. James the Great's bones were kept, and Jerusalem, the most hallowed site of all. Even after it had been taken from the Byzantine emperors by Islamic armies in the seventh century, Jerusalem remained the most sacred destination for Christian pilgrims.

Considering the expense, the dangers, and the unknowns of a pilgrim's journey, it is a wonder that any pilgrimages were actually undertaken. To travel to Palestine from Europe was expensive and hazardous, even before the Muslims began attacking Christian countries. The least dangerous route was by sea, but even here, there was always the risk of piracy or shipwreck. Overland was riskier as it entailed crossing parts of the Byzantine Empire and Islamic Syria. Nevertheless, these perils seemed simply to add to the allure of the pilgrimage and the sense of achievement for those who reached their destinations. Hardships enhanced the notion of penance, which all assisted the salvation of the pilgrims' souls. The Church encouraged pilgrimages, presenting them as the culmination of a faithful life and a reliable way to receive forgiveness of sins—or to escape divine punishment.

Islamic control and conquest

Although the Islamic armies were strong and powerful, single-mindedly sweeping through great swathes of land and overthrowing the inhabitants, all was not peaceful within. Since the death of Muhammad in 632 CE, a major split had occurred between two Islamic sects. The schism between Sunni and Shi'a Muslims initially arose from a disagreement over who should succeed Muhammad on his unexpected death. The Sunni Muslims felt his close companion (and father-in-law) Abu Bakr should become the first Caliph (successor), while Shi'ites believed that his son-in-law and cousin Ali was the rightful heir. Both candidates had compelling credentials: Abu Bakr had been a trusted political and personal adviser to Muhammad, while Ali was the first (male) convert to Islam and was renowned for his unwavering faith. Although Abu Bakr was appointed the first administrative leader by the Islamic community elders, eventually Ali also held the position—but by this time, the rift was firmly in place.

A 17th century Islamic miniature, depicting Muhammad and his trusted adviser and father-in-law Abu Bakr, who became the first administrative leader after Muhammad's death.

The Middle Ages

The term "Middle Ages" corresponds to the same period as the Latin word "medieval." Neither expression was used until the 19th century, when a general interest grew in the era they describe. Although not exactly defined, this period is usually considered to have started with the fall of the Roman Empire, which began in 410 CE, and to have ended with the early 15th century at the start of the Renaissance period, or even in 1453, when Turkish forces captured Constantinople. The end of the Middle Ages is generally described as the start of the Modern Era. This was a time of strong religious belief and fanaticism, which was inflamed by a lack of understanding and communication, and which led to mistrust and brutality. During the period, society changed and developed, with new kingdoms forming in Western Europe. In the seventh century, North Africa and the Middle East, which had once been part of the Roman Empire, were conquered by Arabs and became Islamic. At this time, the Byzantine or Eastern Roman Empire, remained largely independent of Muslim influence.

A 13th-century Arab manuscript of a Muslim warrior on a camel.

Abu Bakr reigned over the Rashidun Caliphate from 632 to 634. During that time he arranged for the first written version of the Holy Qur'an (the "Word of God" in Arabic) to be made. Before Muhammad's life, the Bedouin tribes of Arabia were nomadic people, living in fierce competition with each other to survive. That legacy continued to a certain extent, and from 634 to 641 another of Muhammad's successors, the Caliph Umar, began a military campaign invading several Byzantine-inhabited lands, including Syria, Persia, Palestine, and Jerusalem. After they took control, in general, Muslims continued to allow Christian and Jewish pilgrimages to Jerusalem. But the conquests carried on. Caliph Uthman, Umar's successor, who reigned from 644 to 656, captured Cyprus and attacked Constantinople, setting fire to the Byzantine fleet. The subsequent Umayyad dynasty centered on Damascus and spread Islam as far as Afghanistan in the east and North Africa in the west. In the eighth century, Arab armies began attacking Roman Catholic countries as well and soon overthrew important Christian cities across the Iberian Peninsula. Next, the Arab armies crossed the Pyrenees to France, where they attacked places such as Bordeaux, Carcassonne, and Tours. However, in 732 they were decisively beaten back by Charles Martel, the grandfather of Charlemagne. Within a century,

HOLY WAR

> The leading tribe, the Seljuk Turks, were nomadic, warlike buccaneers and, within a short time, a Turkish Sultan of the Seljuks seized power from the Arab Caliph.

nonetheless, the Arab armies were assailing parts of Italy, and even drove the Pope from Rome. But for all their aggression, the Umayyads and the later Abbasid dynasty allowed the vanquished who remained living in their cities to practice their chosen religions and to continue their pilgrimages—as long as they paid the Muslim rulers an extra tax.

Gradually, Islamic society and culture was becoming remote from the nomadic lifestyles of its ancestors and, after the middle of the tenth century, most Muslims had settled and were no longer keen to fight, even though the Arab government needed to maintain fighting in order to keep control and to continue their forbidding stance over any Christians who tried to fight back. So the government began to rely on foreign immigrants to fight for them. These were mainly Turkish tribes who were newly converted to Islam and extremely aggressive and hostile towards non-Muslims. The leading tribe, the Seljuk Turks, were nomadic, warlike buccaneers and, within a short time, a Turkish Sultan of the Seljuks seized power from the Arab Caliph. By 1065, they took control of Jerusalem and they showed no tolerance to others who were not Sunni Muslims like them. They slaughtered Christian, Jews, and pagans, and they destroyed churches, synagogues and other places of worship. In 1071, they massacred the huge Byzantine army at the Battle of Manzikert (now part of Turkey), captured the Byzantine Emperor Romanus Diogenes, and took Nicaea, one of the most important cities of the Byzantine Empire.

Twenty-four years later in 1095, while in Piacenza, Italy, Pope Urban II (r. 1088–99) received a delegation of ambassadors bearing a letter from the current Byzantine Emperor, Alexius I Comnenus, appealing to the Latin (Catholic) Christians to join forces with them, the Eastern (Orthodox) Christians, to fight back against the Seljuk Turks. The Byzantine Empire had lost most of Anatolia to the Seljuk Turks and Alexius needed military assistance from the West to regain his lands. Although Eastern and Western Christians were divided, in the letter, Alexius described the atrocities suffered by all Christians in Jerusalem at the Turks' hands, explaining that it was no longer safe for any pilgrims to go there. Also promising greater unity between the Church of Constantinople and the Church of Rome, Alexius aroused Urban II's sympathies. Keen to end the divide between the Eastern and Latin Churches and even more eager to save Jerusalem from the devastation being created there by the Turks, in November of that year, the Pope called a Council meeting in Clermont, France.

Call to arms

After nine days of discussion about other matters, on November 27, 1095, French-born Pope Urban II led the Council of Clermont's clerical delegates to an open field, where he had invited the entire population of the city. He sat on his throne in the open air and addressed the huge crowd. Charismatic, good-looking and eloquent, he described the situation across Europe and in the Holy Land, the problems facing the Byzantine Empire and ultimately all of Christendom, and he urged those listening to take up arms to fight "the infidel" alongside their brothers in the Eastern Orthodox Church for the liberation of the holy places. Although the notion of fighting was sinful for Christians, in the fourth century Bishop Augustine of Hippo had written that, with a worthy and honorable purpose and with peace as the aim, violence could be justified.

Believing at this stage that they would only be supporting the Byzantines, Urban spoke of the honor of chivalry and knighthood, reminding everyone that this was what Christendom was once famous for. All who participated in this holy war and turned their weapons on the enemies of Christ, he informed his captivated audience, would receive absolution for their sins. And while they were away fighting, he guaranteed that they, their families and their goods would be protected. Although no contemporary chronicler documented this at the time, it is said that this rousing speech was followed with thunderous, enthusiastic cries from the audience of: "God wills it!" Red cloth crosses were distributed to those who promised to join the campaign and later, after taking their solemn vows, individuals sewed the [red] crosses on the left shoulders of their surcoats as a symbol of their commitment and to indicate their entitlement to certain privileges and exemptions, which the Pope had promised to any who joined the "Holy War." This was the origination of the concept of "Taking the Cross." The word "crusade" developed from "crux", the Latin word for cross.

After Clermont, Urban traveled around France, continuing to preach and urge the faithful to take the cross. Surprised by how earnestly the poor flocked to join up rather than the class of knights he had hoped to attract, Urban made some stipulations. The elderly and the infirm were not allowed to join, and married men had to ask their wives for permission to go. Wives were also invited to accompany their husbands if they chose.

▶
Pope Urban II (c.1035–99) at the Council of Clermont from Sébastien Mamerot's c.1490 lavishly illuminated manuscript *Les Passages d'Outremer* (Journeys to Outremer).

overleaf
Augustine of Hippo by Fra Filippo Lippi (c.1406–69). A Latin philosopher and theologian, Augustine is often declared to be one of the greatest Christian thinkers. While he insisted that Christians should be pacifists, he also argued that it was acceptable to fight in order to restore and maintain peace.

The Byzantine and Roman Churches

Since early Christian times, differences had emerged within the Church. The Byzantine Empire (or Byzantium) was established as the center of the Roman Empire by Emperor Constantine when he converted to Christianity in 312 CE. He settled there and called the capital city New Rome, but it became known as Constantinople after him. It was later the capital of the Eastern Roman Empire for over a thousand years. Meanwhile, the Latin (or Roman Catholic) Church continued developing in the Western Roman Empire. Geographically, the Byzantine Empire included Asia Minor, the Middle East and North Africa, while the Latin Church encompassed Western Europe and northern and western areas of the Mediterranean. The Byzantine Empire was predominantly Greek-speaking, whereas Latin was the principal language of the Catholic Church. The Byzantine Emperor controlled the Eastern Orthodox Church's affairs and appointed its highest official, the Patriarch, while Roman Catholics regarded the Pope as their greatest authority. Unlike priests in Western Europe,

the Byzantine clergy retained their right to marry. Byzantine art focused on the divinity and mysteriousness of Christ, while Roman Catholic art emphasized the humanity of Jesus and the Holy Family. Both sides prayed to images of Christ, the Virgin Mary, and the saints, but in the eighth century, the Byzantine Emperor prohibited the veneration of icons, saying it violated God's commandment against worshipping "graven images." The ban triggered fierce battles within the Empire and, from the West, the Pope excommunicated the Emperor. Although a later Empress eventually restored the use of icons, the conflict left great resentment in Byzantium against the Pope. In their church services, the Byzantines used leavened bread as a symbol of the Risen Lord while Latin Christians used unleavened bread as this was eaten by Jesus at the Last Supper as it was Passover. In 1054, further disagreements led to the Pope and the Patriarch excommunicating each other. This became known as the East–West Schism, or the Great Schism, and it divided the two Churches permanently.

Only healthy, unmarried young men were permitted to become "Knights of Christ" without any of these extra considerations. The Pope invited other Catholic countries to join, including England and Spain, but various issues precluded their wholehearted support. England, for instance, was still struggling for unity after the Norman Conquest of 1066, and the Spanish were fighting the Muslim armies in their own country. In the end, France gained the most recruits and automatically became the leaders of the Crusade, although their king, Philip I, could not accompany them as he had been excommunicated over his bigamous marriage.

The Pope's speech

Like many events of that period, there were no accounts written at the time of Pope Urban's call to arms in Clermont in November 1095. Fulcher de Chartres, Baldric de Dol, Robert the Monk, and Gilbert de Nogent were four contemporary writers who wrote accounts of the First Crusade, but they only include excerpts of the speech in order to enhance the drama of their narratives of the Crusade itself, which are all written years after the event and which differ from each other, so are probably subjective. The closest evidence we have of the original words is believed by most scholars on the subject to have been written in a letter by the Pope himself one month after the speech, at Christmas time in 1095, to those signing up for the Crusade:

> Your brotherhood, we believe, has long since learned from many accounts that a
> barbaric fury has deplorably afflicted and laid waste the churches of God in the
> regions of the Orient. More than this, blasphemous to say, it has even grasped
> in intolerable servitude its churches and the Holy City of Christ, glorified by
> His passion and resurrection. Grieving with pious concern at this calamity, we
> visited the regions of Gaul and devoted ourselves largely to urging the princes
> of the land and their subjects to free the churches of the East.

The People's Crusade

Among the crowd listening to the Pope at Clermont had been a zealous monk in his forties, nicknamed Peter the Hermit, also known as Peter d'Amiens. Filthy, barefoot and wearing a long, coarse robe tied at the waist with a rope, Peter preached—to anyone who would listen—of the need to rescue sacred Christian sites in the Holy Land from

Eleventh-century public relations

The Pope's call to arms was cleverly played to appeal to the sensibilities of devout Roman Catholics across Europe. While he knew that Emperor Alexius was appealing for military assistance against the Seljuk Turks in Asia Minor, Urban purposely channeled the idea to suit his needs. The Latin Church had wanted to secure Jerusalem, with its sacred sites, for a long time. Likewise, Emperor Alexius had intentionally dwelt on the plight of pilgrims in Jerusalem for his own ends as he knew that this was the best way to ensure Western Christians' support.

▲ Peter the Hermit leading "The People's Crusade" from *Les Passages d'Outremer.* This illustration shows the first, unofficial Crusaders, about to be massacred by the Seljuk Turks in a surprise attack.

the Muslims. His passionate appeal attracted a huge number of mainly poor followers, reportedly between 15,000 and 100,000 men, women and children, mainly from France and Germany. Rather than one organized march, the First Crusade evolved as a series of expeditions to the Holy Land, and Peter's enthusiastic followers set off earlier than Urban II's planned date of mid-August 1096. Having withstood floods, plague, and famine at home, these impoverished, largely illiterate people believed that the Crusade would give them the chance to start new lives as well as securing them an assured passage to heaven. With few weapons, little experience of fighting, and no discipline, their ragged march became known as "The People's Crusade." Peter and his assistant Walter

Sans-Avoir (Walter the Penniless) led them overland through Germany and Hungary to Constantinople. On the way the rabble contingent among them began pillaging for food and attacking local inhabitants, and were soon counter-attacked by stronger local armies. Undaunted, the straggling marchers began discharging their religiously fueled passions by calling the Jewish inhabitants of various other districts they passed through "murderers of Christ," offering them the choice of conversion to Christianity or death. By the time they reached the Rhine, one of Europe's major trade routes and an area that had been populated heavily by Jews for centuries, the mob was completely out of control. They began looting and sacking houses and synagogues and massacring entire Jewish communities. Approximately 8,000 Jews died. To be rid of the Crusaders, the horrified Alexius organized their speedy passage across the River Bosphorus. As they reached Asia Minor, they came face-to-face with the Seljuk Turks who completely overpowered and massacred nearly all of them. The People's Crusade was over.

The First Crusade

Meanwhile, the main contingent of the Crusade was traveling to Constantinople. Of the thousands who went, only about a quarter were nobles or knights. The rest consisted of poor men, women and children, plus their donkeys, carts and dogs. Most had never before left their towns and villages. Alexius was appalled by the arrival of this unruly and undisciplined mass, many of whom appeared to be nothing more than ruffians, and who camped outside his capital city's walls through the winter of 1096–7. They were not the small, well-armed force of Christian knights he had envisaged when he had asked the Pope for help, and many began pillaging around Constantinople. Concerned that they could not be controlled and that most were only there to reach Jerusalem on a kind of glorified pilgrimage, he made their leaders swear an oath that they would "restore to the Empire whatever towns, countries or forts they took which had formerly belonged to it." Eventually the Crusader leaders agreed to the oath and they marched on to the ancient city of Nicaea (within present-day Iznik in Turkey), which had been captured by the Seljuk Turks in 1071. Strongly defended by walls and a lake, it was difficult to surmount, but the Christian armies laid siege and within five weeks, Nicaea was regained. Several other battles followed as the Crusaders marched towards the city of Antioch (present-day Antakya in southern Turkey, near the border with Syria). Previously a Byzantine stronghold and famous for never having fallen except by treachery, the city walls of Antioch were almost impenetrable.

Arriving at the city on October 20, 1097, the Crusaders blockaded the main city gates of Antioch, imprisoning the inhabitants and preventing relief forces from getting through. After three months, by January 1098, their own supplies were gravely diminished, many were dying of starvation and others were deserting. Nevertheless, the weakened and much reduced Crusaders managed to gain entry to the city, but they were immediately trapped inside by an external relief-force of 75,000 Seljuk Turks who had just arrived from Mosul (in contemporary Iraq). Meanwhile, some distance away, the Byzantine army was marching towards Antioch to help the crusading Latin army, when several deserters reached them and reported that the Crusaders had all starved to death outside the city. Believing therefore that the situation was hopeless, the Byzantines returned to Constantinople, leaving the Latin army trapped inside Antioch.

The Miracle of the Lance

Finding themselves outnumbered, weakened, and ensnared, it seemed that the First Crusade had ended before it had really started. Then, on 10 June 1098, a peasant called Peter Bartholomew was admitted to the presence of papal legate Bishop Adhemar and Raymond de Toulouse, the most important noble of the Crusade. Before the Crusaders had set off, the Pope had named Bishop Adhemar as his representative and the spiritual leader of the expedition. The idea of the red cloth cross worn on the shoulder had come directly from Adhemar's example. In the presence of these two august men, imprisoned within the city of Antioch, Peter Bartholomew described his recurrent visions. He claimed that Christ and St. Andrew had come to him and told him that the lance that had pierced the side of Christ on the Cross was buried beneath the high altar in St. Peter's Cathedral in Antioch. The Holy Lance, also known as the Holy Spear, the Spear of Christ, or the Spear of Longinus (after the Roman soldier who wielded it), is mentioned in the Bible, but only in the Gospel of John. It was used to make sure that Jesus was dead: "one of the soldiers pierced his side with a spear, and at once blood and water came out" (John 19:34).

Bishop Adhemar was sceptical, as he had seen what had been claimed to be part of the Holy Lance in Constantinople, but Raymond was intrigued and when the story spread among the Crusaders a ripple of hope emerged that had previously seemed unimaginable. The next day, Stephen of Valence, a monk accompanying the Crusade also sought an audience with Adhemar and Raymond. He too reported a vision, this time where Christ

Leaders of the First Crusade

Although they had to organize and discipline many inexperienced Crusaders, the leaders of the First Crusade included some of the most eminent members of European knighthood. Count Raymond de Toulouse headed a band of volunteers from Provence. Godfrey de Bouillon and his brother Baldwin commanded a force of French and German men. Hugh de Vermandois, the younger brother of King Philip I of France; William the Conqueror's eldest son, Robert of Normandy; Count Robert II of Flanders; Bohemond, Prince of Taranto, and his nephew Tancred; and Stephen II, the Count of Blois, all led troops into battle, with varying degrees of courage and ingenuity.

▲

An illumination by the Fauvel Master in 1337, showing the capture of a Muslim city by Christian crusaders led by Godfrey de Bouillon in the First Crusade, from *The History of the Kingdom of Jerusalem* by William of Tyre.

and the Virgin Mary had promised to help the demoralized troops. Adhemar remained suspicious, but when on 14 June, a meteor was seen to fall into the Turkish camp, it was deemed a positive omen by the Crusaders, and Bishop Adhemar gave permission for digging to start in the cathedral. The following day, inside St. Peter's Cathedral in Antioch, Raymond de Toulouse, the historian Raymond d'Aguilers, William, Bishop of Orange, Peter Bartholomew, and a few others began to dig beneath the paved floor under the altar. Nothing was found until Peter jumped into the pit and unearthed a relic of a spear point which he proclaimed was the Holy Lance. When told, Bishop Adhemar continued to believe the object to be a fake and Bartholomew to be a fraud, but Raymond de Toulouse and the others present took this as a divine sign that the Crusaders had God on their side. It is impossible to verify now what really happened. The trusted historian on the dig, Raymond d'Aguilers, reported that he had seen the iron in the ground before Peter Bartholomew exposed it, contesting that Peter had put it there as several sceptics believed. Whatever the object was or how it was found, the excitement in the city was intense as word of the discovery spread. Peter then reported another vision in which St. Andrew instructed the Crusader army to fast for five days (although they were already starving), after which they would be victorious. There was great rejoicing among the Crusaders and they duly fasted. On June 28, they broke out of Antioch led by their best soldier, the Norman warrior Bohemond, Prince of Taranto, with the Holy Lance carried by Raymond d'Aguilers at the front. Although desperately weak from hunger, they were in an exalted mood and some cried out that they could see celestial cavalrymen on white horses riding to help them, bearing white banners and led by St. George. They should have been no match for the far larger and better-equipped Turkish and Arab force, but a great deal of in-fighting had occurred with the Turks and Arabs, leaving their morale as low as the Christians' was high, and they broke quickly under the unexpected Crusader attack. Antioch was once more in Christian hands; but rather than return it to the Byzantines who had deserted them, Bohemond remained there as Prince of Antioch, while the rest of the Crusaders marched on to Jerusalem.

Raymond de Toulouse kept the lance for a time, but rumors of it being a hoax grew as people realized that other Holy Lances were in existence. In the sixth century, a pilgrim, Antoninus of Piacenza had related that in the Basilica of Mount Zion he saw 'the crown of thorns with which Our Lord was crowned and the lance with which He was struck in the side'. After Jerusalem was captured by Persian forces during the following century, according to contemporary writings, a piece of the Holy Lance was taken to Constantinople and placed in the church of Hagia Sophia, and later moved to the Church of the Virgin of the Pharos. Much later, it was sold to Louis IX of France who enshrined it with the Crown of Thorns, but the relics both disappeared during the 18th-century French Revolution. The larger portion of the lance was mentioned as being in the Church of the Holy Sepulcher in Jerusalem around 670, but there is no further mention of it being there. This could be the portion of the lance that was sometimes attributed to being in the Templars' keeping, but there is no clear explanation of how they found it when so many others had not in the centuries between its disappearance and their arrival in Jerusalem.

Although desperately weak from hunger, they were in an exalted mood and some cried out that they could see celestial cavalrymen on white horses riding to help them.

Still, with these objects and about three others that were claimed to be the Holy Lance, several people grew sceptical and Peter Bartholomew became the butt of various accusations. So, in April 1099, he requested an ordeal by fire in an attempt to prove his credibility. On Good Friday 1099, he walked through a narrow passage between two huge piles of blazing wood, wearing only a tunic and carrying the Holy Lance. Although horrendously burned, he claimed to be uninjured because Christ had appeared to him in the fire. Twelve days later, he died in agony and this particular Holy Lance lost its allure. For a while, it was kept in Constantinople and at St. Peter's in Rome. Later, it was linked with the Templars, but by then there were at least four other objects scattered throughout Christendom being labelled "the Holy Lance" and, as it was never seen in the Templars' possession nor found after their end, the idea was soon forgotten.

The Kingdom of Jerusalem

It is believed that 30,000 Crusaders had started out from Europe in August 1096, but fewer than 12,000 were left in June 1099 when they arrived within sight of the Holy City. As they approached, the Muslim governor of Jerusalem closed all exits and entries to the city and poisoned all the wells outside the city walls. A network of underground fresh water systems would keep the inhabitants inside alive, and the city was well stocked with provisions. The outside walls and defenses were virtually impregnable. Coupled with their severely reduced troops and limited provisions, it seemed unlikely that the Crusaders would be successful in their ultimate goal of recapturing Jerusalem. An initial attempt at attack failed, but within a week fresh supplies arrived by sea to the port of Jaffa that had been abandoned by the Muslims. In the following days, the Crusaders built two large siege towers, erecting them after dark and moving them close to the city walls. A desperate and prolonged attack was launched from both sides and, on the morning of July 15, a large faction of the Crusader army commanded by Godfrey de Bouillon captured an inner rampart of the northern wall. The Crusaders poured into Jerusalem and, in a frenzied and unplanned wave of violence and brutality, slaughtered everyone in sight.

The unrestrained and vicious massacre by the Crusaders was not what Urban II had asked them to do in November 1095, and it went against all the values of Christianity. The Pope had wanted them to liberate the Holy Land from the Muslims, not to massacre the inhabitants of Jerusalem. His original call for a return to chivalry had largely been ignored, but it was unlikely that he ever knew of the atrocities, as he died two weeks after the fall of Jerusalem before the news reached Rome.

Despite churchmen in pulpits across Europe condemning the news when they heard it, the Crusaders in the Holy Land believed they had achieved victory. In actual fact, the religious and political conflicts between the Sunnis and the Shi'ites had given the Crusaders greater opportunities for success than they would otherwise have had. Two days after their capture of Jerusalem, the Crusader leaders met to choose someone to take command of the Holy City. Although not everyone agreed, it was decided to turn it into a kingdom with a monarch chosen from among them to remain there and rule. The ideal choice would have been Bishop Adhemar, but he had died the year before at Antioch. So the new crown was offered to Raymond de Toulouse, the eldest, wealthiest, and probably the most chivalrous of the Crusaders. But Raymond did not want to rule in the city where Jesus had suffered. So the crown was offered to Godfrey de Bouillon who had been another powerful leader and was somewhat jealous of Raymond. Godfrey accepted the position, but declared he would not wear a

An image of the Holy Sepulcher from a 15th-century Greek manuscript known as *The Oracle of Leo the Wise*. The Holy Sepulcher is venerated as Golgotha, the site of Christ's crucifixion and resurrection, as well as where a part of the Holy Lance was believed to be at one time.

royal crown in the city where Jesus had worn a crown of thorns. Rather than the title of King of Jerusalem, he accepted the name Defender of the Holy Sepulcher (*Advocatus Sancti Sepulchri*) and he used the Al-Aqsa mosque as his palace, believing that it stood on the site of the illustrious scriptural Temple of Solomon (the *Templum Salomonis*). The Muslim shrine, the Dome of the Rock, adjacent to the Al-Aqsa mosque, which probably is on the site of Solomon's original temple, was given iron railings and a cross and identified as the *Templum Domini*, or the Lord's Temple. The Crusaders also installed an archbishop from Pisa named Daimbert as a Catholic Patriarch, to oversee the Latin Christians who would live in Jerusalem or travel to the Holy Land on pilgrimages. Various other prelates also moved in. Their main goal achieved, most of the Crusaders returned to Europe, taking with them tales of horror, danger, adventure, hardship, and ultimate victory.

Outremer

During the first few years of the 12th century, four different states were established in the territories now controlled by Christians: the County of Edessa, the Principality of Antioch, the County of Tripoli, and the Kingdom of Jerusalem. In Europe, these states became known collectively as "Outremer" which was French for overseas ("outre-mer"). In 1100, Godfrey de Bouillon died and his brother, Baldwin de Boulogne, succeeded as King Baldwin I of Jerusalem, being less reluctant than his brother to take a royal title.

Nevertheless, the name he adopted mattered far less than the overriding problem that had rapidly become apparent in Outremer, which was that there was insufficient protection for the thousands of Christian pilgrims traveling there. The towns were made fairly secure, but travelers beyond the walls were vulnerable to bandits and other assailants. As soon as Jerusalem was in Christian hands once more, an upsurge of pilgrims traveled there from Europe and, with no one to defend them as they journeyed to and from the holy sites, many were attacked and murdered outside the city walls. In 1102, a pilgrim known as Saewulf of Canterbury recorded how pilgrims were often set upon as they traveled on the road from Jaffa to Jerusalem. Specifically targeted by Bedouin nomads, Turks, and Egyptians, such small groups of pilgrims were often killed for the money they sewed into their clothing, and their bodies were left to rot where they were killed. This would have incensed the Christian world, not just because pilgrims were being callously robbed and murdered, but because they were also being denied Christian burials.

Hugh de Champagne

One traveler to the Holy Land at that time was Hugh, the Count of Champagne (c.1074–1125), the third and youngest son of Theobald de Blois. Wealthy, powerful, and pious, Hugh was known for most of his life as Hugh de Troyes, after the land he inherited from an elder brother who died at an early age. Although interested in the First Crusade, he had not joined it, possibly as he had recently married Constance, the daughter of Philip I of France, so remained at home with his new wife and took care of his considerable lands and property. With his wife's dowry and an inheritance from his mother and deceased brother, Hugh seemed to have everything going for him. But his marriage broke down and in 1103, after an attempted assassination from which he narrowly escaped, he spent months being nursed to health by the nuns at the Convent of Avenay. Once recovered, he made a pilgrimage to the Holy Land to give thanks for his life, and while he was gone, his marriage to Constance was annulled on the grounds of consanguinity and failure to produce an heir. In 1107, he returned to Champagne and married another noblewoman, Elizabeth de Varais.

Yet Hugh soon tried to have this second marriage annulled as well. In 1114, when he had returned once more to the Holy Land, Elizabeth went to the Bishop of Chartres and implored him to prevent her husband from rejecting her. As a result, Hugh received a letter from the bishop, remonstrating with him for leaving his wife in order to join "La Milice du Christ" (the Knights of Christ). This was the original name given to the Knights Templar and the name that they were called by Bernard of Clairvaux (1090–1153), but at the time of the bishop's letter, as far as can be ascertained, the Order was not officially formed. This letter seems to have had little effect on Hugh, however. He didn't return from the Holy Land until the end of 1115 and, about two years later, Elizabeth gave birth to a son, whom Hugh immediately denounced as illegitimate. His reasons for this are not confirmed, but they seem to have been valid as the illegitimacy was not disputed at the time (although the boy, Eudes, tried unsuccessfully to claim legitimacy later in life). The official reason that has been recorded, which Hugh insisted upon, was that he was sterile. Whatever it was, Elizabeth and the child were cast aside.

When he had returned to the Holy Land in 1114, Hugh had taken a retinue of knights with him. Before he left, he declared to all that he would be "taking up the gospel knighthood" once there. It is not clear what he meant by this; he may have been implying that he intended to travel to the Holy Land as the Crusaders had done, or he may have planned to protect the sacred Christian sites once there. The conundrum deepens. Hugh stayed in the Holy Land for nearly two years and when he returned to France, he left one of his vassals, Hugh de Payns (c.1070–1136) behind. This was a most unusual course of action. While Hugh de Champagne was back in France, Hugh de Payns was helping to form an order of military monks in Jerusalem. It is possible that Hugh de Champagne returned to France specifically to organize funding for the order in Jerusalem and had left his vassal with instructions about organizing the group of men. With his multiple trips to the Holy Land and later events, it seems likely that Hugh de Champagne was involved in some way. Eventually in 1125, he handed over his land in Champagne to his nephew, Theobald, renounced his worldly wealth and returned to the Holy Land to join the Order of the Knights Templar soon after its official formation. He was probably the only member of the nobility to join at the start of the Order. Even more unusual: to become a Templar, Hugh, the Count of Champagne, had to swear allegiance to his former vassal Hugh de Payns.

Hugh de Payns

Also often called Hugues de Payens, despite his significance in the establishment of the Knights Templar, there is little substantiated about him, apart from his being Hugh de Champagne's former vassal. As far as we know, there is no contemporary biography in existence and so information about him is extremely fragmented. The most detailed accounts come from Archbishop William of Tyre (c.1130–86), who recorded his information over 60 years after the First Crusade, but even these notes are not comprehensive. Born at the family chateau on the banks of the River Seine in the Champagne region, Hugh de Payns (c.1070–1136) is often documented by later chroniclers as being a cousin of Hugh de Champagne and Bernard of Clairvaux, two of the most powerful men in Europe at the time. He is also believed to be related to two other powerful men and leaders of the First Crusade: Raymond de Toulouse and Godfrey de Bouillon.

Several documents state that Hugh de Payns was married to Elizabeth de Chappes or, some later chroniclers assert, to a Catherine St. Clair. There is little evidence about Catherine St. Clair, however, and it seems far more likely that he was married to Elizabeth de Chappes between 1108 and 1111. He has also been attributed with having either one child or three, whose names have been recorded as Guibuin, Isabelle, and Theobald. Theobald is known to have existed as he became abbot at the monastery of La Colombe in 1139, but nothing is recorded about the other two children. There is no written documentation of Hugh leaving his family, nor of what happened to them after he had left France for the Holy Land. In those days, it was not unusual for married people to take holy orders, but

first they had to obtain permission from their spouses, and often the spouses would also enter a convent or a monastery at the same time. This might have happened with Hugh and his wife, but with so few records, it is equally probable that she died, that the child or children were taken in either by wealthy relatives or into the Church, and then Hugh was free to travel with a clear conscience.

It is also probable that, before his marriage, he went on the First Crusade under the leadership of one of his relatives, either Raymond de Toulouse or Godfrey de Bouillon. By his actions and behavior, it can be deduced that Hugh de Payns was a devout and earnest man, inspired by his noble relatives and determined to do what he could to defend the holiest sites in Christendom. He was also poorly educated and lacked intellectual acuity. He was doubtlessly a good fighter and reliable, but it seems that he was also a bit dull and deliberate. With his simplicity of mind, staunch faith and understanding of fighting, he was an ideal choice to lead the first group of Templars. It could also be that he was chosen to help uncover valuable secrets without really understanding their worth.

The start of the Order

In 1118, Baldwin I died suddenly and was succeeded as King of Jerusalem by his cousin Baldwin of Le Bourg, who became known as Baldwin II. The Patriarch Daimbert also died that year and was succeeded by Warmund of Picardy. Perhaps while he was in Jerusalem during 1114 and 1115, Hugh de Champagne had devised with Baldwin I or Daimbert the plan to form a band of knights specifically to protect pilgrims, or perhaps the king or Patriarch had asked Hugh to leave his retinue of knights in the Holy Land for that purpose. Alternatively, it could be that the idea was contrived between the king and Patriarch and Hugh de Champagne several years before, perhaps when Hugh first traveled to Jerusalem in 1104. Or it is possible that when he traveled there ten years after his first visit, in 1114, it was with the distinct intent of organizing a protective body of knights in Outremer, and that could have been what he meant when he declared that he was "taking up the gospel knighthood." Most accounts record that the Templars did not form until 1118, but

the letter to Hugh de Champagne from the Bishop of Chartres that referred to the "Milice du Christ" was sent in 1114. So the concept at least was possibly being discussed at that time. Alternatively, the Bishop of Chartres may have been referring to a small, unofficial group of Christians already in Outremer who were attempting to protect the holy sites independently. The popular account written later by William of Tyre is that the formation of the Order was solely the idea of Hugh de Payns, which seems unlikely. According to William, Payns approached King Baldwin II and Warmund independently in the year of their accessions with his notion of forming a permanent and reputable brotherhood of men to protect Christians and Christian sites in the Holy Land.

The truth might never be known. Most of the information comes from William of Tyre's *History of the Kingdom of Jerusalem*, which he wrote in Latin between 1165 and 1184. The work is sometimes given the title "History of Deeds Done Beyond the Sea" (Historia rerum in partibus transmarinis gestarum) or "History of Jerusalem" (Historia Ierosolimitana), or simply the "Historia." It was translated into French soon after William's death at the end of the 12th century, and then into several other languages. Because it is the only account of Jerusalem in the 12th century written by someone living there, historians have often assumed that it is impartial and objective, but it has recently been realized that William was particularly involved in the kingdom's politics and so some of his information is in all likelihood somewhat biased. Nonetheless, his work is important in that it gives contemporary views on the Crusades and other related events, even though his account of the formation of the Knights Templar was written between 45 and 65 years after he records that it happened. In his account, he asserts that the first Templars were a group of "noble knights" who took the three monastic vows of chastity, poverty, and obedience in 1118 and, at the same time, pledged to protect Christians and sacred sites in Jerusalem, by force if necessary. He recorded that the Order began when Hugh de Payns and a small group of men, including Godfrey de St. Omer and André de Montbard, were accepted by the new King and Patriarch of Jerusalem to form a community of religious knights in the Holy Land:

> In this same year [1118] certain noble men of knightly rank, religious men, devoted to God and fearing him, bound themselves to Christ's service in the hands of the Lord Patriarch. They promised to live in perpetuity as regular canons, without possessions, under vows of chastity and obedience. Their foremost leaders were the venerable Hugh de Payns and Godfrey de St. Omer. Since they had no church nor any fixed abode, the king gave them for a time a dwelling place in the south wing of the palace, near the Lord's Temple. The canons of the Lord's Temple gave them, under certain conditions, a square near the palace which the canons possessed. This the knights used as a drill field. The Lord King and his noblemen and also the Lord Patriarch and the prelates of the church gave them benefices from their domains, some for a limited time and some in perpetuity. These were to provide the knights with food and clothing. Their primary duty, one which was enjoined upon them by the Lord Patriarch and the other bishops for the remission of sins, was that of protecting the roads and routes against the attacks of robbers and brigands. This they did especially in order to safeguard pilgrims.
> WILLIAM OF TYRE, *THE HISTORY OF THE KINGDOM OF JERUSALEM*

◀

A Templar knight ready for battle, from a stained-glass window in the Church of St. Andrew, Temple Grafton, Warwickshire, England, 1875.

At the end of 1119, the nine men of the group were officially given permission to form the confraternity that would be called "The Poor Fellow-Soldiers of Jesus Christ." They were also given quarters in the building that King Baldwin II had used as a palace, the Al-Aqsa mosque. As the Christians believed it to be on the site of the original Temple of Solomon, their name became extended to: "The Poor Fellow-Soldiers of Jesus Christ and the Temple of Solomon." After being lengthened, their title was frequently abbreviated to the far simpler Templar Knights or Knights Templar.

There are writers other than William of Tyre who relate a slightly different story. A scribe from the abbey of St. Bertin, known only as Simon, recorded in about 1135–7 that the first Templars were Crusaders who remained in the Holy Land after 1099. Evidence for this is not forthcoming and, given that so many pilgrims lost their lives in the early years after the First Crusade, this is either not the case or those original Templars were not particularly conscientious. An English monk, Orderic Vitalis (1075–c.1142), based at the monastery of St. Evroul in Normandy, who wrote a contemporary chronicle of 11th- and 12th-century Normandy and England, wrote in the 1120s of the Templars, declaring that they were "admirable knights" who devoted their lives to the physical and spiritual service of God and who "face martyrdom daily." Although he does not describe their formation, his writing affirms that they were in operation by the 1120s. Whatever the actual timing, or whose idea it originally was, the start of the Order remains shrouded in mystery because there is no definitive contemporary account of its beginnings.

It is not apparent why the start of the Brotherhood is so obscure, nor why (according to William of Tyre) only nine men were originally recruited, nor even why that number remained the same or nearly the same for several years, despite the desperate need for far more men to undertake such an important and onerous task as defending the Holy Land. If nothing else, the relative safety of larger numbers of knights on the treacherous roads outside Jerusalem would have been crucial. Some later accounts state that the Templar numbers remained restricted because their existence was so austere, while others assert that it was because the few men had been specifically selected for a secret purpose. Others insist that there were more than nine men within a short time, but the nine original men were briefed to undertake a slightly different role. Some historians have gone so far as to say that the nine is purely symbolic, that there were far more early members, but that nine was used as it is a circular number: it can be divided by three to make three, and no matter how many times it is multiplied together, the resulting number will always be divisible by three. It might even have been simply a round number made up by William of Tyre for tidiness in his account of the early days of the Order.

Bernard of Clairvaux

Born on the outskirts of Dijon in Burgundy to a family of lower nobility, Bernard de Fontaines-les-Dijon (1090–1153) became a Cistercian monk after the death of his beloved mother. At that time, the Cistercian Order was a small, new religious community that had been established in Cîteaux Abbey near Dijon in 1098, expressly to restore the ascetic Rule of St. Benedict, which many felt had become rather lax. A thoughtful and intelligent young man, Bernard was so impressed with the Cistercians that he convinced four of his brothers, an uncle and 26 other young men to join the Order with him. (In the 11th and 12th centuries, entering the Church was a common career for at least one son or daughter

▶

A 1455 French illustration of Jerusalem, from the manuscript *Avis Directif pour faire le Passage d'Outremer* (Information for Making the Journey to Outremer), written in 1332 by Brocart l'Allemand.

of a good family, but it is a measure of Bernard's powers of persuasion that he convinced so many to join with him, including a married brother.)

In 1115, after just three years of being a Cistercian monk, Bernard was asked to found a new abbey in a remote valley known as the Val d'Absinthe, not far from Troyes. The tract of land had been given to the Cistercians by Hugh de Champagne. Bernard took 12 other monks with him and named the new monastery Clair Vallée, or "Valley of Light." The name evolved into "Clairvaux." From his first days of being an abbot, Bernard imposed stringent discipline on himself and his order. His health began to suffer and his monks objected so, reluctantly, he softened his approach—but only slightly. Even with such a severe regime, Clairvaux flourished and expanded rapidly. Word spread about Bernard's persuasive and eloquent homilies and writings, and as the Cistercian Order grew, so did his broader influence and responsibilities. He became the most authoritative and respected monk of his time. A man of many contradictions, he clearly displayed some

Bernard and the banishment of art

St. Bernard of Clairvaux and the Cistercian monks taking possession of the Abbey of Clairvaux, this illustration was created by Paul Lacroix (1806–84) for a book, *Military and Religious Life in the Middle Ages*, published c.1880.

At the time that Bernard joined the Cistercians, monks at Cîteaux Abbey had developed the most advanced style of manuscript illumination in France. Bernard believed that superfluous ornamentation distracted from religious life and insisted that Cistercian architecture was plain and utilitarian, and imagery limited. He was vehemently opposed to any superfluous adornment and his angry letters condemning figurative art and decoration resulted in painting and embellishment being banned altogether in 1154, the year of his death. This is an excerpt from one of his furious writings on the subject:

> . . . what profit is there in those ridiculous monsters, in that marvelous and deformed comeliness, that comely deformity? To what purpose are those unclean apes, those fierce lions, those monstrous centaurs, those half men, those striped tigers, those fighting knights, those hunters winding their horns? . . . In short, so many and so marvelous are the varieties of divers shapes on every hand, that we are more tempted to read in the marble than in our books, and to spend the whole day in wondering at these things rather than in meditating the law of God. For God's sake, if men are not ashamed of these follies, why at least do they not shrink from the expense?

Under Bernard's instruction, Cistercian architecture was extremely simple, logical and balanced, with no excess ornamentation.

extraordinary qualities as he was canonized little more than 20 years after his death. Devout, pious and articulate, he was also charismatic, physically attractive and volatile. While he spoke about the love of God, he also urged Christians to fight and kill Muslims. He wrote of the importance of humility and modesty, and he was asked to advise the popes of his time, so he wielded great power. Pope Eugenius III (r. 1145–53) once complained to him in a letter: "They say that it is you who are Pope and not I.' Bernard claimed to prefer a life of solitude, yet he was almost constantly surrounded by many who asked for his advice or his permission, and his gentle spirituality seemed at odds with his involvement in the often intense politics of the Church. Through his influence, the Cistercian Order became so popular that over his life he founded 163 new monasteries across Europe. Each was built on his command as a plain, geometric structure, devoid of towers, painting, sculpture, or other adornments. Several of these were paid for by Hugh de Champagne and in 1125, just before Hugh left to join the Templars in the Holy Land, Bernard wrote to him, saying how sorry he was that the Count was going to travel so far away to devote himself to God and that, even though it was undoubtedly the will of the Lord, he would still miss his friend who had been so generous to the Cistercians.

> Through his influence, the Cistercian Order became so popular that over his life he founded 163 new monasteries across Europe.

Bernard had close relationships with other reforming orders of his day, such as the Carthusians, but he had particularly close links with the Knights Templar. A friend of the Count of Champagne, he was allegedly distant cousins with Hugh de Payns and the nephew of another of the original Templars, André de Montbard. Two others in that first group of nine, known only as Rossal and Gondemar, had been Cistercians under him. For them to transfer their allegiances from the Cistercians to the Templars, Bernard had to give his authorization. Apart from the Count of Champagne, all the original Templars came from the same background as Bernard, that is, of the lower nobility, and they all grew up in the Champagne region of France.

A devoutly religious man such as Bernard and many of his contemporaries would not have been as shocked at the idea of fighting monks as might be imagined. Since the fifth century when Augustine of Hippo had described the four conditions that could lead to a "just war" by Christians, and even more recently since the First Crusade, the idea of religious men fighting to protect other Christians had become popular. In recent decades in Europe, several groups of lower nobles had banded together and provided themselves with their own (expensive) military equipment, including chain-mail, armor, helmet, shield, sword, lance and a horse (also with armor). These groups of self-appointed knights came together with the aim of protecting churches and monasteries against criminals in their own countries. Several of these groups joined the First Crusade together. Most of these confraternities did not have official recognition, although they usually sought the blessing of a priest before they set off. This could have been Hugh de Champagne's arrangement when he traveled to the Holy Land with his group of knights in 1114.

The Council of Nablus

An order of monks with a distinct purpose beyond simple devotion to God had already been set up in Jerusalem before the Order of the Knights Templar was formed. The Knights Hospitaller, or the Order of the Knights of Saint John the Hospitaller, had been officially established by the Pope in 1113 as a religious order specifically to help sick pilgrims in a new infirmary near the Church of the Holy Sepulcher. The Hospitallers were later called to help protect pilgrims in a more soldierly way, but the Knights Templar was the first specifically military order to be founded by the Catholic Church. In 1120, the Templars received official Church recognition at the Council of Nablus—although this was Church recognition only in Outremer and not in all of Christendom.

The Council of Nablus was an oddity by Western standards. It was a religious council but it included as many lay people as ecclesiastical. This was probably because it was in the Holy Land where the population remained small. The Council was held in Jerusalem to establish the first written laws for the kingdom after the Crusade. Convened by Patriarch Warmund and King Baldwin II, it established 25 rules to deal with both religious and secular affairs. Sixty years later, William of Tyre wrote about it, including why it convened and its official recognition of the Templars, but he did not record any of the canons, as there was a deliberate effort to make Christian-ruled Outremer appear faultless. Nevertheless, the Council of Nablus gives us a date for the Templars' acceptance as respected representatives of the Church in the Holy Land, with this—not particularly specific—canon: "If a cleric takes up arms in the cause of defense, he is not held to be guilty."

King Baldwin II of Jerusalem

After taking part in the First Crusade under the leadership of his cousin, Godfrey de Bouillon, Baldwin of Le Bourg remained in the Holy Land. In 1118, he shot to power as King of Jerusalem, mainly just because he was there. The son of Hugh I, Count of Rethel, and his wife Mélisende, Baldwin had two younger brothers, Gervaise and Manasses, and two sisters, Matilda and Hodierna. In 1101, before he became king, Baldwin married Princess Morphia, the daughter of the Armenian prince Gabriel of Melitene. By all accounts, Baldwin was brave and amenable, and he made great efforts to assimilate with the people he now lived among; unlike his more arrogant predecessors. He was also more forward-thinking than many of his contemporaries. When he and Morphia had only daughters and no sons, he saw no reason why his eldest daughter should not inherit his lands and named her his successor. He also inherited numerous problems. After the

Every Crusader prayed at the Holy Sepulcher before returning to Europe, and significantly, the first Templars swore their monastic vows there.

massacre in Jerusalem at the end of the First Crusade, the city was underpopulated. Pilgrims were visiting, but few Christians chose to live there permanently. Baldwin set about encouraging any Christians, Syrians, Greeks, or Armenians to settle and trade there. He also intended to address the issue of the attacks on pilgrims beyond the city walls. At the time of his accession, pilgrims were the only people bringing money into Jerusalem, so it was important that they still came to the Holy City. One year after he became King of Jerusalem, however, the ruler of Antioch was killed in battle. As the Count of Antioch's heir was only 11 years old, Baldwin assumed responsibility until the boy was old enough. So whether it was his idea, the idea of Hugh de Champagne, or as William of Tyre states, the idea of Hugh de Payns, Baldwin was delighted to pass on one of his heavy responsibilities to the new order of religious knights.

Two sacred sites

On Christmas Day 1119, Hugh de Payns, Godfrey de St. Omer, André de Montbard, Payen de Montdidier, Archambaud de St. Agnan, Geoffrey Bisol, the two former Cistercians recorded simply as Rossal and Gondemar, and one other, who many believe was Hugh, the Count of Champagne, knelt before King Baldwin II and the Patriarch Warmund and made their vows of poverty, chastity, and obedience in the Church of the Holy Sepulcher in Jerusalem. This church had been rebuilt at great expense in 1048 by the Byzantine Emperor Constantine IX and his Patriarch Nicephorus, despite Jerusalem being in the hands of the Muslims at the time. The rebuilding was only allowed after some intense negotiations between the Byzantines and the Arabs. In order for it to go ahead, among other things, the Byzantines had agreed to opening a mosque in Constantinople and to the release of 5,000 Muslim prisoners.

The Church of the Holy Sepulcher was of particular religious importance to Christians. Constructed over two sites, it is revered by all Christians as being on Golgotha, the Hill of Calvary, where, according to the New Testament, Jesus was crucified and where he was subsequently buried and rose again. The church had originally been built by the first Christian Roman Emperor Constantine in about 326. The location was extremely important for pilgrims and it was one of Pope Urban II's greatest concerns when he called for the First Crusade, as the Seljuk Turks were destroying all churches in lands they overran. It was one of the jewels of Jerusalem that the Christians wanted to preserve. Every Crusader prayed at the Holy Sepulcher before returning to Europe, and significantly, the first Templars swore their monastic vows there. It is possible too that, after the first Crusade, the earliest Templars remained based in the Holy Sepulcher as guardians of the building. Godfrey de Bouillon, when accepting the position of first ruler, had taken the name "Defender of the Holy Sepulcher" rather than "King of Jerusalem." William of Tyre wrote about further renovations that were made to the Holy Sepulcher in the mid-12th century, soon after the Templars' formal acceptance at the Council of Nablus.

◀

This illuminated manuscript written by William of Tyre recalls Baldwin II of Jerusalem's death in 1131. The second count of Edessa and the third king of Jerusalem, Baldwin was highly respected by all, and described by William as "a devout and God-fearing man, notable for his loyalty and for his great experience in military matters." Here, the citizens of Edessa pay their respects at Baldwin II's funeral.

CHAPTER 2

The Temple of Solomon

Some of the most enduring legends surrounding the Knights Templar revolve around the location of their first headquarters, believed by many at the time to be the Temple of Solomon. From the time they moved into the Al-Aqsa mosque, stories began emerging about their activities inside the building.

After making their vows, the nine knights returned to the quarters they had been given in the mosque that had been renamed the *Templum Salomonis* under Christian occupation. This was as sacred to Christians as the Church of the Holy Sepulcher, because it was assumed that it stood on the site of Solomon's original Temple. It was of course the Al-Aqsa mosque, which had been built soon after 674, possibly on the site of a Byzantine church. It was also adjacent to the Dome of the Rock, which was most probably built on the actual site of Solomon's Temple. The entire area is known as "Temple Mount." a huge platform on a hill, and the lodgings given to the Templars were large enough to contain them and to stable their horses in a vast underground space. Once they were installed, Baldwin II, his nobles, and Warmund and his priests gave the Templars a small income so that they could buy basic food, clothing and feed for their horses. For the first few years of their existence, they were completely reliant on the benevolence of others.

One of the most enduring legends surrounding the Knights Templar revolves around the location of these first headquarters: the Temple of Solomon. From the time they moved into the Al-Aqsa mosque, stories began emerging about their activities inside the building. It is reported that the Templars were taciturn, which fueled speculation about their clandestine activities, but they were probably no different to other religious orders, and they were undoubtedly busy setting up their organization and aiming for papal approval. As monks, they would almost certainly have been advised to refrain from mingling with the outside world, so this was nothing unusual. The fact that the site of the Temple of Solomon is so important in Jewish, Christian, and Muslim beliefs added to people's fascination about what they might be doing there. They clearly considered their

◀

An icon of King Solomon, part of a 1497 painting from Dormition Church, St Cyril's Monastery of Belozersk, Russia. Solomon was revered for maintaining peace between the newly reunited kingdoms of Israel and Judah.

base to be of great significance, which is why they incorporated Solomon's name into their own, as unlike their vows of poverty, chastity and obedience, Solomon was rich, had many wives and was an unconventional ruler.

As one of the most contested religious locations in the world, Temple Mount has a remarkably busy and varied history. In Jewish and Christian belief, it was where God gathered earth to create Adam; where Cain, Abel, and Noah offered sacrifices to God; where Jacob slept when he dreamt of angels; where Abraham almost sacrificed his son Isaac and where King David set up an altar to God. In Christian teaching, it was the place from which Jesus chased off money-changers, while Muslims believe it was from there that the Prophet Muhammad ascended on his Night Journey to heaven.

During their occupation, the Templars spent a great deal of time excavating beneath Temple Mount, and it is widely alleged that they found something of great significance there. While not conclusive, ideas about what this could have been range from lost religious texts to holy relics, variously claimed to have been: the Holy Grail, the Ark of the Covenant, a fragment of the Holy Lance or Holy Spear, the "True Cross," secret information relating to lost building skills, and even legacies about Jesus. The hypotheses about what this could have been are fueled by the many mystical stories that have emerged about Solomon himself.

> He conquered all surrounding enemies and established an extremely powerful empire. But because he had fought and killed so many in battle, God would not allow him to build the temple.

Mystic, wise man, architect, king

The legendary lost temple built by King Solomon and from which the Templars derived their full name was the first permanent temple in the history of the Jews. Before it was built, the nomadic Jews worshipped in tents and tabernacles, which they carried with them as they traveled. Then King David, the second king of the Jews (after Saul) made Jerusalem the nation's capital and determined to build a permanent house for God where everyone could pray. David had unified Israel and built up the military, the treasury and national pride. He conquered all surrounding enemies and established an extremely powerful empire. But because he had fought and killed so many in battle, God would not allow him to build the temple. In the First Book of Chronicles, David reports:

> But the word of the Lord came to me, saying, "You have shed much blood and have waged great wars; you shall not build a house to my name, because you have shed so much blood in my sight on the earth."
>
> 1 CHRONICLES 22:8

Because of the foundations that David had laid down, his son and successor, Solomon, never had to fight a war, so God permitted him to follow his father's instructions. In approximately 957 BCE, using the site David had selected, Solomon built the Temple. Originally built to house the Ark of the Covenant which contained the stone tablets of the Ten Commandments given by Moses to the Jews, the Temple of Solomon has always been especially revered by the Jewish people. Although it no longer remains, the legendary building has captured the collective imagination probably more than any other structure in the world.

▶

The Judgement of Solomon, Peter Paul Rubens, c.1617, relays the story of Solomon's sagacity when two prostitutes both claimed motherhood of one child. Solomon ordered the child to be cut in two so that the women could share it. When one woman gave up her half to save the child's life, the real mother was revealed.

But Solomon is a problem for historians. Apart from the Bible, the Qur'an, and the Talmud (Jewish law, ethics, customs, philosophy, and history), there is almost no mention of him or proof that he even existed. For centuries it was thought that he lived during the Iron Age. Yet archaeologists have not been able to find evidence of his life from that period and, crucially, nothing of his impressive building projects relating to that time. If, however, he lived during the Bronze Age, then substantiation could be more forthcoming as the remains of Phoenician-style architecture have been found in areas associated with his life. Several historians have worked out that he probably did exist and that his dates were c.961–922 BCE. There are so many legends about him that the stories have become intertwined and it is difficult to unravel authenticity from falsehood. For instance, the 17th-century textbook of magic *The Goetia: The Lesser Key of Solomon*, which developed from medieval books about magic, suggests that Solomon was alive during the 10th century BCE, or the late Bronze Age. Although the author of *The Goetia* is anonymous, the text asserts that it was originally written by King Solomon, although this has been proved to be untrue. The book is essentially a manual that claims to give instructions for summoning 72 different spirits, in particular, the spirits that Solomon is said to have evoked and confined in his bronze vessel. Respected figures such as Sir Isaac Newton (1643–1727) believed wholly in the notion of Solomon being a magician. What this means now is clearly not what it has meant to those living in past eras. Certain legends describe him as having a flying carpet that could travel so fast that it could get from Damascus to Medina

within a day. Clearly some of these concepts are not to be taken literally, but it is possible that Solomon understood various things that many others of his time did not. According to the Talmud, Solomon understood the mysteries of the Qabbalah. He was also believed to be an alchemist and to understand the power of the spirit world. It was said that he could control demons and spirits. A Roman-Jewish historian, Titus Flavius Josephus (37–c.100 CE) wrote, in his *Eighth Book of the Antiquities of the Jews* (c.94) of the magical works ascribed to Solomon, for example:

> Now so great was the prudence and wisdom which God granted Solomon that he surpassed the ancients, and even the Egyptians . . . He composed a thousand and five books of odes and songs, and three thousand books of parables and similitudes, for he spoke a parable about every kind of tree from the hyssop to the cedar . . . There was no form of nature with which he was not acquainted or which he passed over without examining, but he studied them all philosophically and revealed the most complete knowledge of their several properties. And God granted him knowledge of the art used against demons for the benefit and healing of men . . .

Solomon's genie

A Thousand and One Nights is a collection of ancient stories and folk tales written in Arabic, and often called *The Arabian Nights* after the first English translation in 1706. Collected over centuries by various writers and scholars, the tales can be traced back to ancient and medieval Arabic, Persian, Indian, Egyptian, and Mesopotamian traditions. In one of the stories, a genie—or *jinn*—had angered King Solomon who had punished him by shutting him in a bottle and then throwing it into the sea. As the bottle was closed with Solomon's seal, the genie could never free himself. Five centuries later, a poor fisherman found the bottle in his net and noticed the mark of King Solomon. He opened the bottle easily and the genie emerged, furious at having been trapped inside for so long. On seeing the fisherman, he angrily declared that he had made up his mind to kill whoever released him. Thinking quickly, the fisherman said he could not believe that such a large genie could fit into so small a bottle, to which the genie replied: "I"ll show you!" As he disappeared back into the bottle, the fisherman quickly replaced the top and threw it back into the sea.

▶

A late 19th-century illustration of the story of the fisherman and the genie, from *A Thousand and One Nights*.

Solomon (pronounced Suleiman in the Qur'an) is legendary for several things, but most of all for his great wisdom. In both the Jewish Talmud and the Muslim Qur'an, he is an important prophet. Over his 40-year reign, he built on and consolidated his father's achievements: expanding trade and political contacts, weakening tribal affiliations, building a powerful army and fleet, and engaging in an extensive building program, which included, predominantly, his palace and Temple. Because he was such a powerful figure, the Egyptian Pharaoh gave Solomon his daughter as a bride (one of his many foreign wives, but clearly an important one).

Solomon is the hero of many tales, most of them based on his great wisdom and sound judgements, but some refer more specifically to his mystical powers. According to Manly P. Hall in his encyclopedia of 1928, *The Secret Teachings of All Ages*, the name Solomon means "Light, Glory and Truth." Hall writes that medieval alchemists were convinced that Solomon understood "the secret processes of Hermes by means of which is was possible to multiply metals." This could be one of the factors that gave him the reputation of possessing great wisdom. In the Bible, after becoming King of Israel and Judah, Solomon has a dream in which God asks him if there is anything he desires. Instead of saying wealth, a powerful army, or long life, as many rulers would have done, Solomon asked for wisdom. This pleased God who immediately granted his request, and to show his approval, also bestowed riches upon him. The Bible relates that Solomon's wisdom was so great that people came from distant nations to hear his advice. The Queen of Sheba was possibly the most famous of these. It is recorded that she traveled with a train of attendants, carrying much wealth, from southwestern Arabia, to test this great wisdom.

As well as possessing wisdom, the Bible says that Solomon composed 3,000 proverbs and 1,005 songs. In the Qur'an, Suleiman is described as being in communion with nature and also with the spirit world. He commands the spirits or *jinn* (spirits of Arabian folklore) to build his temple. Both Jewish and Islamic histories record him as being a unique figure, possessing extraordinary powers and a personality that demonstrates fortitude and charisma. In several Qabbalistic legends he is portrayed as being both magical and mystical. For instance, the Seal of Solomon, a device he allegedly wore on a signet ring, is said to have come to him from heaven. Consisting of two overlapping triangles, one pointing up, the other pointing down, inside two concentric circles with the words "the most great God" inscribed within, the seal has been credited with various qualities. The ring itself was purportedly made of brass and iron: the brass part enabled him to call upon good spirits, while the iron part allowed him to evoke bad spirits. This legend was especially developed by Arabic writers, who wrote that he also received four jewels from four different angels, and that he set them in his ring which enabled him to control the four elements of earth, wind, fire, and water. In Islamic legends, the six-pointed star that these two triangles made was used to symbolize Suleiman's God-given powers, but once the Jews began using it as the Star of David, Muslims reverted to the five-pointed star.

Temple of Kings

Until David's reign, the Jews had been nomadic people, with no tradition of building for permanence. Taking into account that Biblical numbers are often symbolic, the Book of Kings and the Second Book of Chronicles records that Solomon employed an immense amount of labor over the seven and a half years it took to build the Temple.

This included 30,000 Israelites divided into groups of 10,000 working in shifts, cutting wood in Lebanon, then transporting and building with it. He employed 80,000 more to quarry stone, and a further 70,000 to carry the stone to the site and construct the Temple. There were 3,300 supervisors overseeing the work. The completed building was described as a rectangular stone structure of three stories, divided into three sections: the portico, the main sanctuary and the inner sanctuary, and measuring 60 cubits long, 20 cubits wide and 30 cubits high. Although these measurements are no longer precisely understood, it is believed that this translates to approximately 99 feet (30 meters) long, 33 feet (10 meters) wide and 49 feet (15 meters) high. Further rooms were built around the outside walls of the Temple. Despite the simple structure, it was decorated inside and out with lavish opulence. The inner sanctuary, which was known as the Holy of Holies, housed the Ark of the Covenant. It was paneled with cedar of Lebanon, overlaid with gold and encrusted with jewels. It also contained two huge cherubim made of olive-wood, signifying the zodiac, each with outspread wings of 10 cubits span (approximately 16 feet or 5 meters), which touched the walls on either side and met in the center of the room. A veil of blue, purple and crimson swathed the room, denoting the meeting of heaven and earth. On the altar was a golden candlestick with seven holders, corresponding to the sun, the moon, and the five major planets. Only the High Priest could enter the Holy of Holies, and even then only on certain days of the year.

In the porch were two huge pillars, made of copper, brass or bronze that were named Boaz (meaning "strength") and Jachin (meaning "God establishes"). Their capitals were decorated with carved pomegranates (symbolizing the Jewish people, fruitfulness and hope), and lilies (the eternity of heaven). It is believed that the pillars were made and placed to mark the sun's furthest risings at the solstices, and through their proportions, positions, and ornamentation, they represented the spiritual, material and cosmic worlds. An even more astonishing feature is described in 1 Kings 7, and 2 Chronicles 4, as a large basin filled with a molten bronze (or brass) sea, and in the Qur'an as a "fountain of molten brass" made specifically for the priests' ablutions:

> Then he made the cast sea; it was round, ten cubits from brim to brim, and five cubits high. A line of thirty cubits would encircle it completely. Under its brim were panels all round it, each of ten cubits, surrounding the sea; there were two rows of panels, cast when it was cast. It stood on twelve oxen, three facing north, three facing west, three facing south, and three facing east; the sea was set on them. The hindquarters of each were towards the inside. Its thickness was a hand-breadth; its brim was made like the brim of a cup, like the flower of a lily; it held two thousand baths.
>
> 1 Kings 7:23–6

Most of these spectacular features were produced by methods that were advanced for the time, including smelting, a practice closely associated with alchemy in the ancient mind, while the dyes used in the veil and other Temple fabrics were exceptionally rare. The Temple also allegedly contained thousands of ornately carved columns and pilasters made of pure white Parian marble, quarried on the Greek island of Paros. It was a wonder when it was built, and the impact of its magnificence did not seem to diminish over the centuries it stood. In another unique and advanced feat, every component of the entire Temple was pre-prepared before being transported to Jerusalem. Whether made of stone, wood, or metal, every element was cut, shaped, constructed, and numbered, and then taken to Temple Mount, where it was fitted into its correct place by means of wooden mauls. There was no loud hammering or sawing on the site as this incredible house of God was constructed. "The house was built with stone finished at the quarry, so that neither hammer nor axe nor any tool of iron was heard in the temple while it was being built" (1 Kings 6:7).

Hiram Abiff

According to Masonic legend, as there were no architects in Judea, Solomon employed a man called Hiram Abiff from Tyre as his chief architect. Yet the name Hiram Abiff is not found in the Scriptures. In Freemasonry, however, in the section of the master mason's ritual called *The Legend of the Third Degree*, three central characters are connected with the building of Solomon's Temple. They are: King Solomon, King Hiram of Tyre, and Hiram Abiff. King Solomon and King Hiram of Tyre are mentioned many times in the Old Testament. As Egypt had lessened in importance, Tyre, an ancient city on the Mediterranean coast of Lebanon, had gained strength and independence. It had increased its trading fleet and established commercial

colonies in Sicily and North Africa. In exchange for wheat and oil, King Hiram provided Solomon with cedar wood and craftsmen to panel the interior and exterior of his Temple with wood and gold. Perhaps he also provided Hiram Abiff. With no clear mention of him in the Bible, the closest references seem to be in the Second Book of Chronicles and the First Book of Kings:

> I have dispatched Huram-Abi, a skilled artisan endowed with understanding, the son of one of the Danite women, his father a Tyrian. He is trained to work in gold, silver, bronze, iron, stone and wood, and in purple, blue and crimson fabrics and fine linen, and to do all sorts of engraving and execute any design that may be assigned him, with your artisans.
> 2 CHRONICLES 2:13–14

Hiram is also introduced in the First Book of Kings:

> Now King Solomon invited and received Hiram from Tyre. He was the son of a widow of the tribe of Naphtali, whose father, a man of Tyre, had been an artisan in bronze; he was full of skill, intelligence and knowledge in working bronze. He came to King Solomon, and did all his work.
> 1 KINGS 7:13–14

Huram (in the Second Book of Chronicles) is a variant of Hiram and it can be seen how, through various translations, Freemasonry could have ended up with the name Hiram Abi-ff, also sometimes spelled Abif or even Chiram Abiff. The two passages above describe Huram-Abi or Hiram as an exceptionally accomplished workman and artisan. Someone of his ability would not usually be an architect as well, but it would be possible. He may have been one of the 3,300 supervisors on Solomon's Temple, or he may possibly have indeed been the chief architect. Although magnificently ornamented, the dimensions and layout of the building were not complex, so it might be that this one extremely proficient worker oversaw the architecture as well as the decoration. There was a far greater tradition of building in Tyre than in Jerusalem and there were many similarities between the Temple of Melqart in Tyre and Solomon's Temple in Jerusalem. It seems that Melqart's Temple was possibly used as a prototype for Solomon's Temple and it is

Magical dye

The dyes used on the veil in the Temple were red, blue, and purple. The red was extracted from the blood of beetles and the blue and purple dyes were extracted from sea snails. This dye is believed to have originally been produced by the ancient Phoenicians (the Phoenicians were a race who lived at the eastern end of the Mediterranean and who became an important society between 900 and 700 BCE). The red, blue, and purple dyes were highly valued and

Tyrian purple in particular was prized as it did not fade but grew more intense over time, even if exposed to sunlight. Extracted from the glands of particular sea snails that are found in the eastern Mediterranean, it was extremely costly to produce. This meant that few "ordinary" people had seen such colors on fabrics, so when they were used in Solomon's Temple they were talked about with wonder, as if they were substances acquired by magic or from God.

feasible that Hiram of Tyre could have worked substantially on the Temple of Melqart before working in Jerusalem for Solomon.

Yet scholars continue to debate the existence and importance of Hiram of Tyre. The main issue is not whether he existed, but whether he worked alone as master architect of the project, or whether he was simply one of several artisans. In his *Discourse* of 1737, Andrew Michael Ramsay (1686–1743), one of the first Freemasons, declared that Solomon recorded magical knowledge in a secret book which was later laid in the foundations of the Second Temple. In Masonic legend, three men kidnapped Hiram Abiff and threatened him with death if he did not disclose the secrets he held about the building of Solomon's Temple. When Hiram refused to reveal his knowledge, his assailants murdered him. If they existed, were these the secrets contained in Solomon's book? How did Solomon know Hiram's secrets? Was the book explaining these secrets found by the Templars in the foundations under Temple Mount? Or did they discover the secrets in some other way?

As far as we know, Hiram Abiff's secrets have never been revealed. And Solomon's book, if it existed, has never come to light. But from descriptions of Solomon's Temple, the secrets could have been lost methods of construction, order, and ratio that originated from ancient Greek (Pythagorean) and ancient Jewish (Qabbalistic) systems of numbers and letters, as well as from various philosophies of other ancient peoples, including the Egyptians, Chaldeans and Brahmins. There were certainly multifaceted, mythical and mystical traditions built into the fabric of the Temple. As with most legends, many subsequent layers, theories, and speculations have made uncovering the truth extremely

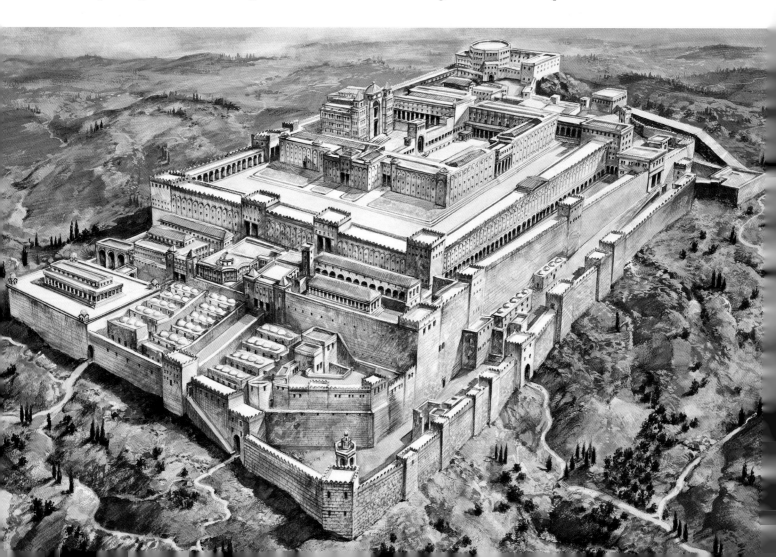

difficult. Hiram Abiff might be significant or he might not. If the account of his attack and murder is true, the secrets he would not reveal might have been the smelting techniques used for the brass fountain, dyes and dyeing techniques, or other advanced methods of production that most masons knew nothing of. Comparisons with Hiram's story and the Egyptian god Osiris can be drawn and links have been made connecting this legend with Jacques de Molay, the last Templar Grand Master, who died maintaining his innocence and refusing to divulge the Order's secrets. Then again, the story of Hiram Abiff could be an allegory; an illustration of the power of secrecy and of honoring a commitment.

The Temple site

The Temple was only one of the major buildings that Solomon constructed on Temple Mount. Adjacent to it, over 13 years, he built a magnificent palace made predominantly of cedar of Lebanon. As well as his dwelling, the palace served as an armory and treasury. He also built a judgment hall and a palace for the daughter of the Egyptian Pharaoh, one of the most important of his 700 wives. Nearly four centuries after Solomon had built the Temple, however, King Nebuchadnezzar of Babylon destroyed it, in August 586 BCE. A Second Temple was started in 520 BCE and later vastly enlarged by Herod (c.74–4 BCE), while he ruled the Jews on behalf of the Roman Empire. The location of this Second Temple was identified by those who ordered its construction, and by many since, as the site of the original Temple of Solomon. This Second Temple was destroyed during the First Jewish Revolt against the Romans, which broke out in 66 CE. When the Roman Emperor Titus finally crushed the insurrection four years later, the Second Temple was accidentally destroyed by fire. Over 600 years later, in 691 CE, the Sunni Umayyad Caliph Abd al-Malik ordered a shrine to be built on the site, to honor Muhammad's Night Journey to heaven. The shrine was called Qubbat Al-Sakhra, or the Dome of the Rock, while the Al-Aqsa mosque, which meant "The Furthest Mosque" as it marked the furthest point from the place where Muhammad ascended to Paradise, was built next to it by 715. The site is the third holiest place in Sunni Islam. After two earthquakes destroyed the original Al-Aqsa mosque, in 1035 the Fatimid Caliph Ali az-Zahir built another, which was the one used by the Templars and which still stands today. Unlike the Dome of the Rock, which reflects the Byzantine architecture of the Church of the Holy Sepulcher, the Al-Aqsa features many characteristics of Islamic architecture, including elaborate enamel-work decoration. The dome of the mosque was originally made of ribbed lead sheeting that glinted silver in the sun. (The lead from 691 remained, but by 1965 it had deteriorated, so it was replaced with a gold-colored aluminum bronze alloy covering. After this rusted, in 1993, the covering of the roof was replaced with gold.)

In 1869, a year after the American author Mark Twain (1835–1910) had traveled to Jerusalem, he published a compilation of letters he had written called *The Innocents Abroad*. He believed that the mosque was made from the pieces left over from the First and Second Temples:

> Everywhere about the Mosque of Omar are portions of pillars, curiously wrought altars, and fragments of elegantly carved marble—precious remains of Solomon's Temple. These have been dug from all depths in the soil and rubbish of Mount Moriah, and the Muslims have always shown a disposition to preserve them with the utmost care.

An impression of Solomon's palace and Temple, made in Italy in the 20th century, by an unknown artist.

At the end of the 11th century, 770 years before these observations, when the Crusaders conquered Jerusalem, they aimed to restore all the places featured in the Bible as holy sites. Along with the Holy Sepulcher, Temple Mount was the most important as the spot upon which the First and Second Temples were built. To demonstrate its importance to them, relatively early in their existence, an illustration of Solomon's Temple was featured on the back of Templar Grand Masters' official seals.

Templar tunnels

Baldwin II was the first Crusader king to live in the Al-Aqsa mosque on Temple Mount, but because he had to spend so much time in Antioch, he neglected it. When the Templars moved in, little had been done to modernize it or simply to make it habitable. So after they had been assigned an area within it, they began restoring the building, constructing quarters suitable for their purpose. Over the 70 or so years of their occupation, they expanded the site, adding an apse, cloisters, a church, offices, and living accommodation, as well as vaulted annexes to the east and west. They used the extensive vaults beneath the building as stabling for their horses and, although the Muslim dynasty of the Fatimids had cleared out these underground chambers when they occupied Jerusalem during the 10th and 11th centuries, the Templars undertook further investigations even deeper within the foundations.

Although the early existence of the Order is vague and William of Tyre recorded that there were only nine knights for some considerable time, in approximately 1170, a Jewish traveler, Benjamin of Tudela (1130–73), recorded that 300 knights lived in the Temple of Solomon "who issue therefrom everyday for military exercise." Almost two decades later, the Muslim chronicler Imad ad-Din (1125–1201) wrote that after Saladin conquered Jerusalem in 1187, he ordered every trace of Templar building on Temple Mount to be removed.

In 1867, a team of British Royal Engineers, led by a Captain Wilson and Lieutenant Warren, investigated beneath the Al Aqsa mosque. They found a vertical shaft through solid rock, approximately 80 feet (25 meters) deep, reaching down to a system of tunnels that radiated out under the Dome of the Rock. In the tunnels, the investigators found various indications of Templar occupation, including the remains of a lance, part of a Templar sword, a spur and a small Templar cross. This discovery inspires more questions than it answers. As they built the tunnels so precisely, did the Templars have a purpose, or know what they were looking for? Were they given their quarters in the Al-Aqsa mosque with the express purpose of digging beneath it? Was the Order established purely for this, rather than their well-publicized undertaking of protecting pilgrims? For what other function could the tunnels have been built? And if they were seeking something, did they find it?

Relics

During the Middle Ages, relics became particularly important aspects of Christian worship. The physical remains of a holy person, their belongings, or other objects closely linked to their lives were believed to have spiritual powers and were revered as a direct

The official Knights Templar seal, showing Solomon's Temple on the back.

spiritual link or accession to God. Stimulated by the Christian belief in the afterlife and the resurrection, in the immortality of the soul, and in the role of saints interceding for humans in heaven, this worship of relics generated fierce controversies within the Church. Such worship gave rise to various feasts, shrines and pilgrimages. Buying, selling, and even stealing bodies or parts of bodies became common. Relics were rarely verified as this would be almost impossible at that time, but it meant that there were often multiple versions of one object, such as several Holy Lances, for instance. Even worse, the stealing of relics from churches became a problem as monasteries and cathedrals sought to obtain the most highly prized objects. The most prestigious relics were those associated with Christ and the Virgin Mary, but because they had both ascended to heaven, this posed a problem as there were no human remains to claim. So the most valued relics soon included such things as the baby teeth of Jesus, a phial of his blood, the nails or wood from the Cross, the Virgin's milk or remnants of her veil. Considered priceless, all relics were usually stored and displayed in highly crafted reliquaries that were invariably covered in gold, silver, enamel, and semi-precious stones. Devout Christians could see and worship some of these relics for a fee, while others were sold by merchants to private individuals, usually at extortionate prices. Religious communities came to rely on the income they generated through charging the faithful to visit their relics. Meanwhile, "relic merchants" often travelled along pilgrims' routes, preying on those who were keen to do all they could to save their souls and charging them for the honor of praying in front of the relics they carried. Charlatans began robbing graves for human bones to sell as the relics of saints, and "relics" brought back from the Crusades were especially revered. Although the veneration of relics was not directly called for by God or explicitly practiced in the Bible, certain biblical passages were interpreted as indications that this was part of Christian belief, such as:

> As a man was being buried, a marauding band was seen and the man was thrown into the grave of Elisha; as soon as the man touched the bones of Elisha, he came to life and stood on his feet.
> 2 Kings 13:21

> Then suddenly a woman who had been suffering from haemorrhages for twelve years came up behind him and touched the fringe of his cloak, for she said to herself, 'If I only touch his cloak, I will be made well.' Jesus turned, and seeing her he said, 'Take heart, daughter; your faith has made you well.' And instantly the woman was made well.
> Matthew 9:20–22

> God did extraordinary miracles through Paul, so that when the handkerchiefs or aprons that had touched his skin were brought to the sick, their diseases left them, and the evil spirits came out of them.
> Acts 19:11–12

Archaeological investigations on Temple Mount

Over the last couple of centuries, although there have been some archaeological excavations at Temple Mount, most have been stopped or prevented. The expedition undertaken by the British Royal Engineers in 1867 was sponsored by Queen Victoria, and although it was restricted because of the religious sensitivities about the location, the men cleared the site of the extensive filth, garbage, and debris that had accumulated over the years. They exposed ancient walls and several architectural surprises, but no mystical secrets. Since 1967, when Israel took control of the Old City, some archaeological excavations have been organized by Israel and the Waqf, the Muslim authority in charge of the Al-Aqsa mosque. But there have been few of these and they have almost always been stopped early as they have sparked angry demonstrations by those who feel that the holiness of the site means that it should not be tampered with.

In the early 12th century, it is highly likely that King Baldwin II, Patriarch Warmund, Hugh de Champagne, and Bernard of Clairvaux would all have been interested in obtaining relics from Jerusalem and any of them may have briefed the Templars to search in the holiest sites for the most sacred relics they could find. It may be that well-educated men such as these had heard of possible locations or where certain relics or secrets could be found. So the Templars could have been specifically searching for lost religious texts, objects or bones, or targeting certain objects, following requests or orders from others.

The Ark of the Covenant

One of the most legendary objects in history, the Ark of the Covenant has inspired perhaps more conjecture than any other biblical artefact. As soon as he had established the city's safety for his people, King David took the Ark to Jerusalem. A wooden box overlaid with pure gold, large enough to contain the stone tablets inscribed with the Ten Commandments, the Ark had been passed down to him for safekeeping and was believed by many to have supernatural powers. Accounts abounded of it bringing victory in battle, bestowing blessings on the worthy, and sending plagues to enemies, although it was not usually seen as a kind of magical talisman, more as a revered—and somewhat feared— object that physically embodied God's communion with Moses when he was leading the Israelites to their own land. As it represented this agreement made directly with God, the Ark of the Covenant is one of the most important objects in the Bible, yet its ultimate fate is unknown. For nearly four centuries, following the building of Solomon's Temple, it is believed to have remained untouched in its inner sanctuary, even though it was worth a fortune with its covering of gold, and later kings of Israel experienced many troubled times and crises. It is not mentioned during the pillage and destruction of the Temple by the Babylonians in 587 BCE, but it is often assumed to have been destroyed at that time. The last time it is referred to in the Bible is in 2 Chronicles 35:1–4:

> What happened to the Ark of the Covenant? Was it still there when Nebuchadnezzar came, or had it been removed previously by the Jews?

> Josiah kept a passover to the Lord in Jerusalem; they slaughtered the passover lamb on the fourteenth day of the first month. He appointed the priests to their offices and encouraged them in the service of the house of the Lord. He said to the Levites who taught all Israel and who were holy to the Lord, 'Put the holy ark in the house that Solomon son of David, King of Israel, built; you need no longer carry it on your shoulders. Now serve the Lord your God and his people Israel. Make preparations by your ancestral houses by your divisions, following the written directions of King David of Israel and the written directions of his son Solomon.

Forty years after this, King Nebuchadnezzar of Babylon captured Jerusalem and raided the Temple. He returned within ten years, took what was left in the Temple and then burnt the entire city. This prompts numerous questions. What happened to the Ark of the Covenant? Was it still there when Nebuchadnezzar came, or had it been removed previously by the Jews? If not, did Nebuchadnezzar take it, or even burn it? An account in the Second Book of Maccabees states that the prophet Jeremiah hid it in a cave before Nebuchadnezzar arrived, but Maccabees is only recognized as part of the authentic Bible

Priceless rubble

A news story reported by various sources, including *The Israel National News*, tells of rubble from Temple Mount that is being investigated by archaeologists. Starting in November 1999, the Islamic Waqf conducted a construction project on Temple Mount, removing vast amounts of rubble, which they dumped in the Kidron Valley. Since 2004, Israeli archaeologists have been working on the rubble, sifting through it painstakingly to ascertain more about the history of Temple Mount. The many artefacts they have found there have included such things as: coins from the Jewish revolt against the Romans that resulted in the destruction of the Second Temple; pottery and a figurine from the period of the First Temple; ceramic oil lamps from the Second Temple period and a Crusader arrowhead. These, and the many other items that have been found so far, are beginning to establish a clearer picture about the history of the site, but they also tellingly demonstrate that there were many artefacts from all significant historical periods present when the Templars were living there.

▲

The Dome of the Rock on Temple Mount in Jerusalem.

by Roman Catholics and Eastern Orthodox Christians, and not by Protestants or Jews. Yet the Maccabees story is not the only mention of this occurrence. The Mishnah, part of the Talmud, ancient Jewish oral traditions that descended from Moses and were written down by rabbis in about 220 CE (often called the "Oral Torah"), gives details about many of the Biblical people and places, from 536 BCE to the first century CE. The Mishnah does not claim to give new messages or laws but, rather, it presents further information about existing traditions. Like the Maccabees account, it mentions that Jeremiah hid the Ark of the Covenant before the Babylonian attack. There is another more tangible reason that makes it unlikely that the Babylonians took the Ark, alongside the many other objects they took from the Temple—they wrote detailed lists of what they took, but made no mention of the Ark. According to some sources, King Josiah, one of the final kings of the First Temple period, learned of the imminent invasion of the Babylonians and hid the Ark. One account states that he dug a hole under the place they used for storing wood on Temple Mount and buried it there. Yet another account states that Solomon anticipated the eventual destruction of the Temple, and so had an underground chamber prepared in the rock directly below his Temple, and it was there that Josiah eventually hid the Ark.

In 1952, an archaeologist found a copper scroll in a cave near Khirbet, Qumran on the shores of the Dead Sea. Accepted as one of the Dead Sea Scrolls, the Copper Scroll differs from the other scrolls, which are written on parchment or papyrus. Between 1947 and 1956, thousands of fragments of biblical and early Jewish documents were discovered in 11 caves near Khirbet, and these proved to be extremely important in helping our understanding of the Bible and in illuminating the cultural and religious background that gave rise to both Judaism and Christianity. The Copper Scroll is written in Hebrew on copper mixed with a little tin and, unlike the other scrolls, which are extra biblical documents, it features a list of locations at which various invaluable treasures are buried or hidden. Dating from c.50–100 CE, the list is an inventory of items that were taken from Solomon's Temple before its destruction—valuables that have not been seen or accounted for since. Among other things, the Copper Scroll claims that the "Tabernacle of the Lord" was hidden in a desolate valley—40 stones deep under a hill on its east side. Through this, it is speculated that the Jewish sect who wrote the Dead Sea Scrolls may have buried the Ark in the Jordanian desert before they were overpowered, or placed it in a carved-out secret chamber "40 stones" under Temple Mount.

Contemporary biblical archaeologist and architect Dr Leen Ritmeyer (1945–) spent 22 years in Jerusalem studying the site of Temple Mount. Through his examinations and available historical resources of the site, he reconstructed the original Temple of Solomon and the Second Temple, plus later additions and expansions. But the Supreme Muslim Council was unwilling to allow further archaeological excavations, so Ritmeyer's proposals about any secrets the site may hold cannot be substantiated. His research, however, confirmed the traditional view that the ancient Jewish Temple once stood in the same place as the Dome of the Rock. Using further historical data supplemented by modern photographs, Dr Ritmeyer also believes that he has identified the exact location of the Ark inside the Temple and its size. Based on his measurement of the Biblical cubit, he suggests that the Ark was exactly 52 × 31 inches (132 × 78.7 centimeters). While scholars and archaeologists do not all agree, all acknowledge that Ritmeyer's suggestions are plausible, and most agree that the Ark was never placed in the Second Temple. It may have been destroyed or taken away and hidden before the Temple was sacked, or it could remain hidden under the ground beneath Temple Mount even now, or somewhere else close by. There is the possibility that it was found by others long after the Jews had possessed it but, if so, what they did with it and where it is now remains a mystery. Ritmeyer believes that it is possibly still buried deep within Temple Mount, in the secret chamber that was built either by King Solomon or by King Josiah. The Mishneh Torah, 14 books of Jewish religious law, compiled between 1170 and 1180, was written by one of the most important rabbis in history, Rabbi Moshe ben Maimon, or Maimonides (1135–1204). It states that the prophet Jeremiah gave instructions to King Josiah that it was imperative for him to remove the Ark of the Covenant from the Holy of Holies in the Temple of Solomon. As Josiah reigned over Jerusalem from 641 to 609 BCE, this was over 20 years before the Babylonians overran the city. The chamber forming the Holy of Holies is purported to be carved out of bedrock with a similarly carved tunnel to reach it. This is not the tunnel found by the team of engineers in 1867, so, with this in mind, in 2009 further investigation was undertaken by several of Israel's leading rabbis. For 18 months, they excavated, but said that they needed a further 18 months of digging to get close to what they were seeking. Unfortunately, owing to religious and political pressure from the Arab world, the Israeli government discontinued their activities and they did not find what they were looking for.

These are not the only theories about the whereabouts of the Ark, however. One belief focuses on western Africa and follows an Ethiopian legend that claims that the Queen of Sheba had a child by King Solomon. The boy was called Menelik, which means "the son of the wiseman." When he was 20 years old, Menelik traveled to Jerusalem to study at his father's court. But Solomon's priests were jealous of him and insisted he leave. While Solomon accepted this, he also ordered that all first-born sons of other elders in his court should accompany Menelik. As they left Israel, Azarius, the eldest son of the High Priest, stole the Ark of the Covenant. Once they reached Ethiopia, Menelik founded the "second Jerusalem" and today, the ancient church of St Mary of Zion is said to house the Ark, which is traditionally brought out every January for a celebration known as Timkat.

▶

The church of Germigny-des-Prés, Loiret, France, built in 806. The central apse features this shimmering mosaic of two cherubim above the Ark of the Covenant.

Other theories maintain that in accordance with the information on the Copper Scroll, along with other temple treasures, the Ark is hidden in a cave near the Dead Sea, believed to be on either the River Jordan's east or west banks. In recent decades, numerous caves in this region have been excavated, including some which contained the Dead Sea Scrolls, but although many other artefacts were also recovered, no evidence of the Ark was found.

Apart from there being no physical or archaeological evidence that the Templars found the Ark of the Covenant, as devout Christians, they would have known of the biblical stories that recounted how dangerous the Ark was. The Bible tells that any unauthorized touching of the Ark of the Covenant resulted in death, as a story in the Second Book of Samuel verifies:

> When they came to the threshing-floor of Nacon, Uzzah reached out his hand to the ark of God and took hold of it, for the oxen shook it. The anger of the Lord was kindled against Uzzah; and God struck him there because he reached out his hand to the ark; and he died there beside the ark of God.
>
> 2 SAMUEL 6:6–7

In the Book of Joshua, the story is told about priests carrying the Ark to the River Jordan, whereupon the river separated, opening a pathway for the Israelites following the priests to pass through:

> When the people set out from their tents to cross over the Jordan, the priests bearing the ark of the covenant were in front. Now the Jordan overflows all its banks throughout the time of harvest. So when those who bore the ark had come to the Jordan, and the feet of the priests bearing the ark were dipped in the edge of the water, the waters flowing from above stood still, rising up in a single heap far off at Adam, the city that is beside Zarethan, while those flowing towards the sea of the Arabah, the Dead Sea, were wholly cut off. Then the people crossed over opposite Jericho. While all Israel were crossing over on dry ground, the priests who bore the ark of the covenant of the Lord stood on dry ground in the middle of the Jordan, until the entire nation finished crossing over the Jordan.
>
> JOSHUA 3:14–17

Later in the Book of Joshua, the Ark of the Covenant is carried by seven priests in a seven-day procession around the walls of Jericho, while they sound the trumpets of seven rams' horns. On the seventh day, the massive city walls collapse. The Ark also killed two sons of Moses, just because they looked at it. It was considered by Jews to be so dangerous to look upon that it was always carefully wrapped up in a veil, animal skins, and a blue cloth.

As devout Christians, the Templars would have known how dangerous the Ark was. The Bible tells that any unauthorized touching of it resulted in death.

A 19th-century painting by Benjamin West, of the Biblical story of Joshua crossing the River Jordan with the Israelites and the Ark of the Covenant. "...The Israelite officers went through the camp, giving these instructions to the people: 'When you see the Levitical priests carrying the Ark of the Covenant of the Lord your God, move out from your positions and follow them.'"

A 20th-century writer (see Chapter 7, pages 179–211) claims that the original nine members of the Templar Order discovered the Ark of the Covenant early in their formation while digging under Temple Mount—and the evidence of this can be seen on a pillar in Chartres Cathedral in France. Known as the Portal of the Initiates, the pillar features a carving of the Ark of the Covenant being loaded on to a wheeled cart, to be transported somewhere. Several historians have suggested that the Templars had connections with Chartres and the later, 20th-century speculation builds on that, claiming that the carving depicts the Templars moving the Ark of the Covenant. The theory is that they found the Ark in Jerusalem, but anticipating the Templar arrests in the early 14th century, they moved their secret, sacred possession to France. There is more on this theory in Chapter 7, but most historians maintain that the carving simply portrays the Ark being transported, either by Moses when it was first made to house the Ten Commandments, or by King David or King Solomon, before it was placed securely in the Temple.

The Dome of the Rock has been refurbished many times since its initial completion in 691 CE, and while living there, the Templars studied many of the materials, proportions and building methods that were used in its construction. Much of this was used in Templar churches across Europe. The Dome of the Rock was built around "the Foundation Stone," or the most sacred site in Jewish tradition, as it is believed to be the location of the Holy of Holies in Solomon's Temple. The Muslim builders of the shrine of the Dome of the Rock echoed the measurements and design of the Church of the Holy Sepulcher. The diameter of the dome is 66¼ feet (20.2 meters) and its height is 67¼ feet (20.5 meters), while the diameter of the dome of the Church of the Holy Sepulcher is 68½ feet (20.9 meters) and its height is 70½ feet (21.5 meters).

A section of the bronze doors of the baptistery in Florence, made by Lorenzo Ghiberti between 1425 and 1452. Dubbed "The Gates of Paradise," this part of the door depicts the story of The Fall of Jericho. Joshua is on a chariot, preceded by Israelites carrying the Ark of the Covenant.

Known as the Portal of the Initiates, the pillar features a carving of the Ark of the Covenant being loaded on to a wheeled cart, to be transported somewhere.

Similar, affiliated legends about the Templars and their excavations have been put forward by various writers but—without real evidence—they remain unverifiable. These include the idea that while digging, the Templars found some biblical documentation, which has been variously described as scriptural scrolls, details of sacred geometry or information regarding long-forgotten wisdom that was understood by the ancient Jewish and Egyptian elders. It would appear by their tunnels that the Templars had a preconceived plan or had been told where to dig, but in the mid-20th century, an international team investigated the Dead Sea Scrolls, and searched every site listed in the Copper Scrolls. The team did not discover anything relating to the Temple of Solomon or any biblical artefacts, but they found further evidence of Templar presence in the 12th century. This has given rise to further speculation that the Templars were looking for certain things and that they knew where to look. However, at this time, nothing further can be ascertained as there still remains a lack of any actual proof that they found anything.

Travel to the West

In 1127, Hugh de Payns, accompanied by a few knights who have been named as Godfrey de St Omer, Payen de Montdidier, Robert de Craon, and André de Montbard, traveled to the West from Jerusalem. Sent by King Baldwin, they were on a mission to recruit new members to the Templar Order and to elicit donations. This was two years after Bernard of Clairvaux had written to Hugh de Champagne when he left France to join the Templars, and nine years after Bernard had allowed his monks Rossal and Gondemar to leave the Cistercian Order and join the Knights Templar in the Holy Land. In 1126, before Hugh de Payns left Jerusalem, King Baldwin had written to Bernard of Clairvaux, explaining that the Templars were seeking papal approval and some financial support for their mission in the East. Bernard, who was probably in communication with Baldwin and Hugh de Champagne, had anticipated the king. In a letter to the Pope in 1125, Bernard had complained that the proposal by a fellow Cistercian abbot, to lead a mission of Cistercians to the East, would be a waste of time and money. What was needed, he wrote, is a "mission of fighting knights, not singing and wailing monks."

As soon as Hugh de Payns arrived in France in the autumn of 1127, donations of silver and armor and grants of land were given to him for the Templar Order. Theobald, Hugh de Champagne's heir, started the donations by giving them land at Barbonne-Fayel, 31 miles (50 kilometers) north-west of Troyes. Other wealthy landowners and church leaders were soon forthcoming with further donations, recording in charters their reasons for donating. For instance, a knight, Baldwin Brochet d'Hénin-Liétard, who is believed to have fought alongside some of the Templars in the First Crusade, gave all his property at Planque in Flanders to the Order, because "the knights of the Temple of Jerusalem abound in the heights of charity and the grace of laudable renown." In the summer of 1128, Hugh de Payns was welcomed with great honor in England by King Henry I, who gave them gold and silver. At the end of his reign, he also gave them land in Holborn, London, where the first Templar church was built. Also in England, Matilda of Boulogne gave the Templars a valuable manor in Essex, which became Temple Cressing. Matilda

overleaf
In this 1840 painting by François-Marius Granet, the Knights Templar are being officially recognized at the 1129 Council of Troyes.

was married to Stephen of Blois, a grandson of William I of England who, among other things, deserted the Crusader army before Antioch, giving rise to the belief by Emperor Alexius that the rest of the Crusaders had perished. Stephen ruled England from 1135 to 1154. Hugh de Payns was given several more tracts of land around England, especially in Lincolnshire and Yorkshire, before he moved on to Scotland and received further donations there. King David of Scotland gave the Templars the lands of Ballantrodoch that became their Scottish headquarters. It is believed that Hugh de Payns also traveled to Rome where he requested an audience with Pope Honorius II (r. 1124–30) who, as could be expected, was particularly sensitive to the situation in the Holy Land and keen for pilgrims to travel there safely. Back in France, Hugh de Payns solicited even more donations as he and his fellow Templars traveled to Troyes to meet Bernard of Clairvaux. Apart from André de Montbard, who was Bernard's [younger] uncle, none of the Templars had yet met the clever and charismatic Bernard of Clairvaux.

The Council of Troyes

On 13 January 1129, a Church Council convened in the town of Troyes, the capital city of the Champagne region. Troyes was close to Hugh de Payns' birthplace and the Council was originally organized to declare "the Peace and Truce of God." This was a

The Champagne region

The birthplace of the First Crusade, the Cistercian Order, and the Templars, during the medieval period, Champagne in the northeast of France, was an important trading area. From the tenth century it was ruled by the self-made Counts of Champagne who created a powerful principality. Popes and kings respected and responded to the rulers of the region and several of these rulers became even more powerful than the French monarchs. The cities of Troyes, Rheims, and Épernay became particularly important commercial centers. The area achieved its greatest strength under Hugh de Champagne's successor, Theobald IV the Great (who was Count of Champagne from 1125 to 1152).

◀

Portrait of Theobald I, who was Count of Champagne as Theobald IV and also King of Navarre, nicknamed posthumously "the Troubadour" (Chansonnier). He was also famous during his life as a brave Crusader, and the first Frenchman to rule Navarre.

contemporary movement of the Catholic Church to attempt to limit the violent in-fighting within feudal societies. It was an organized effort to control civilians through spiritual sanctions rather than by force. The Council was also assembled to settle disputes regarding the Bishops of Paris and to deal with other Church matters of the time, but it was seen by those with interests in the Knights Templar as a way of being heard. Although the Pope convened it, he did not attend, but several of the most eminent churchmen did. These included the papal legate, Matthew, Cardinal-bishop of Albano; ten bishops and two archbishops, Renaud of Rheims and Henry of Sens; and several Cistercians, including Bernard of Clairvaux.

> Who else could look after pilgrims but men of the cloth and who else could defend them, but noble knights?

Once the essential Council business had been dealt with, Hugh de Payns and Bernard of Clairvaux used the forum as a vehicle to gain acceptance for the Templars as an official order, to be recognized by the entire Latin Church and not just those living in or visiting the Holy Land. Hugh was first to address the Council. He spoke about how he started the Order and its mission. Not everyone was favorably inclined towards the notion of holy men taking up arms, as many did not understand the logistics of it and felt the contradiction of faith and fighting to be too great. Hugh's impassioned tale helped to persuade many of those present that it would be the most reasonable and reliable method of defense in the Holy Land. Who else could look after pilgrims but men of the cloth and who else could defend them, but noble knights? As well as the church officials present, the Council included Theobald, Count of Champagne, William, Count of Nevers, and another nobleman, André de Baudemant, who were there specifically to give the clergy a trustworthy understanding of active, combative life. Then Bernard of Clairvaux spoke, championing the Templars' unique situation and their circumstances. Speaking passionately and articulately, he explained why it was imperative that the Church gave the Order its full support. Without them, Jerusalem might as well be in the hands of the infidel, he declared, as no one could visit the holy places. Look how many innocent Christians had been murdered on their way to pray at the holiest of shrines; was it not time, now that Jerusalem was back in the hands of the Christians, that this barbarity and bloodshed was stopped? Eventually, the Council agreed and gave the Templars its full backing.

Until that time, the Templars had worn simple tunics as ordinary knights, and one of the first things Hugh requested was an official habit with a Rule to follow to make them comparable to other monks and mark them as an official confraternity. After much discussion, the Council granted them permission to wear white habits like the Cistercians (white signified purity) and they were given a monastic Rule to follow in line with several other religious orders. The Rule was decided upon mainly by Bernard of Clairvaux, who took into consideration their fighting activities and other specific physical needs as soldiers. So it was with immediate effect that at the Council of Troyes in 1129, the Poor Fellow-Soldiers of Jesus Christ and the Temple of Solomon were officially endorsed.

CHAPTER 3

The Guardians

Within a short time of the Council of Troyes, the Knights Templar were viewed generally as being exceptionally dependable and doing a job that many thought was too difficult to undertake. They quickly established a reputation for being brave and honest, and deserving of the support of good Christians everywhere.

Even before their trip to the West, the Templars had started to receive donations from Europe to assist them in their onerous task in the Holy Land. The first donors were mainly French nobles who either had connections with the First Crusade or who believed that, by being generous to such a cause, their souls would be saved. Donations began coming in more frequently after the Council of Troyes and these varied from small items such as a sword or a saddle, or larger gifts, such as tracts of land, an annual gratuity, or a horse.

When Hugh de Payns returned to Jerusalem after the Council of Troyes, he left some Templars in Europe with the specific task of fundraising and attracting new recruits. One of these men, Hugh Rigaud, avidly canvassed for donations around France and Spain from 1128 to 1136. He and another Templar, Raymond Bernard, were extremely successful at this task, attracting numerous generous donations which included land, vineyards, gold, armor, and servants, as well as some more unusual items, such as rounds of cheese, a pair of old breeches, and a well-worn cloak. Although they were not guarding the Holy Land, these men remained a vital part of the Templar Order, as they traveled across Europe, enlisting new members and encouraging their fellow Christians to generously support their cause. It was an essential task, both at the beginning when the Order had nothing, and later when they had a great deal of property that needed maintaining and enterprises that needed advancing. Some of the donations they attracted were quite astonishing. One of the earliest was a church on the Côte d'Azur, given to them in the early 1120s, although perhaps because of the cost of its upkeep, the Templars gave it back in 1124. In 1128, a married couple from Toulouse, Peter and Borella Bernard, gave themselves and everything they owned to the Order, with a promise that their children would be given the opportunity to become Knights Templar when they grew up. In 1132, an exceptionally powerful family from the Languedoc region, the Trencavels, gave the Templars a small farmhouse in Carcassonne and the services of a man, Pons of Gascon, as well as his entire family. The following year, Bernard de Canet and Aymeric de Barbaira gave the castle of Douzens in the Carcassonne region to the Templars. Aymeric and his brother William Xabert also pledged themselves to the Order. In 1129, a married couple gave the Templars a house, a farm, and further land in the suburb of Troyes-Preize to the south-east of Paris. Other substantial endowments and privileges were granted from nobles, kings and princes in various countries across western Europe. For instance, in 1120,

▼

Two early donations given to the Templars were a farmhouse and castle in Carcassonne, in the Languedoc region of France.

the wealthy and powerful Count Fulk d'Anjou had visited the Knights Templar in Jerusalem and given them an annual revenue of 30 pounds of silver, which was an extremely substantial sum in those days. In an effort to elicit Templar support for their battles against the Moors, the rulers of Aragon, Navarre, and Castile were particularly generous. Although fighting the Moors in Spain was never part of the Templars' brief, the Spanish gifts were so generous that they considered it, although without making any promises. In March 1128, Raymond Bernard was given the castle of Soure and surrounding lands by Queen Teresa of Portugal, the daughter of Alfonso of Castile. She openly gave this in exchange for a promise from the Templars that they would help the Spanish and Portuguese to win back territory from the Moors.

Early expansion

During these first years, as fast as gifts were being bestowed upon them, new recruits mainly from France, Spain, England, Italy, and Germany were volunteering to join the Templars. The endorsement of the Order by the Council of Troyes and the consequent confirmation of this by Pope Honorius II had initiated their sudden rise in prestige and appeal. The original nine men who had started the Order of the Poor Fellow-Soldiers of Jesus Christ and the Temple of Solomon were men of good birth who had abandoned their lands and their families in order to defend the most sacred places of the Bible, and this romantic concept added to the status of joining their ranks. Some joined for just a temporary period, such as Raymond Berenguer IV, the Count of Barcelona, and a group of his vassals, who served for a year. According to Orderic Vitalis, a chronicler of 11th- and 12th-century Normandy and England, Fulk d'Anjou traveled to the Holy Land in 1119 or 1120 and also joined the Templars for a year. He returned to Europe towards the end of 1121, but continued to subsidize the Knights Templar annually, generously maintaining two knights in the Holy Land for a year each. By joining the Order for just a short period, these men of noble birth could experience the discipline of being part of a monastic brotherhood, feel they had helped the Christian cause and still return to their old lives afterward and retain their own wealth.

In spite of their harsh regime that to a great extent mirrored Bernard of Clairvaux's Cistercian Order, official Church recognition and royal connections made the Knights Templar particularly respectable and esteemed by the nobility, monarchs, and ordinary people alike. From the start, they retained close connections with the King of Jerusalem—far closer than they did with the Patriarch—and this set a precedent. Throughout their existence, Templars encouraged and extended a similar closeness with other kings and nobles across Europe. This particularly helped their cause as many who donated did so in order to ingratiate themselves with monarchs or other powerful leaders.

▲

Pope Honorius II, who endorsed the acceptance of the Templars at the Council of Troyes.

▶

The marriage of Queen Mélisende of Jerusalem (1109–60) and Fulk V of Anjou (1092–1143), who insisted on ruling in his own right alongside his wife.

Fulk d'Anjou

In 1127, the mission undertaken by Hugh de Payns to the West was partly a diplomatic assignment on behalf of King Baldwin II of Jerusalem. Along with their immediate issues of establishing the Order with the Pope and raising money, Hugh was directed to persuade Fulk, the Count of Anjou, to accept a proposition. Baldwin had no sons, so had named his eldest daughter Mélisende as his successor to rule Jerusalem after him. Baldwin wanted Fulk to return to Jerusalem and marry her. In agreeing to his proposition, Fulk would be Mélisende's consort when she ruled Jerusalem.

Fulk V of Anjou was born in Angers in western France between 1089 and 1092, the son of Fulk IV of Anjou and Bertrade de Montfort (who later bigamously married King Philip I of France, which was why he could not go on the First Crusade). On his father's death in 1109, Fulk became the Count and the following year he married Erembourg, the Countess of Maine. They had two sons and two daughters, but Erembourg died in 1126 when their youngest child was 13. In April 1128, Fulk entertained Hugh de Payns at Le Mans. The idea of marrying the beautiful, half-Armenian Mélisende was not abhorrent to him, but he did not want to be consort to a queen; he wanted to rule alongside her as king in his own right. Baldwin did not need long to consider Fulk's demands. Jerusalem

needed a strong ruler and Fulk was wealthy, intelligent, and brave. He would help Mélisende in the difficult task of ruling Jerusalem. In February 1129, Fulk gave Anjou to his 16-year-old son Geoffrey and left France for Jerusalem with Hugh de Payns. In Jerusalem that June, he married Mélisende. Meanwhile, Baldwin had married his second daughter, Alice, to the new count of Antioch, Bohemond II, and his third daughter, Hodierna, to the Count of Tripoli. The youngest daughter, Yveta, chose to take holy vows, and Mélisende had the convent of Bethany built for her sister. As Abbess of Bethany, Yveta wielded great power in the Church and at the Court of Jerusalem. By the time Fulk died in a hunting accident in 1143, he and Mélisende had two sons: Baldwin, who would carry on the line in Jerusalem, and Amalric. Baldwin II had died in 1131, the year before his second grandson was born, leaving the Holy Land in the hands of his offspring.

Geoffrey d'Anjou

The powerful royal line of Plantagenet kings who ruled England from 1154 to 1485 descended from Fulk and Erembourg's elder son, Geoffrey d'Anjou. Although Geoffrey and his predecessors were known as the Angevins (from Anjou), when he became founder of the line, his heraldic device of a sprig of yellow broom known in Latin as *planta genista* became the family emblem and name. Geoffrey and the Angevins were French but Geoffrey's wife, Matilda, was Henry I of England's daughter, and so granddaughter of William the Conqueror. In 1154, Geoffrey and Matilda's son, William the Conqueror's great-grandson, took the throne as Henry II, and began the rule of the Plantagenet dynasty.

The Templar Rule

In the early days of the Knights Templar before the Council of Troyes, they pledged their vows of "poverty, chastity and obedience." For this, they gave up worldly goods, wore simple tunics and ate what food they were given or could afford with their small allowance from the king and Patriarch of Jerusalem. They did not womanize, or fraternize unnecessarily with anyone outside their community, and they strictly adhered to the wishes of their Grand Master (of whom Hugh de Payns was the first), who took his lead mainly from King Baldwin II and to a slightly lesser degree, Warmund the Patriarch.

However, once they were accepted as an authentic monastic order at the Council of Troyes, Bernard of Clairvaux worked out a number of suitable regulations by which they should live, known as the Rule. Basing this on his own Cistercian Rule, with some additions and slight changes to accommodate the fighting element of the Order, Bernard drew up 73 clauses for the Templar Rule. It decreed that, on joining the Order, every Templar gave up all worldly goods and renounced his will. They were required to be prepared to fight in defense of Christians and sacred Christian sites, and to be prepared to die for this cause if necessary. In relinquishing their wills and worldly goods, they could either give it all to their heirs and descendants, or to the Order (which many did). Married men could only join the Templars as sergeants and their property was then bequeathed to the Order rather than to their wives upon death. Knights were to wear white habits as a symbol of their mental purity and physical chastity, but for the many other Templars who joined as squires, chaplains, sergeants, farmers, servants, or temporary members, brown or black habits were regulation. No fur or other finery was permitted to be worn by any of them, not even to decorate their horses' bridles. There was one concession; because of the heat in the Holy Land, and later in their dwellings in other Mediterranean countries, they were allowed to wear light linen shirts from Easter to All Saints' Day on 1 November. The Rule, while strict, also gave them some strange concessions. If they were washing their hair, for instance, when the bell rang to call them to prayer, they were allowed to be late. They were to remain frugal in all things. Although at first their poverty precluded this, as the Order grew, each knight was permitted to have three horses and one squire to take care of them. The Rule often seemed a little illogical, but every order originated from a considered reason and careful thought. For instance, no Templar was allowed any form of lock to secure anything personal, to prevent any secretiveness; they were not allowed to sleep in total darkness—some form of light always had to be illuminated so there could be absolutely no clandestine behavior at any time. Falconry and hunting, two of the secular knights' main pastimes, were also prohibited.

The Rule was not just about discipline; it was also a guide, giving instructions on a wide range of considerations, such as how to admit and treat novices to the confraternity, what kind of conversation was suitable (or unsuitable) between them, with too much discourse being discouraged. Templar brothers were required to cut their hair, keeping it short with the usual monk's tonsure, but they were not allowed to shave their beards—which was unusual. Conventional religious orders were forbidden to have facial hair, so the insistence on beards singled them out. While this was different, many of the clauses in their Rule were the same as for other religious brotherhoods, such as eating in silence, not losing one's temper, attending regular daily religious services, and eating meat only on three days of the week. Templars were requested to limit their speaking

From *The Story of Godfrey of Bouillon*, 1499, showing the Knights Templar before Jerusalem.

and conversation and to behave "decently and humbly, without laughter." The Rule was so controlling that they were even told how to cut cheese and under what circumstances they would be allowed to leave a meal table early (only in the event of a nosebleed). They went to bed at midnight and rose again at 4 a.m. Although they were forbidden any private possessions, collectively the Order was allowed land, property, and servants. The care of their horses was of fundamental importance and the Rule gave strict instructions about this. All members of the Order were responsible for the horses—and the weapons, and although they had servants and squires to do this, knights had to oversee the tending of their horses and the cleaning of their equipment at least twice every day. Horses and other animals kept by the Templars were also allocated according to the Rule. Knights had strong, powerful warhorses; turcopoles (locally recruited mounted archers) had lighter, faster horses; men at arms and other working Templars who were not knights had access to palfreys (well-bred riding horses), mules, donkeys, camels, and packhorses.

Overall, discipline was enforced by the Grand Master, or once there were many different chapters in various countries, the second in command, who was known as the Master, was in charge. The Rule set out appropriate punishments for all kinds of misdemeanors, from penances to expulsion, but also other, somewhat crueller penalties were enforced for certain offences. These included beatings, being put in irons or being made to eat off the floor. Rules of discipline differed for knights and other members of

the Order. For instance, if a knight lost his weapons in battle, he had to remain and fight on, while in similar circumstances, a sergeant or servant was allowed to retreat. The Rule was written in Latin, but as most Templars, particularly early on in their history, could not read Latin, it was soon translated into French. This in itself showed up ambiguities and discrepancies in the Rule and gradually, new clauses were added. Eventually, the number of clauses increased to several hundred.

In Praise of the New Knighthood

After Pope Honorius II died in 1130, a conflict arose between the supporters of the new Pope, Innocent II (r. 1130–43), and his enemies who declared his election to be illegitimate. At the forefront of his defense was Bernard of Clairvaux who was highly instrumental in gaining greater support for Innocent and assisted in eventually securing his position. In gratitude, at the Council of Pisa in 1135, Pope Innocent II ratified the Rule of the Templar Order. Yet despite the Templars' growing consequence, there were many who still opposed them. Critics, who included theologians, wrote impassioned essays against the idea of military monks, declaring that it was irreconcilable for men of religion to fight. According to Christian beliefs, monks should be prepared to die rather than take up arms, even in self-defense.

To defend the Templars against these critics, Bernard, who understood the dangers of the situation in the Holy Land and recognized that fighting but honest and trustworthy men were needed there, wrote a long document entitled "In Praise of the New Knighthood" (*Liber ad milites Templi: De laude novae militiae*). It took him two years to pen the open letter that justified the existence of a group of monks whose only real purpose was to fight and kill, contrary to other, traditionally gentle monastic endeavors. In his usual articulate and persuasive manner, Bernard passionately compared the devout and godly Templars with secular knights who, he declared, fought only for greed, vanity and self-aggrandizement. He declared that this new knighthood humbly served God and he outlined the virtues of a holy war, explaining that a religious order of knights was necessary to take up both spiritual and physical swords in the Holy Land. He proclaimed that if any of the Templars were to die in battle for Christ, their deaths would be especially glorious, while ordinary knights who fought for secular causes were in danger of damnation:

> The knight of Christ, I say, may strike with confidence and die yet more confidently, for he serves Christ when he strikes, and serves himself when he falls. Neither does he bear the sword in vain, for he is God's minister, for the punishment of evil-doers and for the praise of the good. If he kills an evil-doer, he is not a man killer, but, if I may so put it, a killer of evil. He is evidently the avenger of Christ towards evil-doers and he is rightly considered a defender of Christians. Should he be killed himself, we know that he has not perished, but has come safely into port. When he inflicts death it is to Christ's profit, and when he suffers death, it is for his own gain . . . I do not mean to say that the pagans are to be slaughtered when there is any other way to prevent them from harassing and persecuting the faithful.
> Bernard of Clairvaux, "In Praise of the New Knighthood," c.1135

With this essay, Bernard may have succeeded in his purpose, but he also irritated several people. Many were angered that so saintly a monk should be openly encouraging fighting and killing. After his death, another Cistercian, Walter Map (c.1140–1208/10), wrote equally vehemently against him and the Templars. Although not as influential by any means as Bernard of Clairvaux, Walter Map planted one particularly negative thought about the Templars being proud or arrogant and greedy—and this stuck. It was a small thing at the time, and Map's words were not published, but this perception of the Templars adhered to them for the rest of their existence.

Friend or foe?

As soon as the Templars were established in Jerusalem, they began their policing duties along pilgrims' routes. Naturally this did not mean that they immediately began fighting with any non-pilgrims they met beyond the walls of Jerusalem, but they set up a rota for patrolling the vulnerable areas around the city. They also worked on other methods of peacekeeping. As each perceived the other as evil, it was initially inconceivable to any Christians or Muslims that friendships should occur between them, and considering the Templars' task was to overcome any marauding infidels, it would have seemed incongruous to most that they could ever communicate civilly with each other. But the Templars pursued a cautious policy, aiming for peaceful control of the menace beyond Jerusalem's walls. Accepting that most of the attackers were intractable and violent, the Templars approached some of the Arab leaders with a view to establishing treaties. The plan was to persuade Muslim rulers to restrain their own miscreants. This would make the Templars' job far simpler. By even speaking civilly to the Arabs, the Templars were breaking new grounds in diplomacy. For some considerable time, this proved a fairly successful solution to the problems.

It took him two years to pen the open letter that justified the existence of a group of monks whose only real purpose was to fight and kill.

The first treaty made between the Christians and the Muslims was with the leader of the Assassins, a fanatical Shi'ite sect that formed in approximately 1091 in fierce opposition to the Sunni Seljuk authority. The name Assassin possibly derived from the word Asasiyun, which essentially means the foundation of the faith. Also known as the Hashshashin, Assassins were generally young men with great physical strength and endurance. Necessarily intelligent and well-educated, they worked by gaining knowledge about their enemies' culture, native language and personalities. Trained to disguise themselves, to steal into enemy territory and to murder stealthily rather than openly in battle, they were shrewd, furtive and cunning. This is the origin of the word assassin. Although they were the Christians' adversaries, in sharing their common hatred of the Seljuks, the Assassins were not as averse to dealing with the Templars as many other Muslim forces were. However, it was not the Templars themselves but the King of Jerusalem who first approached the Assassins with the offer of a treaty. After this, the Templars made several more military alliances with surrounding Muslim rulers, learned the language and about the culture of Islam, and so strengthened their guard in the Holy Land.

More than mere treaties, however, some Templars and Muslims even became friends with each other. For instance, Usama ibn Munqidh (1095–1188), a poet, author, warrior, and diplomat from northern Syria, recorded that he had become friendly with several Christian knights and even stayed with the Templars "who were my friends" in Jerusalem. The Templars allowed him to pray in a chapel they had built in the Al-Aqsa mosque.

▶
A portrait of Gregorio Papareschi, Pope Innocent II from 1130 to 1143, by Giuseppe Franchi (1731–1806).

INOCẼT. II.s
EX BÑTINI.
P. M.

While it seemed a rational approach in the Holy Land, this behavior was viewed by those living in Europe as going against all that the Christians had fought for. Other monastic orders and ordinary Muslims and Christians who were based elsewhere would neither have understood nor condoned what they would have perceived as duplicitous behavior. When word spread back to Europe of the Templars' secret dealings with the infidel, many suspicions were roused about their motives and their true faith and loyalties. This notion subsequently fueled several conspiracy theories about the Knights Templar.

Meanwhile, the situation in Outremer remained fraught with difficulties, and although minorities befriended each other and a few treaties were made, there was little trust between the various factions. William of Tyre refers to the Templars in Tripoli taking payment from the Assassins, and the Assassins negotiating with the King of Jerusalem for another form of alliance in order to stop the payments. Nearly a century later, another chronicler, Jean de Joinville (c.1224–1317), recorded that the Assassins were making regular payments to both the Knights Templar and the Knights Hospitaller as reparations for murdering members of the Christian orders. In 1197, Henry II de Champagne, ruler of Jerusalem from 1192 to 1197, sought an alliance with the Assassin leader, which was immediately reported to Christians in Europe and caused outrage. Although diplomatic relations were necessary where these religious people lived in close proximity to each other, most writers were wary of relating too much about them for fear of provoking anger in Europe.

The relationships between the Templars and the Muslim and Jewish communities in the Holy Land were more complex than Christians living beyond Outremer would understand. Despite his pressure on them to fight the infidel, Bernard of Clairvaux always insisted on tolerance, and even on the benevolent treatment of Jews. He only wanted Jerusalem and other important Christian sites to be under Christian control, but beyond that, he told the Templars to try to tolerate other religions. When the Templars acquired more land and property in the Holy Land, in several cases they became landlords to many Jews living there and were allegedly friendly and respectful.

Privileges and growth

In 1139, in an unprecedented show of approval, largely due to his indebtedness to Bernard of Clairvaux, Pope Innocent II granted the Templars numerous privileges in a papal bull. Among other things, he made them responsible only to the Holy See, which was an enormous privilege. It gave them strong papal protection and local or any other clergy had no command over them, which was unprecedented. No one but the Pope could excommunicate them, or give them any form of penance. This annoyed many who did not have such advantage and it irritated some bishops and priests who had no authority over the Templars as they had over other orders. The privileges continued. Templars were absolved from feudal duties, entitled to keep any spoils of war, allowed to collect tithes, to build their own churches, to bury their own dead, and to try and execute criminals. They were given the right to choose their own Grand Masters and Masters, and Templar properties and revenues were free from taxation to the Crown or the Church. All

> When word spread back to Europe of the Templars' secret dealings with the infidel, many suspicions were roused about their motives and their true faith and loyalties.

Depiction of Mary with Child and Saints from 1486 by Filippino Lippi (1457–1504). The inclusion of John the Baptist with Bernard of Clairvaux and two other saints is a demonstration of Bernard's importance in the Church.

these concessions were almost unique and certainly singled the Templars out as a particularly favored order. In 1144, Pope Celestine II (r. 1143–44) declared another bull that became called *Milites Templi* (Knights of the Temple) and caused even greater resentment within the clergy. Pope Celestine urged Christians everywhere to donate as much as they could to the Templar Order. If annual donations were made to the Templars, he declared, any penance subsequently given to the donor for any sins would be reduced by one-seventh. This was galling for almost all other orders and local churches, as it encouraged the faithful to donate to the Templars all the time rather than to their local churches.

▶
A 17th-century portrait of Guido Ghefucci da Castello, Pope Celestine II from 1143 to 1144. A controversial pope, he particularly favored the Templars, causing huge rancor within the clergy.

This, however, was not the biggest insult to other members of the Church. *Milites Templi* also decreed that when any Templars entered a town, city, village, or castle to collect contributions, even if the place was under interdict, the churches should be opened "in a friendly manner in honor of the Temple and in respect for these knights, and divine offices should be celebrated" *(Milites Templi*, 9 January 1144). Interdict was one of the few—and the strongest—methods the Church could use to enforce the obedience of its followers. It was the only way of punishing rulers and their parishioners for grave sins and it was generally effective. If a location was under interdict, usually due to the ruler's wrongdoing, then no one could attend Mass, receive communion, or go to confession. In the medieval period, this was particularly frightening to God-fearing Christians. By the *Milites Templi* insisting that, for any period in which Templars were present, that interdict would be lifted and everyone could rush into church and receive all the sacraments needed for the salvation of their souls, then the interdict would lose its power and it would not matter too much if it was re-imposed once the Templars had left. This took the gravity out of the interdict and also meant that grateful worshippers would be as generous as they could to the Templars, and any money they might have given to their local church would no longer be forthcoming.

The rite of sepulture

In 1146, according to William of Tyre, Pope Eugenius III granted the Order the right to wear the splayed red cross on their tunics, symbolizing their willingness to suffer martyrdom in the defense of the Holy Land. It was a great honor as it marked them out once again as being specially selected. Sixteen years later, Pope Alexander III (r. 1159–81) issued another papal bull confirming and endorsing all the grants and concessions that previous popes had bestowed upon them. With such advantages, it facilitated their rapid expansion. Almost inevitably, the Templars were criticized for taking advantage of their favors, but they would have been criticized

The Splayed Cross

It is believed that the splayed cross, also known as the cross pattée or crux gemmata, had been worn by members of the ancient tribe of Benjamin, one of the biblical tribes of Israel. It was later used in early Christian art and made popular in Christianity after Empress Helena claimed to have found the True Cross in the early fourth century, when she had a piece of the True Cross placed in an elaborate, cross-shaped reliquary with splayed ends. When the Templars adopted it, they did not use it consistently, nor did the design remain the same. In general, the lines making up the Templar cross are of equal length, unlike the more common Christian crucifix symbol that has a longer vertical line. It is believed that the Templars adopted the equal-length cross with splayed ends after seeing it in churches of the Coptic faith, an Eastern Orthodox branch of Christianity founded in Egypt. The splayed cross was not their exclusive symbol, although they have become known for it in recent centuries, and they did not all wear it as an official emblem. Among others, the Knights Hospitaller and the Teutonic Knights also wore other forms of the splayed cross, as did St. George.

CÆLESTINVS II P.M.

equally had they not done so. Although other religious orders were also given privileges, it seemed that the Templars were being given more than their fair share. Eventually, there were few areas left where they did not receive special advantages. In 1162, Alexander III even gave them the "rite of sepulture," which meant they could administer last rites and actually bury their own dead.

> We . . . concede to you the power of constructing oratories in the places bestowed upon the sacred house of the Temple, where you and your retainers and servants may dwell; so that both ye and they may be able to assist at the divine offices, and receive there the rite of sepulture; for it would be unbecoming and very dangerous to the souls of the religious brethren, if they were to be mixed up with a crowd of secular persons, and be brought into the company of women on the occasion of their going to church.
>
> Excerpt from Pope Alexander III's papal bull, 7 January 1162

In giving last rites and burying their own dead, once again the Knights Templar subverted the power and authority of local clergy. It was a bonus for the Templars but it exacerbated rancor elsewhere. Presumably reflecting the fact that both brotherhoods were based in the Holy Land and had specific functions to fulfil, the Hospitallers received similar grants and privileges. At the Third Lateran Council held in 1179, Pope Alexander received several complaints from priests and bishops that the Templars and the Hospitallers were abusing their privileges and undermining the authority of local clergy:

> Now we have learnt from the strongly worded complaints of our brethren and
> fellow bishops that the Templars and Hospitallers . . . exceeding the privileges
> granted them by the apostolic see have often disregarded episcopal authority,
> causing scandal to the people of God and grave danger to souls.
> EXCERPT FROM THE THIRD LATERAN COUNCIL, 1179

The Council decreed that the Templars and Hospitallers were to amend their behavior or they would find themselves under interdict. In 1207, Pope Innocent III (r. 1198–1216) wrote to the Knights Templar, complaining that they had grown proud and were misusing their prestigious position. He wrote that virtually anyone with money in their pockets was permitted to join the Order, including those who had been refused access to the Church, even wrongdoers. It seems that in their eagerness to raise as much money as possible, some Templars were perceived to be greedy and not always honest.

Commercial activities

With so many donations and new members pledging their worldly goods to the Templars, their expansion was rapid and, from the start, they ran the Order like a business. By the early 1140s, they had acquired enough new members, land, and money to be able to initiate and uphold military operations in both the Holy Land and the Iberian Peninsula, as they conceded to Spanish and Portuguese rulers that they would help to fight the Moors in exchange for valuable land and castles. They were also given properties in other parts of Europe. So while their main priority was always the protection of Jerusalem, their farms, vineyards, mills, mines, barns, houses, chapels, castles, and preceptories (known as *commanderies* in French) all over Europe meant that they could open chapters in various countries. By 1150, they owned areas stretching from the Holy Land to Tuscany, from Spain to Portugal, from Provence to Occitan (now known as Languedoc/Roussillon), from Normandy to England and Scotland, and from Denmark to the Orkney Islands. A huge amount of personnel was needed to maintain this vast amount of property and land, in the form of servants, farriers, laborers, blacksmiths, carpenters, farmhands, armorers, and herdsmen, and, without any prior experience, the Templars quickly became an efficient and extremely well-organized enterprise. This maximized their capital, which in turn increased their efficiency and strength.

From the middle of the 12th century to the beginning of the 13th, increasing international trade and social stabilization occurred throughout Europe, as the feudal system changed and agriculturalists, bankers and merchants gained wealth and status. A network of roads was being built across Europe, and although their vow of poverty meant that they owned nothing personally, the Knights Templar played an active part in the creation of this new, business-led society. They had started to generate substantial

A fresco by Luca Spinelli (1332–1410), showing Alexander III entering Rome with the Germanic Emperor, Frederick Barbarossa (1122–90).

PP III

✠ INNOCENTIVS ẼPS SERVVS SERVORṼ DI. DILECTIS FII
SPECṼ BEATI BENEDICTI REGLARẼ VITÃ SERVANTIBVS
VIRTVTṼ NVLLṼ MAGIS EST MEDVLLATṼ QVÃ ꝙ OFF
CARITATIS. HOC IGIT ATTENDENTES. CṼ OLI CAVSA DEVOTIC
VRE QVE BEATVS BENEDICT SVE CONVERSIONIS PRIMORDIO CONS

income through trade, farming, industry, and shipping. Their farms, fields, and vineyards yielded grain, wool, fruit, vegetables, wine, and olives. They received rents and tithes from numerous properties in the form of land and buildings; they rented these to workers and farmers and for regular markets and fairs that were common at the time, and they mined coal and metal ores. They were also involved with smelting metal, which was used in tool and armament production. As they expanded, they necessarily used commercial shipping companies, but by the early 13th century they began building up a fleet of their own, another undertaking that they developed carefully and conscientiously, taking advice from experts. With so many members now of all different nationalities, they could research the best practice for any of their enterprises in each country. In a relatively short time they owned a large fleet of well-made ships, with bases in Italy, France, Spain, and the Holy Land. Templar ships carried travelers, including pilgrims, merchants and troops, as well as provisions and supplies, horses, and many commercial consignments including wine, olive oil, wheat, wool, cloth, armaments, and various other foodstuffs across Europe and possibly even further afield. Much of this was for their own use, but even more was for their commercial enterprises. Among other ports, they based their ships in England at Bristol, Dover, Portsmouth, and Rye, in France at La Rochelle and Marseilles, in Italy at Bari and Brindisi, and in Outremer at Acre, Caesarea, Sidon, Tortosa, and Tripoli. For many years, their main port was Acre, a walled city built on a promontory with a double harbour. It was very important for the Christians who lived in and around Jerusalem, but after Saladin took Jerusalem in 1191, it became even more so; and the Templars moved their headquarters there.

Within 50 years of their foundation, the Knights Templar had become a strong and prosperous commercial force, while they still continued to maintain their primary role of defending pilgrims in the Holy Land. Within 100 years of their humble beginnings, they had developed into the medieval equivalent of an international corporation, with interests in almost every form of commercial enterprise of the time.

Medieval markets and fairs

As a consequence of the rapidly growing economy across Europe, markets and fairs became extremely popular, providing an opportunity for people to buy and sell goods. Markets took place on the same day each week or month. Traders paid tolls to the landowners where they set up their stalls. The same happened at annual fairs, which were held in practically every town. Usually beginning on the day of a religious festival, they attracted visitors from all over the country or further. As well as staple goods, they also offered luxury products, including silks, oils, perfumes, jewelry, and spices from distant locations. Fairs also attracted entertainers such as jugglers, acrobats, and fortune tellers, all of whom had to pay the landowners for their sites. Fairs were the result of new trading links and they expanded as new roads were built. They became important events on the calendars of local towns and villages, as popular and thriving social events and meeting places, and the Templars made good profits by renting their land for the purpose.

◀
Late 13th-century fresco of Pope Innocent III, who complained to the Templars that they were too proud and arrogant for holy men.

Banking

Traditionally, monasteries had provided safe deposit facilities for holding important documents and valuable belongings, but once the Templars had a large number of properties across various countries, they were in a unique position to do this and more. As they gained resources and achieved successes in their various ventures, they also invented new ways to manage their finances and to help others do so too. They began forming an institution that many regard as the origin of modern banking. Pilgrims were targets for bandits mainly for the gold and silver coins they carried, so, from about 1150, the Templars introduced arrangements for looking after the pilgrims' money. This in effect was the introduction of bank accounts (although some bankers already existed in Italy, they looked after papal funds and other extremely wealthy patrons, not the finances of ordinary people). With so many preceptories throughout Europe and the Holy Land, the Templars were well placed to start a system of safety deposit boxes, whereby pilgrims could deposit their cash in one preceptory and receive coded receipts—or credit notes—to redeem their money for a modest fee at any other preceptory. These were, essentially, the first traveler's checks. Largely due to their meticulous banking transaction record-keeping, the money was reimbursed with few problems and they quickly developed the reputation of being dependable and safe. In general, it was far safer to deposit money with Templar bankers than to keep it almost anywhere else. The Templar bankers kept scrupulous accounts, enabling them to run an effective, reliable, and accountable concern, where they were able to trace and keep watch over transactions with ease and remain completely transparent and trustworthy. As money could be handed in at one Templar preceptory and cashed at another, whether in the same country or abroad, it was exceptionally convenient, and the Templars soon offered many further financial services as well. These included current accounts; safe deposits for documents, money, gold, jewelry, and other precious items; loans, credit and pensions; and they acted as tax collectors and receivers. Although

▲

A view of the Port of Acre, used extensively by the Templars. It lay in the bay of Haifa and was protected on one side against the open sea by the city and by a strong dyke wall on the other two sides.

initially they had started providing banking facilities just for pilgrims, within a short time, they had gained a broad range of customers. The Templar banking system grew rapidly, and later, their Paris preceptory became their main financial center. As their wealth increased, the Templars also began lending money to European rulers—which augmented their own importance and perceived trustworthiness. For instance, in 1147 King Louis VII of France (1120–80) borrowed a large amount of money from them and repaid them with tracts of land in Paris (where they subsequently built their Paris preceptory). At the time of the Magna Carta in 1215, King John of England gave them his Crown jewels for safe-keeping and borrowed money from them; and, as soon as it was built, the Paris Temple came to be used as a stronghold for monarchs' important jewels and money. The Templar bankers soon became involved in large and complex transactions that were usually only undertaken by merchants and bankers in Italy.

This fast-growing early system of international banking that soon became indispensable, arose mainly through several unique advantages held by the Templars. Firstly, their reputation as pure, determined, honest and restrained religious brothers seemed to be unshakeable. Secondly, their preceptories were as impregnable as forts, and as knights who were protecting the innocent in the Holy Land, they offered unparalleled security and protection, both when money was locked away safely and if it was being moved around for customer convenience. Thirdly, they used codes on their traveler's checks, based on Latin, so if any thief stole them, they would be exposed as soon as they tried to cash the check. Finally, the Templars were extremely parsimonious themselves as this was part of their Rule—and the financial burdens of the organization were huge. But this was open to certain corruptness, as some took advantage of the rights bestowed on them by popes and sold the right for ordinary people to be buried in Templar cemeteries.

But the banking system had a great and positive effect. Individuals felt confident leaving their money with Templar bankers, pilgrims in particular felt safer and when they no longer carried large bags of money on pilgrimages, they became less tempting to assailants. Consequently, over time, not only did pilgrimages become safer, but the Templars also became highly respected international financiers. In this way, they also helped to change the Church's attitude towards money lending, which contributed to the rise of capitalism.

> This early system of international banking arose mainly through several unique advantages held only by the Templars.

Paris and London preceptories

Based on the round plan that followed the Byzantine design of the Church of the Holy Sepulcher with Arabic features styled on the Dome of the Rock, Temple Church in London was moved from its original location to its current site near Fleet Street when the Templars needed more space. The necessary enlargement was primarily because of the success of their banking activities, so by 1160 they began building a church closer to the River Thames along with various other buildings and facilities around it, including military training grounds and an impregnable preceptory. The church was consecrated by Heraclius, the Patriach of Jerusalem, on February 10, 1185, probably in the presence of King Henry II of England. At the time, the round church would have been colorfully decorated; even the gargoyles were painted in bright colors. The Templars' Paris preceptory was built in a similar way to the London buildings, with a church, training grounds and living accommodation built adjacently. The Parisian structure was completed by 1147 and was a large complex, fortified like a castle with strong crenellated perimeter walls, towers and vast vaults, built on land the Knights Templar were given by Louis VII in what is now known as the Marais district. The Paris Temple became the headquarters of Europe's finances. Today, only the London church remains and nothing is left of either the London or Paris preceptories.

The white slave trade

Before the Templars were established, one major fear of pilgrims travelling to Jerusalem was of being kidnapped and taken as slaves. While slavery did not occur in most of Europe, in parts of the Mediterranean and the East, the trade was rife. Coupled with their devout Christian beliefs ("love thy neighbor as thyself") it might seem incongruous that the Templars could be involved with the slave trade themselves, but while in the Holy Land, both the Templars and the Hospitallers often used slaves to help them build their preceptories and castles. It is even thought by some scholars that they used slaves to row their galleys and shipped others to places such as Sicily and Aragon, where they needed more workers. Although unverified, this is plausible, as it was an easy method of gaining free labor. The slave trade had existed for centuries among many different nationalities and was not suppressed either by the perpetrators or by the Crusaders. As it was such a huge concern, those who lived in Outremer seem to have overlooked the horrors and realities of the business.

By the time the Templars had achieved success, wealth and power during the 13th century, the white slave trade was a long-established and thriving business. Slaves were taken as spoils of war, or plucked from poor areas across Europe. This could occur in any country, but it happened particularly in Turkey, Greece, and what later became Russia. In some countries where slavery was common, if not kidnapped, the poor and destitute often even sold their own family members as slaves. Slave traders made plenty of money by shipping men, women, and children from their native countries to distant shores to be attached to wealthy households, work as prostitutes or be converted to Islam and trained to fight in Muslim armies. Without the indignation that later arose over this trade, it was not stopped, even though it was not condoned. Only one major uprising occurred and that was by the slaves themselves. In Egypt in the 1240s, slaves who had been converted to Islam rose up and killed their masters. They became the Mamluk rulers in Egypt and Syria.

Mamluk slaves had become a powerful caste in some Muslim societies before their uprising, and they later fought and overcame the Crusaders at the end of the 13th century. They were an unusual caste of slaves who were expensive to purchase originally and had never been allowed to carry weapons or perform certain tasks. In some places, Mamluks held a social status above freeborn Muslims.

Life in the Order

Unlike other orders, Templar knights generally did not practice self-denial through fasting or abstaining from certain foods (although they were only allowed meat three times a week and never on Fridays), nor did they punish themselves with hair shirts or beatings for example. As their number was made up predominantly of knights, the Rule accepted that they needed to be strong and healthy and one of their main duties was to be ready to fight at any time. This was another reason why some Templars joined for short periods—the training and discipline was good for the body, while being in a religious environment and partaking in regular prayers was good for the soul. This kind of retreat became quite popular and both parties gained, as all the temporary Templars were expected to donate heavily for the privilege of joining the Order for a short time. Some married men joined briefly, but they did not undergo monastic training and, although their wives did not accompany them, as the Rule insisted on chastity, to prevent any bad influence, their sleeping quarters were kept separate from the permanent, celibate Templars. The Rule's insistence on chastity was so strict that Templars were not even permitted to kiss their female relatives. Yet although the Templar knights did not fast or abstain, the ordinary monks in the Order did. Generally, for most of their existence, the Poor Fellow-Soldiers of Jesus Christ were recognized by outsiders as being particularly devout and abstemious, true followers of Christ who adhered to the asceticism of the Cistercians.

Every item of clothing and equipment, even down to the cloth used, was specified for each member of the Order. Fabrics used for their habits were of poor-quality linen; only slightly better-quality fabric was used for knights' habits than for the other Templars. Unusually for the standards of the time, every Templar was given changes of under-garments and outer-garments. This was because hygiene was important—even though they had to ask the Commander of their chapter for permission to have a bath. Too many baths were forbidden as this was believed to weaken the health and strength. While secular knights wore hose to show off their shapely calves, fashionably pointed shoes and short tunics, the Templars were not allowed to wear hose of any kind, nor pointed shoes, and their habits were longer than the popular short tunics worn by other knights—short enough to allow manoeuvrability, but not so short as to be immodest. Their clothes were checked regularly to make sure that everything was neat and clean; it was against the Rule to be unkempt or slovenly. For cold weather, they were each allowed a feather-lined cloak. Each knight was given a hauberk or chain-mail tunic, a chain-mail vest, and leggings, a linen shirt, a helmet, a cassock and a surplice, and they had the use of a spear, a lance, a shield, and a mace. Weapons had to be plain and not embellished, unless they were received as donations—but even then, only certain gifts were permitted to be used on the battlefield. Every Templar had a towel, a straw mattress, a sheet and blanket, or a quilt stuffed with wool.

Each day, two meals were served and Templars were expected to attend seven services, although most of these were shorter prayer meetings, such as matins, prime, compline, or vespers, and not full-length Masses. In contrast with other orders, new Templars had a short probationary period, although there was no regular or official period of trial and training—recruits tended to be accepted into the Order at the discretion of the Master or Grand Master. Every new member was required to meet certain simple requirements: he should be of legitimate birth, free of debt, fit to fight, and unmarried. The initiation ceremony was undertaken in secrecy, and this caused a great deal of speculation outside the Order, leaving the Templars open to all kinds of accusations. It is believed that the ceremony usually occurred among few other members. Behind closed doors, in the presence of the Master, the postulant simply knelt with his hand on a Bible, declaring his obeisance to God, the Virgin Mary, and the Templar Rule, but this has never been completely established, and it became a huge element in their later persecution. Often, the only training or period of instruction that new recruits received was a recitation of the Templar Rule. Brothers who could read were given a copy to read and in case anyone forgot, over many meals, the Rule would be read out as the monks ate in relative silence. It was a strict way of life, but whoever he was, whatever role he performed within the Order and from wherever he had come, once a man had joined the Knights Templar, solidarity, support, and discipline were paramount. It was a cohesive, efficient and innovative confraternity, with everyone working towards its collective aims. Witnesses of battles claimed that of all the fighting forces, the Templars were always the most disciplined, brave, and orderly in the face of danger and chaos. They were the first into battle and the last to retreat. Their courage, resolve and comradeship became legendary. As the Templar Rule declared:

> No one must leave his position without the permission of the commander, not even if he is wounded; and if he finds himself unable to request leave, he must send a comrade to do it for him. And if by chance it should happen that the Christians are defeated—God save us!—no brother must leave the field of battle as long as the banner of the Temple is still flying, and anyone in violation will be expelled forever from the order.

For all their activities the Templars needed a huge workforce. Following the Council of Troyes, and almost unrelentingly for many years after, recruits joined in droves, partly due to religious fervor, partly because of the passion so many felt about reclaiming and defending the holy sites, and later perhaps because they wanted to be part of a successful and exciting international organization. While many young men of good family pledged themselves to be Templar knights, many more were needed to perform all kinds of jobs and help keep the vast concern running smoothly and efficiently. Men of all ages and abilities from across Europe joined, and everyone's strengths were used to advantage. Unlike many religious orders of the period, however, the Knights Templar did not recruit children or young boys. They considered them to be too immature to be able to participate in the fighting and so could not be of any real assistance. Young boys were also seen to be unsure of their own minds and the Templars did not want to expend time and money on a boy's education, only to be abandoned when he grew up and decided that he did not want to spend his future as a Templar. So young, healthy men were encouraged to join to train for combat and older men were also welcomed, as they added considerable benefits in the forms of experience, dedication, and solemnity. Widowers who could leave

their worldly goods to their heirs—or to the Order—and join with no attachments were often encouraged to do so. In the first few years of the Knights Templar, only knights were allowed to be fully committed brothers of the Order, while sergeants and servants were employed by the Templars, but not permitted to become brothers. After some years, however, this changed and sergeants were authorized to take their monastic vows alongside the knights, assuming the full responsibilities of the Poor Fellow-Soldiers of Jesus Christ, even though they did not fight. For the rest of their existence, Templar brothers were divided into four main categories:

- knights, who fought, mainly as cavalry;
- sergeants, who came from a lower social class than knights and were usually equipped as light cavalry;
- chaplains, who were ordained priests and addressed the spiritual needs of the Order;
- farmers, who managed the Templars, property.

Then, of course, as they grew, many more Templars took up new positions to manage their vast financial infrastructure and others managed their building work and maintenance of land and property, while still others oversaw the production, upkeep, management, and use of their fleet. After the early days, for most of their existence, there were approximately 300 knights and 1,000 sergeants based in the Kingdom of Jerusalem, and when Jerusalem was lost, this main contingent moved to their new headquarters in Acre and then Cyprus. In Europe, chapters were considerably smaller, although a fairly large number was based in the Iberian Peninsula, and from the time the huge preceptory was built in Paris, a large number of men lived and worked there.

Diverse recruitment

As the Templars had so many diverse undertakings that did not apply to other monastic brotherhoods, new recruits were enlisted from all backgrounds and nationalities, even though from the start, the majority were French. Templars needed to be strong, committed, healthy, and full of stamina. Piety was a bonus, but not as important as strength and energy. Thoughtful maturity was preferable to the impetuousness of youth, honesty was more favored than cleverness, and dependability was more valued than zealousness.

▲

Built by the Knights Templar and consecrated in 1185 by the Patriarch of Jerusalem, Temple Church in London is in two parts: the Round Church and the Chancel. The Round Church was designed to model itself on the circular Church of the Holy Sepulchre in Jerusalem.

If the concept of dealing with the enemy through political agreements and even friendship was incomprehensible to outsiders, then the idea of recruiting non-Christians or those from small, alternative Christian sects into a Catholic religious order was equally difficult to understand. Nonetheless, in their need for so many members, it soon became logical or even necessary for the Templars to look beyond their immediate circle and to recruit where they could. Languedoc in southwestern France had for many years developed as a fertile region, noted for its rich and abundant produce, its wealthy, powerful families, and its mix of religions. The name, Languedoc, evolves from "the language of Oc" or "Occitan," a name that was also used for the area. Many Templars were located in the region, and they built churches, forts, castles, and villages there. They owned the villages of Théziers and La Couvertoirade and a farm at Orgnes du Rhône, for example, and they were given the church Saint-Martin-de-Tréveils near Ponteils, as well as a farm at Caissargues.

Although the idea was not accepted by the Catholic Church, living alongside each other under the protection of the leading families in the region were Roman Catholics, members of small Christian sects and nonconformists. These included Arians, Waldensians, and Cathars.

Arianism evolved from closer consideration of the Holy Trinity: God the Father, God the Son, and God the Holy Spirit. Arians were concerned that, since Jesus, the Son of God, was created by God the Father, he had not always existed, which made him subordinate to God the Father—whereas orthodox Christians believe that the three divine persons of the Holy Trinity are equal. The Waldensians were another small Christian sect, also called Vaudoise. Following a merchant from Lyons, France, named Peter Waldo, the Waldensians began their movement in Lyons in the late 1170s and gradually migrated to the Languedoc region. The Waldensian movement proposed a return to the vows of poverty and the preaching of the Gospel, as Jesus and his apostles had advocated. Originally a reform movement within the Catholic Church, the Waldensian sect was declared heretical by 1215, after it disputed the sole authority of ordained priests to preach and interpret the Gospels. Catharism was another Christian religious movement that flourished from the 11th to 13th centuries. The Cathars' beliefs are thought to have evolved originally from Eastern Europe and the Byzantine Empire, although they are believed to have emerged first of all as a sect in Bosnia before settling predominantly in southern France and Spain. Catharism soon became a large and

The word fair comes from the Latin word "feria" which translated as holy day. So the "fair" was originally a day when people gathered for worship. Soon, the Church recognized the moneymaking opportunities and began actively to sponsor fairs on feast days. Here a bishop is blessing the annual market that was held for two weeks in June outside Saint Denis in Paris. Commerce and religion had become closely entwined.

well-organized concern and, once again, most settled in the Languedoc region, where the rulers were tolerant of them and their beliefs. Although they believed in many of the same things as Christians, Cathars had their own clergy and they did not accept that one God was the creator of all. They reasoned that if he was, he would not allow so much suffering, illness and death in the world.

Two gods and two worlds

Cathars believed that there were actually two gods and two worlds parallel to each other. They believed that Jesus Christ was not really part of this world as he had never been an actual human and that his life and resurrection from death were all simulated somehow. They believed that the angry and judgmental God of the Old Testament was the "bad" God and that Jesus had been sent by the "good" God as his messenger. They also believed that the only way to salvation was to follow Christ's teachings. Like the Waldensians, they also disputed the authority of priests, but they believed that no human could perform God's work. Cathars openly voiced their criticisms of the corruption they saw in the Catholic Church. Similar to the Cathars were the Gnostics who also had a fairly large presence in the Languedoc region. Like the Cathars, Gnostics believed in dualism and declared that they knew the secret of salvation. This contradicted Christian teaching, and was viewed as heretical by the Church, but the Templars owed much of their expansion to the wealthy and noble families of the Languedoc region, and several of their greatest supporters came from these religious sects, so although they were part of the Church, they were not averse to recruiting members of their Order from within these small groups, as well as the usual orthodox Christians. As they worked and built up their Brotherhood with all its many varied pursuits, the notion of recruiting widely seemed logical to them, if not to other Christians who heard rumors of these recruitments. The men they recruited from the sects were often intelligent, well-positioned and able to assist in the efficient running of various Templar interests. Some were able to take on important responsibilities in their farming, manufacture, business, or shipping ventures. Some helped with the care of horses or armaments, or in the banking sector. Some became courageous soldiers, while others were put to use as squires. Whoever the Templars recruited, once they were in the Order, it seems that their qualities were made the best of. All adhered to the Rule and through outstanding levels of organization the entire, vast scope of the Brotherhood functioned like a well-oiled machine.

Templars needed to be strong, committed, healthy and full of stamina. Piety was a bonus, but not as important as strength and energy.

Further legends tell of the Templars recruiting from groups of people living in the Holy Land, including some from the religious group known as the Essenes, who lived communal, austere existences abstaining from worldly pleasures—perfect for the monastic existence. Inevitably perhaps, the Templars are also believed to have recruited some Assassins from the East, but none of these unusual recruitments are verified. If they did recruit from their Muslim neighbors, they seem to have chosen judiciously, as the Order was more successful than any other during the main years of its existence, in terms of efficiency and accomplishment. But of course, at a time when religion was such an important aspect of life, it must have seemed exceedingly suspect that men of the Church were closely fraternizing with heretics. Accusations that the Templars were secretly Cathars,

or even Muslims, were generated, but most of these ideas were quashed, largely because of the effectiveness of the Order. While the Templars were doing such a good job in Outremer and beyond, few wanted to question them. Additionally, glowing reports came from non-permanent members and, ultimately, all Templars had to answer to the Grand Masters, who were nearly all highly devout and honest men.

Grand Masters

Although the entire enterprise of the Knights Templar was kept running smoothly by an organized network of efficient men across the various headquarters, in absolute charge, answerable only to the Pope and making the ultimate decisions, were the Grand Masters. Grand Masters were elected by the Templars themselves and assumed a similar role to abbots in other religious orders. Both abbots and Grand Masters were perceived as representatives of Christ within their confraternities, and in the same way as an abbot, the Grand Master was expected to observe humility and compassion, following Christ's example. Nevertheless, Grand Masters did not work completely alone. As with every other aspect of the Order, the roles within were organized for efficiency. Grand Masters had a hierarchy of men beneath them to call upon. Although there was only ever one Grand Master, living in the main headquarters (Jerusalem until 1191, Acre until 1291, and after that on the island of Cyprus), next in line were the Masters, who lived in the Templar headquarters or chapters in other countries. Each Master was in charge of his chapter, but he still reported ultimately to the Grand Master at the main Templar headquarters, and the Grand Master could delegate work and decisions to any of his Masters. Succeeding the Masters were the Grand Commanders or Seneschals, who as with all Templars, were ultimately accountable to the Grand Master, but they also had to obey the Master. Grand Commanders lived in chapter houses and worked for the Masters. They administered all the lands belonging to their chapter and, in war, managed the army's movements and provisions.

▲

Peyrepertuse, meaning "pierced rock" is a ruined Cathar castle in the Languedoc region of France. Built in the 11th century, the main part of the castle overlooks the sea and resembles the prow of a ship. It was surrendered by the Cathars in May 1217.

By the time the Templars had risen in prominence in the eyes of all Christendom, most Grand Masters were treated as the equivalent of royalty. Overseeing and endorsing the Templar Rule, overseeing and managing all Templar activities, including military operations, industrial and agricultural enterprises, and all else, to be a Grand Master was a vast undertaking. Most Grand Masters held their position for life, but a few abdicated, usually to join other monastic orders. For instance, the third Grand Master, Everard des Barres (1113–74), left the Templars in 1151 and joined the Cistercians at Clairvaux. In view of their elevated status, despite being a "Poor Knight of Christ," Grand Masters were also entitled to a large entourage that could consist of four horses, one chaplain, one clerk with three horses, one sergeant with two horses, one gentleman valet with one horse, one farrier, one Saracen scribe, one turcopole, one cook, two foot soldiers, and two knights as companions.

At the beginning of the Order when they were living on the beneficence of the king and Patriarch of Jerusalem, Hugh de Payns did not have any of these privileges. After he died in 1136, the Templars in Jerusalem gathered to elect a new Grand Master. Robert de Craon, the preferred candidate of Fulk d'Anjou, was chosen. Craon was acknowledged as an intelligent man and an exceptionally astute administrator, which was what was needed from the leader of such a growing concern. Within a short time, Craon proved himself by obtaining the extra privileges from Pope Innocent II in *Omne Datum Optimum*, the papal bull of 1139. From the start of the Order until its end, there were 23 Grand Masters. Some of their histories are not known, while others are more accessible. Odo de St. Amand, for instance, was the eighth Grand Master, at the end of the 12th century, who came from Limousin in France. As a headstrong leader, he was both praised and resented. Fiercely loyal to his men, he took part in several military expeditions and achieved many victories. At the Battle of Montgisard, his knights routed the stronger Muslim force.

Grand Masters often traveled to Europe, visiting regional preceptories and European rulers in efforts to generate larger donations and assistance for the Order. The Grand Master was assisted by an elected council from members of the Order. A brother, known as the Visitor, regularly toured all regional preceptories to make sure that standards were being maintained and to take any requests or complaints back to the Grand Master and the council.

The House of Toulouse

One of the most powerful, influential, and tolerant dynasties of the medieval period was the family of St.-Gilles who became known as the Counts of Toulouse, Dukes of Narbonne, and Marquises of Provence. Through marriage, they were related to other leading families of Europe and they owned a vast area of land in the Languedoc region. In medieval times, St.-Gilles was a major commercial center and the fourth most important pilgrimage site in Europe. An important member of the family was Raymond of Toulouse, a highly revered leader of the First Crusade, who founded a new dynasty as Count of Tripoli in the Holy Land. Unlike the leaders of the Catholic Church, the Counts of Toulouse were all religiously tolerant, refusing to discriminate against Jews, Cathars, or other religious dissenters living in their region. Under their control, women enjoyed more freedom than in most parts of the world at the time, and learning and literacy flourished. Languedoc was in a thriving position geographically. Merchants crossed it regularly and new cities sprang up around the new roads. Yet, although they gained the respect of the people, the Counts of Toulouse attracted the condemnation of the Roman Catholic Church for their religious tolerance, which eventually resulted in a religious war, the fall of the House of Toulouse and the extinction of their line.

CHAPTER 4

Sacred defense

Templar property in western Europe was divided into provinces and organized by groups of officials, which changed over the course of the Order's history. Their northern European provinces were added to by 1143, with a province covering "Provence and parts of Spain," and by 1220, they had their first province in Germany.

Once the Templars had established chapters and preceptories all over Europe as well as in Outremer, they continued in their main objective of protecting pilgrims. No longer limited to the Holy Land, they soon patrolled nearly all the major international shrines. Although Jerusalem was the most notorious, other routes and sites were also extremely vulnerable and accessible to assailants. These included established routes such as the Via Francigena, which passed from Canterbury in England to France, then through Switzerland and Italy to Rome, or the Camino de Santiago ("Way of St. James"), which was one of the most important pilgrimage routes of the time to Santiago de Compostela in northwestern Spain. The Templars also guarded many actual shrines including those at the Cathedral of St. James of Compostela, Canterbury and Chartres Cathedrals, Mont St. Michel and Rocamadour in France, as well as several other sites where black madonnas were worshipped. Templar protection was so thorough that for the first time in years, pilgrims, merchants, and other travelers felt comparatively safe along the major routes of Europe, and traveling and trade increased vastly as a result. The Templars were succeeding in the role they had been given beyond all original expectation.

Black madonnas

In medieval Europe, the worship of material objects, from relics to artwork, was an important aspect of the Christian faith. Any objects relating to saints were envisaged as having supernatural powers and almost anything relating to Christ or the Virgin was believed to have particularly miraculous attributes. The Templar Order was officially dedicated to three things: the protection of pilgrims, the Virgin Mary, and all of Christendom. The Virgin Mary was their patroness and protector, and novices were told that "we were established in honor of Our Lady." So images of the Madonna were particularly significant for them. From approximately the 11th to the 15th centuries, largely because of reports of miracles emanating from them, the black madonna became a phenomenon of general Catholic devotion.

◄

A black Madonna and Child, from the Church of Saint Pierre, the Pyrenees town of Prades. These Madonnas were especially venerated and were often the object of pilgrimage from the 11th to 15th centuries. Yet little is known of their origins or the relevance of their color.

In many shrines and churches, particularly in areas with Templar, Cistercian or Cathar connections, numerous images of the Virgin Mary had dark rather than white skin. These statues and paintings were not created to appear ethnically black, as they often are in African countries. They were either created intentionally to appear European but with dark skin or they were simply conventional portrayals of the Virgin that had darkened over time for various reasons. Many darkenings were caused by a reaction of the pigment with the air. Some darkened from constant candle soot and incense smoke, and others appear dark simply because they are painted on dark wood, such as ebony, which showed through the paint. Generally found in Roman Catholic rather than Eastern Orthodox environments, the paintings nonetheless resemble Byzantine icons in their stylization, while the painted wood or stone statues are usually standing or sitting on a throne, which also reflects the Byzantine style. It is estimated that there are about 500 black madonnas in existence, mainly in churches or shrines in France, Spain, Italy, Germany, and Switzerland, with a few beyond Europe.

> As devout Christians it was quite acceptable for the Templars to revere black madonnas, but after their downfall, they were accused of "wrongly" venerating these images.

As devout Christians it was quite acceptable for the Templars to revere black madonnas as well as the paler versions, but after their downfall, they were accused of "wrongly" venerating these images. With no surviving texts to explain whether these blackened madonnas were made deliberately or by accident, analysis of their purpose remains ambiguous. This was a time of ignorance and superstition. If some of the icons were darkened deliberately, there are at least two theories that have been put forth by scholars about their purpose. One is that they were made to illustrate a text from Solomon's biblical "song of Songs": "I am black but beautiful" (*negra sum sed formosa*). Bernard of Clairvaux wrote many essays on this aspect of the Bible and he was also known to visit several shrines to black madonnas. There is a black madonna in Chartres Cathedral and in the medieval period it was one of the most revered of all the black madonnas in France. In 1150, Bernard of Clairvaux was asked to lead a new Crusade from Chartres Cathedral and, although this never happened, he remained vaguely associated with Chartres. Many claim that the Templars helped to construct the cathedral, and some have speculated that the genre of the black madonna developed from the Templars' links with the Cathars. Another theory is that black madonnas developed from images of ancient earth-goddesses, many of whom were portrayed as black, such as Artemis, the ancient Greek goddess of the hunt; Ceres, the Roman goddess of agricultural fertility; or Isis, the ancient Egyptian goddess who represented the ideal mother and wife as well as being the patron of nature and magic, whose son Horus was born on December 25.

Despite the horror expressed in the 14th century about the notion of worshipping images of pagan gods, however, this was not unheard-of. When Emperor Constantine converted to Christianity, to help his people understand the new faith they were to follow, much of the art and customs of his empire were simply transferred. This was not seen as sacrilegious; images and customs were always simply a way of helping the faithful to focus; the images were never intended to be substitutes for the real thing. So, for instance, early images of Jesus were almost identical to those that had been created of Apollo, the most important Roman god, who was created as a continuation of the image

▶

An ancient Egyptian statuette of Isis and her son Horus, 330–30 BCE. In common with black madonnas, Isis was perceived as the ideal mother and wife.

of the Greek god Zeus. In this way, ordinary people could understand that this was an important figure to whom they should pray. Images of the Virgin Mary and her child were also based on previously recognized pagan gods, simply to help the illiterate to continue worshipping in their national religion with as little confusion or disruption as possible. Many early Christian works of art are deliberate amalgamations of pagan and Christian symbolism for this reason.

The Reconquista

From early in the 1140s, through their massive increase in revenue, men and land, particularly across the Iberian Peninsula, the Templars were firmly established, with thousands of properties reaching through Europe and Outremer. As well as protecting pilgrims, they were trying to regain the entire Iberian Peninsula for Christianity. The Reconquista was a protracted period of fighting with the specific aim of recapturing land in the Iberian Peninsula from the Muslim invaders of the region, known as the Moors, who had originally invaded and conquered lands there in the ninth century. Since then, the Moors had become established and spread. After the First Crusade, the Pope acknowledged that the fight against the Muslims in Andalusia was a legitimate crusade and he granted those who fought in the Reconquista the same redemptions as had been given to the First Crusaders. The Reconquista lasted many years, and by the mid-12th century the Templars became involved, by which time the strength and unity of the Moors was beginning to break down and, after their success in the First Crusade, the Christian fighters were feeling confident and aggressive. The Templars fought in a series of wars with their legendary determination, and by the mid-13th century, most of Spain was back in Christian hands.

Further fighting orders

From small beginnings, the idea of warrior-monks protecting Christians became more valued and in demand, as the 12th century progressed. Gradually, more armed brotherhoods were formed with similar aims to the Knights Templar, particularly in the Iberian Peninsula where the fight between the Christians and the Moors was perpetual. So the first three of these new orders were Spanish: the Knights of Santiago, the Knights of Alcántara, and the Knights of Calatrava. While the Knights of Calatrava were founded to protect pilgrims on their journeys to and from the shrine of Santiago de Compostela,

the Knights of Santiago and the Knights of Alcántara were established specifically to fight the Moors. Like the Templars, they aligned themselves with established monastic orders. The Order of Santiago was founded in 1175 and followed the Rule of St. Augustine. The Orders of Calatrava and Alcántara followed the stricter Rule of the Benedictines. The Order of Calatrava received papal approval in 1164, and the Order of Alcántara, which was confusingly also called the Knights of St. Julian, was founded in 1166 although not sanctioned by Pope Alexander III until 1177. Later orders based on the same concept included the Order of Montesa, established in the Kingdom of Aragon in 1317, the Order of Christ, founded in Portugal in 1319, and the Teutonic Knights, founded at the end of the 12th century. The Teutonic Knights were officially called the Order of Brothers of the German House of St. Mary in Jerusalem. Modeled on the Knights Hospitaller and the Knights Templar, the Teutonic Knights were formed to establish hospitals and to aid German Christians on their pilgrimages to the Holy Land. Initially Catholic, this small but effective order later became Protestant.

King Alfonso's will

King Alfonso I (1073/4–1134), known as "the Battler" or "the Warrior," ruled Aragon and Navarre from 1104 for 30 years. As a second son he succeeded his brother and after marrying Urraca, Queen of Castile and León, he began using the title Emperor of Spain. Known for his prowess in battle, he set up his own military order at Monreal del Campo, which was not successful, and he spent most of his reign at war with the Moors in his own country. His marriage was dissolved in 1114 and he remained childless. In a move that he did not explain to anyone, in October 1131, three years before his death at the Siege of Bayonne, he wrote his will, leaving his kingdom divided equally to three religious orders: the Knights Templar, the Knights Hospitaller, and the Order of the Holy Sepulcher. The Order of the Holy Sepulcher had been initiated directly after the First Crusade by Godfrey de Bouillon when he became the first ruler of the Kingdom of Jerusalem in 1099. Like the Knights Hospitaller, it was not a military order until some years later.

> Therefore, after my death I leave as heir and successor to me the Sepulcher of the Lord which is in Jerusalem and those who observe and guard and serve God there, and to the Hospital of the poor which is of Jerusalem, and to the Temple of Solomon with the Knights who keep vigil there to defend the name of Christendom. To these three I concede my whole kingdom. Also the lordships which I have in the whole of the lands in my kingdom, both over clerics as well as over laity, bishops, abbots, canons, monks, magistrates, knights, burgesses, peasants and merchants, men and women, the small and the great, rich and poor, also Jews and Saracens, with such laws as my father and I have had hitherto and ought to have.
> ALFONSO I THE BATTLER, OCTOBER 1131

However, when Alfonso died in 1134, his will was deliberately overlooked by his successors and none of the beneficiaries could enforce it. Ten years later, after prolonged negotiations, the new ruler of Aragon, Raymond Berenguer IV (c.1113–62) begrudgingly gave the Templars six castles, exemptions from certain taxes, a fifth of all the land captured from the Moors, a fifth of all they plundered during campaigns against the Moors, an income of 100 sous a year, a tenth of all royal revenues, and assistance in

Detail of an illustration from a 13th-century manuscript of a battle between Christians and Moors, during the Reconquista of Spain.

constructing the castles and fortresses they built as defense against the Moors. Until that point, the Templars had not been involved in the Reconquista and they remained reluctant to be involved in the struggle against the infidel on a second front, but this situation propelled them into it. From then on, they took a major role in the conflict. Disciplined, brave, and united, they were an asset to the cause and Raymond was delighted. He continued to favor them and, in 1153, he gave them the castle of Miravet in Aragon, but his successors did not adhere to the agreement and demanded more assistance from the Templars. Annoyed at this treatment, the Templars reconsidered their position, and decided to focus once more on defending the Holy Land as their most important mission.

Living in the Holy Land

Life for Europeans dwelling in the Holy Land was very different from that in the West. Numerous Christians had remained there before the Muslims took it and even more remained after the First Crusade. The heat, the flies, the scarcity of water, and reduced availability of food were challenging. Maintaining good hygiene was difficult and mortality rates were high, particularly among the vulnerable young and elderly. Church leaders frequently appealed for more Christians to emigrate there, but Eastern Orthodox Christians always outnumbered the Roman Catholics. Apart from that, Islamic culture had developed rapidly while European culture had slowed over the last few centuries, and it was apparent to many Europeans living in the East, how far certain Islamic dynasties had developed in art, architecture, science, and medicine. While many Europeans had been exposed to aspects of Islamic culture for centuries through developments in the Iberian Peninsula and Sicily, it was not until others had settled in the Holy Land after the First Crusade that they began truly absorbing new ideas in these disciplines. By traveling abroad, ideas and learning were shared and discovered, heralding the development of the Renaissance in later years.

Continuing conflicts

While Hugh de Payns was Grand Master, the Emir of Aleppo and Mosul, Imad ed-Din Zengi (c.1085–1146), a Seljuk Turk, began making efforts to take Damascus by force, but was frequently countered by its governor Unur, who allied with the Franks against him. Even more than fighting the Christians, Zengi was intent on defeating the Shi'ites of Egypt and Damascus. In 1139, three years after the death of Hugh de Payns, Zengi successfully attacked and conquered the town of Baalbek in Lebanon. According to Ibn al-'Adim (1192–1262), a biographer and historian from Aleppo, Zengi did not keep his word to protect his captives there. Zengi "had sworn to the people of the citadel with strong oaths and on the Qur'an and divorcing (his wives). When they came down from the citadel he betrayed them, flayed its governor, and hanged the rest."

In 1140, King Fulk organized an alliance between Jerusalem and Mu'in ad-Din Unur, the newly appointed ruler of Damascus. So when Zengi attacked Damascus, the united forces of King Fulk, Prince Raymond of Antioch, and

By digging tunnels beneath the city, Zengi's army brought down its fortifications. They massacred all the male citizens of Damascus and sold all the women into slavery.

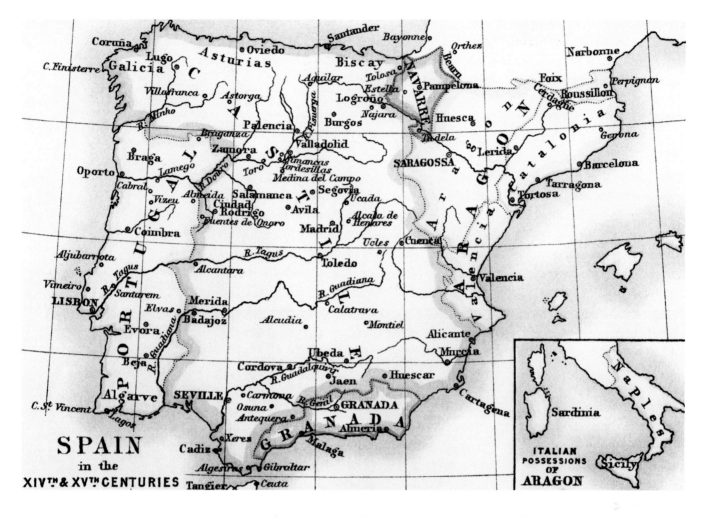

A map of the Iberian Peninsula in the 14th and 15th centuries.

Mu'in ad-Din Unur overpowered him. But in 1143, Fulk was killed in a hunting accident and his successor was his 13-year-old son. Raymond and Mu'in ad-Din Unur were no match for the determined Zengi and, in 1144, he attacked Edessa in Mesopotamia. By digging tunnels beneath the city after he had lured away its governor, he brought down its fortifications. His army massacred all the male citizens of Damascus and sold all the women into slavery. Within two years, however, when Zengi was in a drunken sleep, his own eunuch stabbed him to death. He was succeeded by his two sons, Saif ad-Din Ghazi and Nur ad-Din (1118–74), who divided their father's kingdom between them. Nur ad-Din governed Aleppo, while Saif ad-Din Ghazi ruled Mosul. Particularly fanatical, Nur ad-Din employed Kurdish tribesmen and Mamluk slaves (who had a reputation for cruelty) to swell his army. Nur ad-Din was determined to eliminate the Christians in the Holy Land and to gain overall power there. With this ruthless determination, within weeks of his father's death, Nur ad-Din seized several castles in the north of Syria and prevented Count Joscelin de Courtenay of Edessa from winning the city back.

In order to strengthen the Muslim front against their common enemies from the West, like the Christians before him, Nur ad-Din sought to make alliances with his Shi'ite neighbors. In 1147, he signed a treaty with Mu'in ad-Din Unur and also married his daughter, to be sure that Unur did not side again with the Christians. Together, Mu'in ad-Din and Nur ad-Din besieged the cities of Bosra and Salkhad. Their alliance was not comfortable, however, as Mu'in ad-Din was never sure of Nur ad-Din's motives and he was also concerned about offending his former Christian allies who had helped him to defend Damascus against Nur ad-Din's father. Meanwhile, Nur ad-Din turned towards Antioch, seizing cities and towns along the way.

The Second Crusade

Furthest east of all the Crusader lands, and far from aid, Edessa had always been a Christian city, and the news of its loss and the massacre horrified Christians everywhere. King Louis VII of France immediately declared he would take the cross, and Pope Eugenius III issued a bull calling all Christians to march together to fight the infidel in another Crusade. King Louis VII was the first to sign up. A hot-tempered, volatile young man, his reign (1137–80) was dominated by feudal struggles (particularly with the House of Anjou), and saw the start of years of conflict between France and England. It also witnessed the beginnings of the building of the Cathedral of Notre-Dame and the

Eugenius gave the
Order permission
to wear the splayed
red cross as a sign
of "the red blood
of the martyr."

founding of the University in Paris. Meanwhile, Pope Eugenius hoped to be as appealing as Urban II had been in 1095, but he did not have the same personal magnetism. Originally one of Bernard of Clairvaux's Cistercian monks, he began enthusiastically, traveling around France and calling all to arms, but when he realized he was not having the desired effect, he asked his more charismatic former Abbot, Bernard, to step in. This was the sort of issue that Bernard of Clairvaux thrived on. On Easter Day in 1146, King Louis, accompanied by his court and many ordinary people from miles around crowded into the church of Mary Magdalene at Vézelay in the Burgundy region of France, to listen to Abbot Bernard of Clairvaux. His charm and powers of persuasion were as strong as ever and, as with Pope Urban half a century before, almost everyone in the huge crowd listening vowed to join the next Crusade. Led by Queen Eleanor of Aquitaine, even the women declared they would go on the Crusade as well.

As preparations began, Bernard rushed to enlist Conrad III of Germany (1093–1152) to the cause. Yet, unlike Emperor Alexius in the First Crusade, Conrad had not asked for the West's help and he was suspicious of the motives of his French neighbors. Although agreeing to join with his army, he was not enthusiastic. In a measure of their increased status, rather than calling the Templars to a meeting, King Louis and Pope Eugenius traveled to visit them to ask for their help in the cause. Nine years before, Louis had given the Templars a house in a swamp area north of Paris. By 1146, they had drained the swamp and many were living there while a program of building was being carried out around them. In response to the request by the king and the Pope, Everard des Barres, the Master in Paris, assembled 150 of his finest knights and their sergeants. It was at that time that Eugenius gave the Order permission to wear the splayed red cross as a sign of "the red blood of the martyr."

Meanwhile, the German army led by Conrad had proceeded before the rest of the Crusaders and, in October 1147, they were on a direct route across Asia Minor, close to the border of Seljuk Turk territory. In spite of its vast size, when set upon by the more experienced Turks, the German army was heavily defeated. Those who survived, including Conrad himself, retreated to travel with the predominantly French Crusaders who were taking a safer coastal route. But on reaching Ephesus on the west coast of Asia Minor, Conrad was taken ill and returned to Constantinople with his remaining forces. The French, however, were experiencing their own difficulties. As they followed on after the huge German army, the townspeople and villagers they passed had grown weary of the demands of hungry marchers, and they retracted their generosity. This in turn angered the Crusaders, who plundered the land they traveled through. Everard des Barres stepped in to take control, artfully smoothing the explosive situation, and he put Templar knights at the front and rear of the marchers, to keep the disorderly army in some form of disciplined shape.

But it was a motley crowd that marched on. The many women who had followed Queen Eleanor's lead had also taken their maids and often their children and other servants, so numerous families, pedlars, pilgrims, and other stragglers accompanied the soldiers. As the months passed, many of the marchers became ill and weak from weariness, the cold, and lack of food. In January 1148, when they reached the Cadmus

◄

Taken from a history of France in illuminated manuscripts, the *Grandes Chroniques de France*, made between the 13th and 15th centuries, the marriage of Eleanor of Aquitaine and Louis VII of France is depicted on the left, and on the right their embarkation for the Second Crusade 1147–9.

Mountains (today part of western Turkey), it was decided that the stronger members of the army would go on ahead. They would set up camp on the far side of the mountain, leaving the sick and tired to follow on more slowly. With the Seljuk Turks following closely on their heels, these slower marchers were in an extremely vulnerable situation. On the steep, rocky slopes of the mountain, they and their horses lost their footings as the Seljuks nimbly galloped past, firing arrows rapidly as they did so. When the Crusaders eventually all met up again, most of the slower group had been annihilated. Horrified and remorseful, King Louis asked Everard des Barres to take complete control of the army. He wasted no time in dividing the vast army into smaller units, placing a Templar in charge of each unit, and he made the members of these units swear to obey their Templar leaders without questioning. In this way, the Crusaders reached the city of Attalia (now Antalya) on the Mediterranean coast of Turkey in relative safety, where they waited for the Byzantine ships that they had been promised would take them to the Holy Land. But when the fleet arrived, it was far too small to take them all, so only Louis, Eleanor, their nobles, and a small contingent of the army set sail, leaving the others to cross the hostile Seljuk lands on foot. The majority were either killed or died of exhaustion or hunger on the way.

SACRED DEFENSE

By the time Louis arrived at Antioch early in March 1148, he had run out of money. He abandoned his original plan of retaking Edessa and instead marched on to Jerusalem where he visited the holy shrines as a pilgrim rather than as a conquering soldier. He sent Everard des Barres to Acre to raise money from Templar resources there to pay for the cost of the journey so far, which resulted in him owing the Templars the equivalent of about half his annual income. The remaining Crusader army, which consisted of a number of French and German survivors (along with Conrad who had recovered and arrived by sea from Constantinople), was not completely depleted, so between them they considered making an assault on Aleppo, but soon abandoned the idea in favor of attacking Damascus instead. It was an ambitious and ill-considered plan.

In June 1148, a Council was called in Acre, attended by Louis of France, Conrad of Germany, the 17-year-old King of Jerusalem Baldwin III, Raymond of Antioch, Everard des Barres, and a large number of Templars, Hospitallers and other knights from the area. Raymond of Antioch wanted to attack Aleppo and recapture Edessa, others wanted to attack Egypt, but that was not deemed possible as the city of Ascalon in between was still ruled by the powerful Fatimid dynasty. So the discussion focused on Damascus. Because it had been one of the Muslim powers that had allied with the Christians previously, the Crusaders perceived that it might be an easier target. An ancient and wealthy city, Damascus was famously conquered by Alexander the Great in the fourth century BCE. It was in a particularly strategic position, north-east of Jerusalem, Nazareth, and Acre, and south-west of Tripoli. After a long meeting, the Crusaders decided that Damascus would be their target. The following month, they marched to Damascus and, in preparation

for a siege, set up camp in a location that was naturally supplied with fresh flowing water and orchards that gave shade and fruit. However, they had not noticed that the trees in the orchards also served as cover for the Damascene army, who repeatedly attacked them as they camped. Apart from that, however, the siege was beginning to move in their favor, but Louis and Conrad decided to relocate their troops on open ground. Their new camp lacked water and shade and was close to a section of the city walls that was of a greater height than in their former camp. Within a short time, these elements defeated them; the Crusaders were dying of thirst and exposure, and the walls were too high to surmount. Forced to retreat without a fight, the Crusaders' efforts had been a total failure. Humiliatingly, the Crusaders had gained nothing and the Second Crusade was recognized by all as a fiasco. Six years later in 1154, Nur ad-Din took control of Damascus without a fight, strengthening the power of Muslims in Outremer once more.

cedente. Laquelle fut tant prouf-
fitable quelle entendra leuisor
au Roy z a ses barons dentre
prendre plus auant contre leurs
enemis. Et par ce quilz sca-
noient les grans maulx descla-
sonne leur auoient fait. Ilz
conclurent quilz yroient comme
par course soudainne estreper bi-
thies z arbres hore leur Cite.
Et de fait eulx partans de

Ihrlm a tout bien petite armee
pour executer leur conclusion.
aterent deuant ceste Cite descla-
sonne. dont les citoyens les ter-
ans furent tant espointz quil
ny eust aucunne doulx qui o-
sast saillir hore des murs. Po-
quoy le Roy z ses aultres y-
ens de larmee. hame la condi-
se des escalomois entreprirent
et iurerent quilz assiegeroient

The Siege of Ascalon

During the winter of 1149–50, the young King Baldwin III of Jerusalem asked the Templars to take control of Gaza, a city on a strip of land surrounded by Egypt, Ascalon, and the Mediterranean Sea, 48 miles (78 kilometers) south-west of Jerusalem. Baldwin had rebuilt the ruined city of Gaza and intended that the Knights Templar would defend it against continual raids by the Fatimids, who had kept control of Ascalon, a small patch of territory ten miles to the north of Gaza, after the First Crusade. Ascalon was an important base for the Muslims and they had used it for centuries. From there, they attacked pilgrims as they traveled from Jaffa and Nazareth to Jerusalem.

After the Second Crusade, Conrad III of Germany had attempted to besiege the fortress in Ascalon, but as he had no support from anyone else, he was forced to withdraw. It was not until Baldwin III had rebuilt the city of Gaza, and invited the Templars in to defend it, that he, too, decided to make an assault on Ascalon. At the end of January 1153, the entire army of Jerusalem, with Patriarch Fulcher holding the relic of the True Cross aloft, plus the Templars, Hospitallers, and a number of powerful barons, marched towards Ascalon with as many siege towers as they could gather. Situated on the Mediterranean coast, the port of Ascalon was shaped like a basin, protected by the sea on one side and strong, curved man-made walls on the other. The Crusader siege was therefore undertaken both by land and by sea, with the fleet commanded by Gerard Grenier, Lord of Sidon, who strangely often raided both Muslims and Christians at sea. Sidon was one of the Crusader states, having been captured in 1110. In the 13th century, one of Gerard's descendants sold the land to the Knights Templar, but it was later destroyed by the Mongols. The Mongols, sometimes called the Tartars, were pagans from central Asia who began as nomads, divided into tribes and brutally attacked and conquered several civilizations.

> Siege towers were constructed and for five months many clashes between the two sides left things at stalemate. Ascalon was virtually impenetrable.

On its way to Ascalon, the Crusader force was also augmented by a large group of pilgrims who were on their way to Jerusalem at the time. Siege towers were constructed and for five months many clashes between the two sides left things at stalemate. Ascalon was virtually impenetrable and behind its massive walls and gates were twice as many defenders as there were besiegers outside. Within the walls, the inhabitants had food supplies that would potentially last for years. In May, the powerful Egyptian fleet arrived to resupply the city, and while it was there it destroyed Gerard of Sidon's far smaller fleet. Then in August, a group from within Ascalon tried to burn down one of the Crusader siege towers. The wind blew the fire back against the walls of Ascalon causing a large section to collapse. Written over 25 years later, William of Tyre's account described Templar knights rushing through the opening in the wall without King Baldwin's knowledge. The Templar Grand Master, Bernard de Tremelay, stopped others from following, but subsequently he and about 40 of his Templar knights were killed by the larger Egyptian force within. Their bodies were displayed on the ramparts and their heads sent to the caliph in Cairo. This has not been verified, however, and other accounts do not mention it. William of Tyre disliked the Knights Templar, so his report has to be treated with caution, but it is known that Bernard de Tremelay was killed during the fighting.

◀

The Siege of Ascalon by King Baldwin III of Jerusalem, from an illuminated manuscript by Sébastien Mamerot, *Les Passages d'Outremer* (Journeys to Outremer).

By August, eight months after they first set out, the Crusaders were exhausted and it was suggested that they abandon the siege, but King Baldwin was convinced that they were on the verge of victory. Three days later they made another assault and another breach was made in a different part of the wall. Bitter fighting ensued but eventually the city fell to the Crusaders. By the end of August 1153, the fortress was officially surrendered. The Muslim inhabitants were allowed to leave in peace and most fled back to Egypt. Ascalon was turned into a diocese directly under the Patriarch of Jerusalem and the city was added to the County of Jaffa, which was ruled by Baldwin's brother Amalric. The city's mosque was reconsecrated as a church. The fall of Ascalon contributed to the downfall of the Fatimid dynasty in Egypt; in 1162, Amalric succeeded his brother as King of Jerusalem and, throughout the 1160s, he led numerous expeditions from Ascalon into Egypt, but he never succeeded in his aim of bringing Egypt under his control.

Building for defense

When the disasters of the Second Crusade were reported in the West, the reaction was one of shock and outrage, closely followed by anger over the cost. It was apparent that a more robust and permanent defense of the Holy Land was needed. Knights of the military orders already established there would have to become more secure, better equipped and more prepared to fight and attack on many levels to form a greater defense where it was most needed.

In the 1130s, the Templars had been made responsible for guarding the region between Cilician Armenia, a principality that was formed by refugees escaping invasions of Armenia by the Seljuk Turks from the 11th to 14th centuries, and the Principality of Antioch. Since then, they had also been building or reinforcing castles across Europe and Outremer. Being an international organization, the Templars could draw on the building practices and best techniques employed by the many nations they were involved with. In particular, they learned quickly from both their friends and adversaries in Outremer and created massive structures that were able to withstand heavy bombardment or siege. The ability of the Templars to learn and apply what they saw around them was one of their major attributes. Templar castles served as protective fortresses as well as living quarters and administrative centers. After the Second Crusade, castle building took on an even greater importance and urgency. More were built strategically across the Crusader states and enhanced by the latest military advances. The Crusader states made up a long narrow strip of the Principality of Antioch, the County of Tripoli, and the Kingdom of Jerusalem, with the Mediterranean coast on one side and mountain ranges on the other. Beyond the mountains, the cities of Aleppo, Homs, Hama, and Damascus were controlled by Muslim rulers. So the earliest Templar castles were built during the 1130s in the mountains to guard the passes for Christian travelers.

The first Templar castles

Built in the Amanus Mountains, northwest of Aleppo, the first Templar castle was probably Baghras Castle, also known as Gaston Castle. It was originally constructed by the Byzantines during the tenth century but the Templars took it over in about 1131. Built on a rocky peak with steep slopes running away from it on either side, it overlooked the road to Antioch and the south approach to the Belen Pass (also known

The ruins of the castle of
Ponferrada in León, Spain,
built by the Knights Templar
in the 12th century on the
pilgrim route, the Way
of St. James, to Santiago
de Compostela. In 1178,
Ferdinand II of León donated
the city to the Templars for
protecting the pilgrims on
their journeys. The name
Ponferrada derives from a
nearby iron pilgrim bridge
built at the end of the
11th century.

as the Syrian Gates), through the Amanus Mountains. Other castles soon followed Baghras, including Trapesac (or Darbsak) Castle, which guarded the north approach to the Belen Pass. Then there were Banyas, Calamella, Roche Roussel, and Tortosa Castles, all built or in Templar possession by the mid-12th century.

Situated to the south of Antioch, Tortosa had become part of the County of Tripoli after it was conquered by Raymond of Toulouse in 1099. It was an important town, used as a landing point for pilgrims and also a busy port serving mainly Genoese and Venetian ships. In 1152, Nur ad-Din captured Tortosa, but within months it was regained by the Christians and immediately assigned to Templar protection. They built a large fortress there and raised impregnable walls around the whole town. In the Kingdom of Jerusalem, the Templars were given the castle of Latrūn, also called Toron des Chevaliers. After the Second Crusade, the Templars were given the fortress of Gaza. This had been built by King Baldwin III on the main north–south coastal road. The Templars used it as a base for raids against the Muslim-held city of Ascalon and for protecting the southern side of the Kingdom of Jerusalem against Egypt. In the 1160s, they were given the castle of Safed in Galilee, but less than 30 years later, after a bitter siege, it was taken by Saladin. In 1240, through a treaty made with the Muslims, the Templars regained Safed Castle, but in 1266 it finally fell to Baibars (1223–77), a Mamluk slave who became Sultan of Egypt and whose reign marked the start of an age of Mamluk dominance in the Eastern Mediterranean.

During the castle-building program, in 1217, the Templars began erecting Atlit or Athlit Castle, also known as the Pilgrims' Castle, south of Haifa. Building of this castle lasted until 1221. Even before it was completed, Atlit became one of the major Crusader fortresses, where up to 4,000 troops could live (and did during a siege in 1220). There were three freshwater wells within its enclosure, and with a protected harbor on one side, the castle served both as a port and as a guard over the pilgrimage road from Acre to Jerusalem. Additionally, as the castle dominated the coastal route and surrounding countryside, the Templars could draw revenue on it from tolls and rents, which helped to pay for its upkeep and their equipment and food.

Castle building in Outremer

During the 11th century, Norman masons built massive stone castles in Europe, replacing former earth and timber defenses. Many Normans were involved in both the First and Second Crusades and several remained in the Holy Land to build castles there for the Templars. Because the land in Outremer was so inconsistent, castle

La Couvertoirade; the remains of a village with a castle situated in the valley of River Dourbie near Lodève in France. It was originally a stopping place for pilgrims on the road to Santiago de Compostela and was given to the Knights Templar in 1185 so that they could protect the pilgrims on their way to that shrine.

design was necessarily varied and often experimental. Building techniques and styles often borrowed from surrounding influences, such as the Byzantine use of small bricks, or Armenian, Byzantine, European, or Islamic methods of cutting and shaping stones. Variations in mixtures of cement and mortar also reflected different cultural influences and an understanding of requirements in warm climates. Castle building in the Holy Land developed more rapidly than in the West. For example, the first concentric castles were built in Outremer in the late 1160s, over a century before they appeared in Europe. After the Second Crusade, towers became larger and more closely spaced and castle walls became thicker. The originally Islamic concept of the talus (an additional sloping front on a castle) along the lower parts of walls and towers was adopted. The number of embrasures for archery or observation was increased and various forms of projecting machicolation appeared, to allow arrows to be shot out or missiles to be dropped on to enemies below. These also followed Byzantine and Islamic fortification styles.

Safety and practicality

By the 1180s, there were approximately 600 Templar knights in Jerusalem, Tripoli and Antioch, and approximately 1,000 sergeants, and these were involved in every battle fought in the area. All their castles were under a Commander in charge of supplies and the sergeants who guarded the gates. The Templar Order was the only organization capable of building these great castles at the time and they were all solid and robust, whether they were vast strongholds or small simple lookout towers. As well as drawing on ideas from local Byzantine and Islamic styles and methods, the Templars also hired expert masons from Europe to assist in their castle-building program. Pilgrims often worked as laborers in return for their protection. From the second half of the 12th century, most Templar castles were concentrated in the northern part of the Principality of Antioch and in the south of the Kingdom of Jerusalem, where they were used primarily to guard pilgrim routes. Portraying an image of strength and impregnability, they were predominantly used as bases from where Templars could ensure that passing pilgrims had enough food, tents, and mules.

As they spread across Europe, the Templars built castles in other locations as well, mainly in the Iberian Peninsula. But their building program concentrated more on barns, preceptories, and churches. Templar church and domestic architecture features some of the finest of their craftsmanship, and throughout Europe they built approximately 9,000 preceptories, comprising farms, barns, strongholds, and other practical buildings. Totally different from either their castles or their churches, Templar barns are usually timber framed and functional. Theodorich, a German monk who went on pilgrimage to the Holy Land in 1172, wrote about the Templar buildings he saw in Jerusalem:

> . . . on the other side of the palace, that is on the west, the Templars have built a new house, whose height, length and breadth, and all its cellars and refectories, staircase and roof, are far beyond the custom of this land. Indeed its roof is so high that, if I were to mention how high it is, those who listen would hardly believe me. There indeed they have constructed a new palace, just as on the other side they have the old one. There too they have founded on the edge of the outer court a new church of magnificent size and workmanship.

For these holy men, their churches and other places of worship were possibly the most essential aspects of the Templars' daily existence. Large castles were built to contain a chapel, refectory, halls, stables, dormitories, and other chambers and storerooms that could be used to store enough provisions in the event of lengthy sieges. If the castles were not large enough for a separate chapel, the Templars used part of the inner baileys as their chapels. Further churches were built by them across Europe and Outremer, as this was one of the unique privileges granted to them by Pope Innocent II in 1139—other religious orders were not allowed to build their own churches. As a result, within the first century of their existence, the Templars had built approximately 150 churches and cathedrals. These churches reflect the Order's collective, humble devotion to their religion. In the Holy Land in particular, they seem to have felt their religious responsibilities keenly.

Gothic architecture

Within a few years of the Templars' formation, a new style of church architecture appeared in Western Europe. Becoming known later as Gothic, the first examples were built in France in around 1140 and the style flourished during the crusading period. Characterized by large towers and spires that soared high into the sky, Gothic churches were physical examples of an improved knowledge of engineering and a reverence for God. It has been speculated that the Templars were involved in the invention of the Gothic style of architecture. The basis for this theory included the fact that the development of the style began in Europe just after the Order was established at the Council of Troyes and it became more widespread when the Templars were becoming extremely successful, and expanding in many different directions, including becoming proficient in building for several different purposes. Another reason for the theory is that many elements of the style seem to emerge from Byzantine and Islamic traditions, which would not have been familiar to established European architects and masons, but were accessible to the Templars in the East. Yet there are other facts that counteract these claims, including: if they invented it, why did the Templars not create Gothic style churches for themselves?

The overall appearance of Gothic architecture was unique and served to glorify both the Catholic faith and, it is claimed, the French royal family—the Capetian dynasty. Gothic architecture was tall, light, and airy, with high vaulted ceilings in web-like designs that balanced on soaring stone pillars. The Byzantine and Islamic methods that feature in Gothic churches in turn developed from earlier Egyptian techniques, such as making use of solid walls and pillars rather than hollowing them out as had been done previously. In this way, they could support greater weights. Other Eastern methods included precision cutting of stone, so that everything slotted together and exactly matched other stone blocks. These were just two of the new building innovations that enabled the new churches to be far larger than previously built European churches. Soon the use of buttresses and flying buttresses allowed the stonework to be supported from the outside, so huge, heavy glass windows could be fitted into the solid walls, and this made Gothic churches vast, high-ceilinged

> Gothic churches were vast, high-ceilinged places, that filled with sparkling jewel colors as the daylight shone through the stained-glass windows.

places, that filled with sparkling jewel colors as the daylight shone through the stained-glass windows. Gothic architects were creating the loftiest interior spaces the world had ever seen, while outside, spires soared high into the sky as if reaching up to heaven and God. The technical innovations of the style enabled buildings to be constructed on a skeleton framework, which enormously increased architects' flexibility.

The key features of Gothic architecture that also reflected Eastern building practice included the pointed arch that originated in the Byzantine and Sassanid (Persian) Empires and subsequently became a distinctive feature of Islamic architecture. Another was rib vaulting that originally appeared in ancient Egypt as barrel vaulting, then in ancient Rome as two barrel vaults intersected at right angles to form groin vaults, which were also used in Byzantine and Islamic buildings. Gothic builders modified the concept into the rib vault, which was a skeleton of pointed arches, or ribs, on which masonry was laid. Buttresses used in Gothic architecture were also previously used in Byzantine, Sassanid, and Islamic architecture, and window tracery also appeared originally in Byzantine buildings. But the notion that the Knights Templar were the instigators of the Gothic style seems improbable when considered in the context of their structure. Bernard of Clairvaux, who was so important in their formation, advocated greater simplicity and the eradication of embellishment and expense in art and architecture. Gothic architecture was far too ornate and decorative for his tastes and

Gothic architecture in the abbey on Mont Saint-Michel in Normandy, which was built over five centuries. The style became widespread at the time of the Templars' expansion, and many aspects seemed to derive from eastern traditions, but their involvement was not apparent.

the Templars adhered strongly to Bernard's other beliefs, so it would have been singular for them to have contradicted him in this area. Many of the characteristics of Gothic architecture had been used in the architecture of the Romanesque period, which began in Europe long before the Order of the Knights Templar was formed. Certain elements, such as pointed arches and large stained-glass windows, did not appear in Romanesque churches, however, but pointed arches and ribbed vaults did appear in Durham Cathedral in England, which was begun in 1093, before the foundation of the Knights Templar, or even the First Crusade.

Another common assumption that denies any Templar link is that Gothic architecture was invented by Abbot Suger (c.1081–1151) of Saint-Denis. An influential French cleric, chronicler, and statesman who believed that art enhanced religious

experience, Abbot Suger started an enlargement program of the Abbey-Church of Saint-Denis in Paris in about 1140. A highly literate man, he was close to kings Louis VI and Louis VII of France, served as regent for Louis VII during the Second Crusade and lived at the court of Pope Calixtus II (r. 1119–24) for a year. After being made abbot of Saint-Denis in 1122, Suger soon instigated its rebuilding. Since the seventh century, Saint-Denis had been the royal abbey of France where kings were both educated and buried. When Abbot Suger's new basilica was consecrated in 1144, the innovations in the architecture astonished and inspired many others.

Following Suger's belief that beauty and art honored God, the design of Saint-Denis resembled the opulence of Byzantine churches. He wrote two accounts about it: *Liber de rebus in administratione sua gestis* ("The book on what was done under his administration") and *Libellus alter de consecratione ecclesiae sancti Dionysii* ("The other little book on the consecration of the Church of Saint-Denis"). In the books, Suger gave details about the construction of the church and its symbolism. He explained that, by 1133, he had collected artists and craftsmen "from all lands," including a group of Arabic glass-makers. Colored glass was originally produced by the ancient Egyptians and the Romans. The tradition continued in the East where it was produced mainly for use in mosques; for example, by the 12th-century, the Fatimid dynasty in particular had been using stained glass in their mosques for over a hundred years. Fatimid scholars and mystics used colored glass in geometric patterns to assist their meditation. Some stained glass had been used in the windows of European churches and monasteries from the seventh century, but these had been small. It was not until the engineering of Gothic architecture made it possible to incorporate large windows in churches, that stained glass became a meticulous and expressive art form. It is credible therefore that the first stained-glass window makers of the Gothic period in Europe learned their skills from Islamic glass-makers. Further contemporary independent reports about Saint-Denis explain that Suger was involved with many ideas behind the architectural designs, but there is no evidence that he was active on the technical side, so it remains uncertain just how much he actually influenced the development of the style. That he was an active participant in the building of Saint-Denis is clear; he wrote about losing sleep over many aspects of the work and how he even sourced some raw materials himself. As abbot, he probably had the final say about whether or not designs were acceptable, and he must have been receptive to and encouraging of new ideas and innovative styles, materials, and methods, but it is unlikely that the actual plans and methods were of his making or even of his instigation. He was not trained in either architecture or engineering and, although he clearly appreciated the final outcome, the church was built to exacting standards that required the expertise of skilled, trained architectural engineers and masons.

After 1144, Saint-Denis became the model for other churches and cathedrals across France, England, the Low Countries, Germany, Spain, northern Italy, and Sicily, but no Templar churches followed the Gothic style, and although both Bernard of Clairvaux and the Templars have been linked with the rise of Gothic architecture, there is no definitive proof of this. While Templar builders were extremely sophisticated and remained aware and knowledgeable of current architectural fashions and developments, they continued to follow Bernard of Clairvaux's preference for simplicity without unnecessary adornment. There was no standard form of Templar church. From the time they were

A 12th-century stained-glass window in the Basilica of Saint-Denis, which had been a place of pilgrimage since the 10th century. Abbot Suger, a powerful political figure, had the basilica rebuilt according to new architectural techniques at that time, and this is said to be the first Gothic building and the prototype for all other Gothic cathedrals and abbeys across much of Europe. The brilliantly colored stained glass windows depict Christian stories. Here, it shows St. Maurice urging the officers of the legion to suffer martyrdom with him and below, refusing to sacrifice to Pagan gods.

given permission to build their own churches in 1139, they built many types, including rectangular, cruciform, octagonal, polygonal, and round. Many recalled the shape of either the Dome of the Rock or the Church of the Holy Sepulcher. As Bernard of Clairvaux advocated, Templars sought functionality and quality rather than beauty, and their churches remained modest in comparison with the massive Gothic cathedrals and abbeys being constructed across parts of Europe during the same period. Although strong and harmonious in style, there is nothing particularly unusual for the period about any Templar building. As their wealth and influence grew, however, so Bernard of Clairvaux's instructions for "simple architecture" began to be forgotten, and later Templar buildings, particularly the churches, became a little more ornate. But, although all their buildings were constructed with great precision using the latest technology and methods, none featured any of the design elements that were later called Gothic. So if they had any involvement in the building of the great cathedrals, it remains indistinct and difficult to establish.

> Although they acquired many previously constructed buildings, the Templars always enhanced or rebuilt for their own purposes.

Although they acquired many previously constructed buildings, the Templars always enhanced or rebuilt for their own purposes. Their preceptories, for example, were like miniature towns, complete with chapels, armories, refectories, training grounds, barns, dormitories, and offices. Some were fortified, some were fitted and equipped ready to host guests and pilgrims, and all were built for practicality within their particular country. The Templars employed expert builders from outside the Order, including local stone masons and architects, as well as masons from within the Order, who were known as "Mason brothers." Apart from priests, the Mason brothers were the only other members of the Templar Order allowed to wear leather gloves. Section 325 in the Rule stated that: "No brother should wear leather gloves, except the Chaplain brother . . . the Mason brothers may wear them sometimes, and it is permitted them because of the great suffering they endure and so that they do not easily injure their hands; but they should not wear them when they are not working." Mason brothers were not Templar monks, but it appears from this statement that the Templars did not simply hire outside workers for their construction work, as has been suggested by many, but used trained artisans and craftsmen as part of their organization.

Sacred geometry

Little has been documented about Templar Mason brothers, but this was not unusual. Medieval masons in general were secretive, which has stimulated the beliefs that many of them practiced "sacred geometry." The notion of sacred geometry in architecture arises from the perfect proportions and ratios and geometric shapes found in some ancient religious buildings. These have been recognized in buildings constructed by various different cultures. As certain proportions and ratios have been used in Byzantine, Gothic, and some Templar churches, these have been claimed by many to have been constructed on the principles of sacred geometry, although this has not been substantiated. The Templars learned much about building from the Byzantine and Islamic architecture they were familiar with in the East, and both Byzantine and

Islamic buildings standing at that time were constructed with complex and balanced proportions. The principles of sacred geometry are believed by some to have been handed down from ancient builders, including the architects of Solomon's Temple. Some claim that after the fall of Jerusalem in 70 CE, the knowledge of sacred geometry was lost until the Templars rediscovered it when they excavated beneath Temple Mount in around 1127. It was soon after this time that Gothic architecture developed, which has inspired some to make links with these concepts. Others suggest that many of the advanced developments and proportions of Western architecture evolved from European builders learning from their previous counterparts in the East.

Various undeciphered symbols have been found carved on the walls of some Templar buildings and these have given rise to the theory that they are also linked with the ancient understanding of geometry and proportion. The pentagram is a particular symbol that has given rise to speculation that the Templars had secret links with Islamic masons, who also used pentagrams in their architecture, but pentagrams have been used by many diverse cultures for different reasons. Some geometric symbols have been found on the walls of a tower in Chinon Castle where 60 Templars were imprisoned in 1308. The symbols include stars, grids, and hand shapes with hearts on them. Similar carvings have been found at Domme in France where further Templars were imprisoned at the same time. Although still not understood fully, it has been conjectured that these are connected with sacred geometry, or they could simply be a code used by the Templars. Some have speculated that the symbols are linked with Templar knowledge and admiration of Islamic and Byzantine architecture, but again, nothing has been proved. As the Templars learned much from their Islamic neighbors about medicine, mathematics, architecture, and literature, this is plausible, but—apart

The pentagram

Since ancient times, the pentagram has been used as a symbol by various cultures and endowed with various meanings. Its earliest known use was on Mesopotamian potsherds from around 3500 BCE. Later, it was used by the Hebrews to symbolize the Pentateuch, or the first five books of the Bible: Genesis, Exodus, Leviticus, Numbers, and Deuteronomy. The Hebrew pentagram is believed to have changed at some point to the hexagram, becoming the Seal of Solomon or the Star of David. The shape was important to the ancient Greek followers of Pythagoras, who used it as a symbol of recognition among themselves. The ancient Greeks called it the pent-alpha, as it appears to have been formed from five letter "A"s. Early Christians attributed the pentagram to the Five Wounds of Christ, and Emperor Constantine used it in his seal and amulet. Any evil associations with the symbol came after the time of the Inquisition; before that, the pentagram had often been used as a protection against demons. Perhaps most significantly, it is believed that the shape was used as the seal of the City of Jerusalem, which makes it possible that the Templars adopted the pentagram as one of their key symbols to make a visible link with their early connections with Jerusalem and the Temple of Solomon.

▲

A 13th-century pentagram here carved in stone was used as a funerary relief.

from the pentagram—the Templar symbols and symbols found in other culture's buildings do not correspond.

Fundamentally, the term "sacred geometry" encompasses certain religious, philosophical, and spiritual beliefs that have been used by various cultures in their religious architecture. It is described as geometric shapes and ratios used in the planning and construction of churches, temples, mosques, monuments, altars, tabernacles, and consecrated outside spaces, which have derived from the philosophies and mathematical theories of the ancient Greeks, mainly Pythagoras (c.575–c.495 BCE), Plato (424/3–348/7 BCE) and Euclid (325–265 BCE). Pythagoras, a philosopher, mathematician, mystic and scientist, explained the inherent sacredness of numbers and how geometry is intrinsic to the design of the Universe. Plato, a philosopher, mathematician, writer and founder of the Academy in Athens, began the first institution of higher learning in the Western world. Along with his mentor Socrates and his student Aristotle, Plato helped to lay the foundations of Western philosophy and science. Euclid, a mathematician, became known as the "father of geometry," as he was responsible for assembling almost all the world's knowledge of geometry in one book. His work, together with the work of Pythagoras, forms the basis of sacred geometry. They worked out that the entire universe is shaped according to set geometric values that can be seen throughout the natural world. Simple examples of sacred geometric shapes include circles, triangles, squares, pentagons, and pentagrams, while three-dimensional examples include the sphere and the five Platonic solids: the tetrahedron, hexahedron (cube), octahedron, dodecahedron, and icosahedron. Euclid discovered the ratios of "Pi," a formula for dividing circles, while Pythagoras and Plato determined the Golden Ratio or Mean, the balance between excess and deficiency using symmetry, proportion, and harmony. The architecture—and art—of many ancient cultures involves the repetition of numerical relationships and the use of shapes, placement, and proportion that clearly derive from the theories of these ancient Greeks. Sacred geometry was accepted by many ancient scholars and the term *prisca sapientia* (sacred wisdom), became quite commonly used during the 15th to 17th centuries to describe this accepted but elusive theory.

As sacred geometry is complex and multifaceted, it cannot be seen in one single form or design, but emerged in different cultures, interpreted through different design styles. For instance, the spirals on the Ionic capitals of ancient Greek temples follow the perfectly balanced order of sacred geometry, while the spires of much Gothic architecture also follow the theories. The notion of creating surroundings that enhance prayer and spirituality was not well known

> As sacred geometry is complex and multifaceted, it cannot be seen in one single form or design, but emerged in different cultures, interpreted through different design styles.

Preceptories

In addition to castles and churches, the Templars' vast building program included preceptories, mills, bridges, city walls, agricultural structures, and other buildings related to their commercial enterprises. The preceptories were the hub of the organization, usually where all administration was undertaken. Rather like an amalgamation of monastery, farm, village, and offices, most preceptories contained a smithy, breweries, bakehouses, stables, a kiln, an orchard, a vegetable garden, fields, and livestock, as well as a strong chest that held their legal records including charters of donation. Within each preceptory were cells for the Templar monks and servants as well as for monks from other orders who could stay there in isolation for short periods of prayer and contemplation.

during the medieval period, but became important to the Neo-Platonic Society of the Renaissance period and flowered in the art and architecture of that time. The fact that the harmonious proportions and geometric shapes and ratios can be seen in many Templar and other Christian buildings of medieval Europe inspired a great deal of conjecture about where they learned this. It is clear that they had a more complex relationship with various groups in the East than was originally thought and that they employed indigenous builders and craftsmen, but whether they learned about sacred geometry from Islamic or Byzantine builders has not been established. The most popular suggestion returns to the notion that they learned about it when excavating under Temple Mount. It has also been observed that cathedrals, churches, and abbeys produced by the Cistercian Order were built on measurements based on 12 squares of equal length by 8 squares of equal length, which corresponds to the Golden Ratio. Bernard of Clairvaux was involved with much of the Cistercians' building programme during the 12th century and, of course, he was particularly involved with the Templars. In 1134, it is said that he was also involved in the building of the north tower of Chartres Cathedral. It was a soaring, impressive structure that is believed by many to be based on the pivotal dimensions of sacred geometry. Bernard once described God as "length, width, height, and depth," and it has been conjectured that his belief in the godliness of number and proportion in design came directly from the influence of the Knights Templar. Without concrete evidence, however, speculation and investigations continue.

◀

One of the soaring towers of Chartres Cathedral in France. Chartres is considered by many to be one of the finest examples of the French High Gothic style. Constructed in the main between 1193 and 1250, it became a milestone in the development of Western architecture with its pointed arches, rib and panel vaults, and flying buttresses. Additionally, Chartres has many stained-glass windows and sculptures. It is often said, but has never been verified, that the Knights Templar were involved in the building of Chartres.

The Albigensian Crusade

In the midst of all these developments, the Cathars continued to thrive and because the Templars are believed to have employed some of them in their building program, when the Church turned directly against the sect, rumors about the Templars' real leanings began circulating in several quarters.

Although never openly tolerated by the Catholic Church, at first the Cathars were largely ignored by the authorities, although they were always viewed with suspicion since their ideas were controversial. The main differences in their beliefs and those of Christian teaching were that God was not all-powerful as there were two: one good and one evil, in constant watch over humanity. They believed that the evil god was responsible for the world itself, while the good god was in heaven, waiting for souls to return. In effect, these beliefs gave the devil a more prominent role. Catharism is believed to have originated in Bosnia in the mid-tenth century, but many adherents had traveled and settled in the Languedoc region of France by the early 12th century. They became known as Albigensians, probably because the 1176 Church Council was held near Albi. It was there that the Catholic Church declared the Cathar doctrine to be heretical.

Unlike most religious sects, the Cathars, or Albigensians, were extremely organized, and as their numbers increased, they established priests and bishops, collected funds, distributed them to the poor and lived off the land, making them effectively a greater threat to Christianity than many other, less organized fringe factions. They did not recognize the authority of either the French king or the Catholic Church, but they were protected by the powerful Counts of Toulouse who refused to persecute them. For many years, they were disregarded by Church authorities, but almost as soon as he became Pope in 1198, Innocent III resolved to deal with the Cathars. Initially, he sent Catholic priests and friars to try to persuade them to convert to Christianity, but after great concerted efforts, the priests were categorically unsuccessful. While trying to convert the Cathars, however, the priests discovered more about their beliefs and behavior: they were chaste and honest, but they did not believe in the intercession of priests. To the Church, this was heresy and the Pope determined to take decisive action. But he needed the assistance of the rulers of the Languedoc region, and the powerful Count Raymond VI de Toulouse refused to support the Church against the Cathars. The Pope was furious. The papal legate Pierre de Castelnau was appointed by the Pope to suppress the Cathars, but in 1208, while in Languedoc, he was assassinated—this was believed to have been by some of Raymond's friends. Pope Innocent immediately excommunicated Raymond and placed an interdict on his lands. This made things extremely difficult for Raymond, so eventually he apologized and complied with the Pope's wishes.

Meanwhile, despite their obligatory loyalty to the Pope, the Templars strove to maintain neutrality. They remained reluctant to take up arms against their neighbors in France, as some of their patrons were known Cathar supporters and it is probable that some Cathars worked for them. But by 1209, Innocent prepared to instigate a military campaign to completely wipe out Catharism in Languedoc. He promised

> They believed that the evil god was responsible for the world itself, while the good god was in heaven, waiting for souls to return.

A 13th-century miniature showing the Albigensian Crusade—the persecution and annihilation of the Cathars—in the Languedoc region of France.

any knight who fought against them the same spiritual rewards that had been promised to the Crusaders in the Holy Land, and he promised to give the lands of Cathar "heretics" to any French nobleman who took up arms against them.

Over the next few years, swelling Catholic armies marched through the Languedoc region, storming the dwellings of the Cathars, slaughtering them indiscriminately, even massacring those sheltering in churches. Any captured Cathars were burned. Innocent III died in July 1216 but the crusade continued, and for over 20 years the Cathars were oppressed and fought. From 1233, the Inquisition was called in to crush what remained of Catharism. Their final destruction came in 1244 at the fortress of Montségur on top of a high hill in the eastern Pyrenees. Over 200 Cathars held out for nearly two years against assaults and sieges by the 10,000 troops besieging them below, but in March 1244 they finally surrendered. Approximately 220 men, women and children who refused to renounce their faith were bound together and set alight on a huge pyre that had been prepared for them. During the Albigensian Crusade, methods were developed by the Church that were later taken up and refined by the Inquisition.

CHAPTER 5

Shifting Sands

Throughout their history, the Knights Templar remained a paradox to many. Devout monks who were also fighting soldiers; individually poor yet collectively wealthy; Christians who befriended many Cathars, Jews, and Muslims. Yet despite these contradictions, their courage and gallantry made them extremely popular and successful—for a while anyway.

Approximately a century before the Albigensian Crusade, when Bernard of Clairvaux spoke and wrote "In Praise of the New Knighthood," he aimed to convey the originality of the idea. The knights of the Templar Order, as opposed to other Templar brothers, were necessarily brave, disciplined and, as Bernard explained, determined to devote all their "energies to the struggle on both fronts, against flesh and blood and against the evil spirits in the air." It was a completely new concept. The duty of a knight was to kill his enemies and fight in the name of his lord. The duty of a Christian was to love his neighbor as himself, and to turn the other cheek when confronted with aggression. The Order of the Knights Templar was somehow an amalgamation of the two conflicting concepts. In defending the Templars, Bernard condemned the behavior of secular knights, proclaiming that Templar knights fought for the glory of God and not themselves. To further the cause of the Church, he promoted the Order as an option for secular knights to join and so redeem themselves in the eyes of God. He saw this "new knighthood" as a solution to the prevalent sins of pride, vanity, and desire for personal glory among ordinary knights, as well as a method of solving the problems of defense against the infidel in the Holy Land. Although no actual chivalric code was written, Bernard's Rule gave the Templars instructions to govern their behavior both on and off the battlefield.

So, the Knights Templar were contradictory in many ways. As soldiers as well as monks, they could not renounce the world as most monks did. The work they undertook required them to have relationships with many from the outside world, from the king and Patriarch of Jerusalem to the many pilgrims they defended, from the knights and nobles of other armies and countries to the many Muslims with whom they came into contact. Fasting and penance, usually an important aspect of monastic brotherhoods, were forbidden for the knights of the Order as they had a duty to maintain their strength and energy, to be permanently prepared for battle, so any practice that weakened them

◄
A c.1180 print of a rare contemporary portrait of Saladin, who became the first Sultan of Egypt and Syria and the founder of the Ayyubid dynasty.

was discouraged. Similarly, most monks were encouraged to study, but this aspect of the religious life was largely disregarded for the Templars. Few Templars were well educated, although as most of the knights came from fairly aristocratic backgrounds, the rudiments of education had been attended to as they grew up. When drawing up their Rule, Bernard considered and included the most honorable aspects of lay knights' behavior, and the most dishonorable, which he ensured would be avoided by the Templars. Medieval knights were obligated to a "chivalric code" or unwritten law of behavior. Bernard's personal chivalric code was governed by his strong Christian morality, and this also became part of the Templar Rule. There were four main knightly virtues that all knights were supposed to adhere to, and these were Christian values that were shared by the Knights Templar. They were: physical strength, courage with honor, loyalty to fellow knights, and the spirit of sacrifice.

First used at the end of the 13th century, the word "chivalry" arose from the French word *chevalier* meaning horseman. The accepted chivalric code at that time developed among lay knights as basically a moral system, or code of behavior. It comprised a duty to: fight for the welfare of all; protect those who could not protect themselves, such as widows, children and the elderly or infirm; obey those in authority; guard the honor of fellow knights; persevere to the end in any enterprise once started, and never turn one's back on a foe. All knights were expected to be strong, disciplined, loyal, generous, and honest. The Templars aimed to meet these ideals, but they also had a duty to put God and the Church before all. In the second half of the 12th century, an anonymous pilgrim observed:

> The Templars are most excellent soldiers. They wear white mantles with a red cross and when they go to war a standard of two colors called a balzaus is borne before them. They go in silence. Their first attack is the most terrible. In going they are the first. In returning—the last. They await the orders of their Master. When they think fit to make war and the trumpet has sounded, they sing in chorus the Psalm of David, "Not unto us, O Lord" . . . These Templars live under a strict religious rule, obeying humbly, having no private property, eating sparingly, dressing meanly and dwelling in tents.

In his treaty "In Praise of the New Knighthood," Bernard set out to describe the new type of knighthood that—unlike secular knights, who fought inspired by pride, anger, greed or yearning for glory or power—was inspired by honorable motives and a wish to defend the holiest sites on earth as well as their fellow Christians, and a genuine wish to overcome evil:

> This is, I say, a new kind of knighthood and one unknown to the ages gone by. It ceaselessly wages a twofold war both against flesh and blood and against a spiritual army of evil in the heavens . . . He is truly a fearless knight and secure on every side, for his soul is protected by the armor of faith just as his body is protected by armor of steel. He is thus doubly armed and need fear neither demons nor men . . . Gladly and faithfully he stands for Christ.
> BERNARD OF CLAIRVAUX, "IN PRAISE OF THE NEW KNIGHTHOOD," C.1135

A French illumination, of the future Baldwin IV as a boy showing William of Tyre his sores. It illustrates how William of Tyre recognized Baldwin's leprosy from an early age.

Secular knights traditionally underwent a special ceremony before they were invested and this involved them laying their swords on an altar, which showed that they were God's knights, but Bernard's vision for the Knights Templar went even further. Although this concept of knightly culture was often contradictory (and the Templars' role at first had seemed especially so), it became particularly popular during the period in which the Templars were gaining their respectability.

Saladin

Salah ad-Din Yusuf ibn Ayyub (1137/8–93), better known as Saladin, was the son of a Kurdish Muslim who worked for Nur ad-Din as a soldier and politician. Allegedly, in 1132, his father saved the life of Nur ad-Din's father Zengi, by helping him across the River Tigris when he had been defeated in a battle against the Caliph of Baghdad. From these humble beginnings, Saladin eventually became the first Sultan of Egypt and Syria, who plotted the Islamic reconquest of the Holy Land and the expulsion of the Christians there. A legendary hero of folk tales among Muslims and Christians alike, Saladin founded the Ayyubid dynasty and, leading his Muslim forces in the Holy Land, he became renowned for his courage, chivalry, and magnanimity. A devout, courteous and merciful man, Christian chroniclers related stories of his benevolence and humanity. He was an astute and able ruler who could also be ruthless when he believed it to be politic. Although he had many Christian friends, he believed they were all damned. Described as small in stature with a round face, black hair, and dark eyes, he was literate, cultured, and skilled in combat. As well as Christian enemies, he also had many jealous Muslim rivals who made alliances with the Christians in efforts to arrest his rise to power. Saladin began his ascent by ruling Egypt on behalf of Nur ad-Din as vizier. In 1170, he invaded Jerusalem and took the city of Eilat, severing Christian-ruled Jerusalem's connection with the Red Sea. In 1174, when Nur ad-Din died, he declared himself sultan in Egypt, and rushed to seize Damascus. Egypt's enormous wealth enabled him to build a vast empire that included Damascus and Aleppo, and stretched from Cyrenaica in present-day Libya to the River Tigris in present-day Iraq. His power and determination earned him the support of several other influential Muslims, including the Caliph of Baghdad and the Sultan of Anatolia.

Amalric I and Baldwin IV

King Baldwin III, the eldest son of Mélisende and Fulk of Jerusalem who had become king while still a child, died childless and was succeeded by his younger brother Amalric. Amalric I was King of Jerusalem from 1163 to 1174 and the father of three future rulers of Jerusalem: Sibylla, Baldwin IV, and Isabella I. In 1157, Amalric had married Agnes de

Courtenay, the daughter of Joscelin II of Edessa. The marriage had been accepted until Baldwin III died childless, then Patriarch Fulcher and others objected to Agnes de Courtenay on grounds of consanguinity, as the two shared a great-great-grandfather. Although Agnes and Amalric had three children: Sibylla, Baldwin, and Alix (who died in childhood), opposition to Agnes increased and many refused to endorse Amalric as king unless his marriage to Agnes was annulled. Eventually Amalric agreed and ascended the throne without a wife, although Agnes continued to hold the title Countess of Jaffa and Ascalon, and received a pension. She soon married the man to whom she had been engaged before her marriage with Amalric. The Church ruled that Amalric and Agnes's children were legitimate and preserved their place in the order of succession.

Amalric established himself as a good ruler, alternately attacking or creating treaties with Muslim neighbors in efforts to keep the peace. In 1167, he married Maria Comnena, a descendant of the Byzantine emperor Manuel I Comnenus. They had a daughter Isabella, and another stillborn daughter. Over the next few years, Jerusalem continued to be threatened by Nur ad-Din, and then by Saladin and also by the Assassins. It is not clear why, but when Amalric was first on the throne, a band of Templars murdered the emissary of the Assassins. When Amalric, who was trying to keep the peace, demanded that the leader of the Templar band be surrendered to him for punishment, the Templar Grand Master, Odo de St. Amand, refused. Instead, the Grand Master took the Templar in question and imprisoned him at Tyre. What happened to the prisoner after that remains a mystery, but relations between Amalric and the Templars became ambivalent. Two years later, when Nur ad-Din died in 1174, Amalric besieged Banias between Lebanon and Syria, but after giving up the siege he fell ill from dysentery. He reached Jerusalem but died a few weeks later, within a few months of Nur ad-Din. Baldwin succeeded his father and immediately brought his mother, Agnes de Courtenay, back to court.

Saladin continued to work to unite the Islamic states surrounding the Holy Land, and gradually managed to encircle the Kingdom of Jerusalem with Muslim-held territories.

Baldwin IV of Jerusalem (1161–85) was educated by the historian William of Tyre, later Archbishop of Tyre and Chancellor of the Kingdom of Jerusalem. It was William who recognized the symptoms of leprosy in the child, before he was crowned at the age of 13. A year into his reign, Baldwin's father's cousin, Raymond III of Tripoli, acting as regent for Baldwin, aimed to make a treaty with Saladin. Raymond was supported by the noble families established in Jerusalem and by the Knights Hospitaller, but opposed by the Templars and others in the Holy Land, such as Reynald de Châtillon (1125–87), who were eager to fight for more land rather than make compromising treaties. Raymond's regency ended on the second anniversary of Baldwin's coronation, when he was 15 years old. Noting the disunity within the Christian camp, according to William of Tyre, Saladin led a force of 26,000 men across the Sinai Desert towards the Templar fortress at Gaza. The Templars gathered to counter-attack, but Saladin and his army continued past them and laid siege to Ascalon, which the Christians had controlled since 1153. Young Baldwin IV raised an army to defend it, leaving Jerusalem unprotected. Saladin immediately left a minor force to restrain Baldwin at Ascalon and marched on to Jerusalem. Realizing his mistake, again according to William of Tyre, Baldwin summoned the Knights Templar from Gaza and broke out of Ascalon. In November 1177, Baldwin, Reynald de Châtillon, the Templars and

A watercolor on parchment, c.1460, from William of Tyre's "Historia," illustrating the death of Amalric I of Jerusalem and the Coronation of Baldwin IV.

overleaf
The Battle of Montgisard, November 25, 1177, painted by Charles-Philippe, c.1842. This dramatic and dynamic work shows the blind king, Baldwin IV, being carried on a litter into battle. The Crusaders are vastly outnumbered, but show no fear as they approach the massive Muslim army.

a secular army of about 2,000 men fell upon Saladin's huge army as they were crossing a ravine at Montgisard, near to the Jaffa–Jerusalem road. Taken completely by surprise, Saladin's force was overwhelmingly defeated, with 90 per cent killed. Saladin narrowly escaped and fled back to Egypt.

United under Islam

Undaunted nevertheless, Saladin continued to work to unite the Islamic states surrounding the Holy Land, and gradually managed to encircle the Kingdom of Jerusalem with Muslim-held territories. Persuaded by the Templars to reinforce the route to Damascus, King Baldwin IV began building the castle of Chastellet, 50 miles (80 kilometers) north of Jerusalem on the River Jordan at Jacob's Ford; the place where Jacob had wrestled with an angel, described in the Old Testament Book of Genesis. The building of Chastellet Castle was overseen by the Templar Grand Master, Odo de St Amand. The castle's location and impregnability induced Saladin to offer Baldwin considerable amounts of money to have it demolished, but no amount of money could convince Baldwin to destroy it. The more Saladin offered, the more determined Baldwin was to keep it, as it was clearly a big threat to the Muslims. In the summer of 1179,

before it was finished, Saladin attacked the castle. Baldwin, Raymond III of Tripoli, the Knights Templar led by Odo de St. Amand, and the Knights Hospitallers led by Roger des Moulins counter-attacked. A fierce fight ensued and the Muslims suffered heavy losses, but as usual, Saladin would not submit. He regrouped and decimated the Christian forces. Baldwin escaped with the relic of the True Cross, but Odo de St. Amand was captured and died in captivity the following year. A few weeks later, Saladin returned and laid siege to Chastellet Castle. Within six days he had overwhelmed the castle's defenses by sapping, a traditional method of assaulting castles. Saladin's men built tunnels beneath the 33-foot-high walls, filling them with wood and then setting the timber alight. At the time, there were 1,500 knights, architects, and builders inside the castle; 700 were killed and the other 800, overpowered by smoke, were taken captive. The next year, Baldwin and Saladin signed an uneasy two-year truce. In recounting the battle, William of Tyre, whose brother was killed in the conflict, blamed Odo de St. Amand for his arrogance and impetuosity. Naturally, William of Tyre was exceptionally biased because of the loss of his brother, but as he was the only chronicler of the events, our knowledge and understanding of them are incomplete.

Saladin gains ground

A year after the truce between Baldwin and Saladin, in 1181, Reynald de Châtillon attacked some rich Muslim caravans as they traveled to Mecca and Medina. Reynald had served in the Second Crusade and remained in the Holy Land after its defeat. He ruled as Prince of Antioch from 1153 to 1160 and through his second marriage became Lord of Oultrejourdain, an eastern extension of the Latin kingdom in the Holy Land. Saladin complained to Baldwin about Reynald's attack and demanded recompense for his breaking of the treaty. Baldwin complained to Reynald about his behavior, but Reynald refused to make amends. Early in 1182 before the truce was over, he launched a fleet of ships into the Red Sea where they raided Egyptian and Arabian ports, including Mecca and Medina. Saladin's brother gathered a force and drove them back. In May 1182, at the end of the peace agreement, Saladin rode out with an army from Cairo ready to fight the Christians. Because of his leprosy, Baldwin was now almost blind and had to be carried into battle on a litter. Accompanied by Heraclius, the new Patriarch of Jerusalem, and the relic of the True Cross, the Christians fought as hard as the Muslims and the result of the battle was inconclusive, with both sides claiming victory. The following summer, Saladin captured Aleppo, gaining control of the whole of Syria, essentially enclosing the Latin kingdoms with powerful Muslim territories.

With Outremer surrounded, Roger des Moulins, Heraclius, and the new Templar Grand Master, Arnold of Torroja, traveled to Europe to muster support. In London, Heraclius consecrated the Templars' new church. The Templars had recently benefited from a tragedy in England. In 1170, four of King Henry II's knights had murdered the Archbishop of Canterbury, Thomas Becket, in his cathedral. Their punishment was that each knight was to serve 14 years with the Templars in the Holy Land, and King Henry, who had incited them to Becket's murder, promised to provide the Templars with enough money to pay for 200 knights for a year. When Henry had died in 1172, he left 20,000 marks towards a crusade: 5,000 for the Templars; 5,000 for the Hospitallers; 5,000 to share between them, and 5,000 for miscellaneous religious houses, lepers and hermits

▶
A 12th-century illustration of a Templar knight galloping forward with a lance in battle. This is in the Templar Chapel in Cressac-Saint-Genis, France.

in Outremer. Apart from this, few others in Europe felt compelled to help the situation in the Holy Land at this time. The expense and failure of the Second Crusade was still fresh in everyone's minds and the travelers could muster little else in the way of donations. When Arnold of Torroja died in Verona in 1184, a new Grand Master, Gerard de Ridefort, was elected in Jerusalem. By then, the brave young King Baldwin IV was close to death through his debilitating disease.

Dissension in Jerusalem

In March 1185, Baldwin IV died and was buried in the Church of the Holy Sepulcher. His named successor, his eight-year-old nephew Baldwin V, also died the following year, leaving a power struggle for the throne of Jerusalem. Raymond III of Tripoli was the chosen regent until a suitable king could be found, but Sibylla, Baldwin IV's sister, claimed the throne for herself and her husband, Guy de Lusignan. Backed by Reynald de Châtillon, Gerard de Ridefort and the Knights Templar, and Patriarch Heraclius, Sibylla and Guy were crowned in August 1186. The Knights Hospitaller and their leader Roger des Moulins, however, supported Raymond of Tripoli, who, angry to be robbed of his

When Saladin learned that Raymond had made peace with King Guy, he amassed a huge force and attacked Raymond's city of Tiberias.

regency, had withdrawn to his northern territories. Raymond was also Prince of Galilee and Tiberias through his wife Eschiva. Distancing himself from the court of Jerusalem, he made an independent truce with Saladin and allowed a Muslim army to cross his territory, which aroused anxiety in Jerusalem that Raymond was about to ally himself with Saladin against them.

Throughout the winter of 1185–6, Gerard de Ridefort implored King Guy to march on Raymond and take Tripoli, to force Raymond to reconsider his loyalties. However, after considering this, by the spring of 1186, Guy and Sibylla were keen to make peace with Raymond instead of attacking him, so Gerard of Ridefort, Roger des Moulins, and a group of other carefully chosen men went to negotiate with Raymond. At the same time, by coincidence, Saladin's son al-Afdal, took some of his men to Tripoli. Upon hearing that Muslims were gathering there, Gerard de Ridefort immediately summoned as many of his Templars as he could and Roger des Moulins did the same with the Hospitallers. On May 1, an army made up of about 90 knights from the two orders, another 40 local knights, 300 foot soldiers, and the 2 Grand Masters arrived at the Springs of Cresson, north of Nazareth. Below them, a huge army of Muslims had gathered. Greatly outnumbered, Roger des Moulins and the Templar marshal James de Mailly urged Gerard de Ridefort to retreat; but he refused, taunting James de Mailly for being a coward. In the ensuing battle, both James de Mailly and Roger des Moulins were killed alongside almost every Christian knight. Of those who had entered the field, only four Christians survived, one of whom was Gerard de Ridefort.

The massacre at Cresson was a disaster undoubtedly brought on by Gerard's arrogance and impetuosity. The one good thing that emerged from it was the unification of the Christian factions, as Raymond of Tripoli and Sibylla and Guy were reconciled. When Saladin learned that Raymond had made peace with King Guy, he amassed a huge force and attacked Raymond's city of Tiberias. In response, Guy similarly summoned every Latin soldier in the Holy Land. King Henry II's money was used to pay for weapons and mercenaries and, by the end of June 1187, the medium-sized Christian army was ready.

The Battle of Hattin

On July 1, Saladin crossed the River Jordan near Lake Tiberias with 30,000 foot soldiers and 12,000 cavalry. He sent half his force up into the hills and took half to the shore of Lake Tiberias. While he was laying siege to Tiberias, the Christian army were settling into a good defensive position elsewhere. Their army included a large number of Templars and Hospitallers, Raymond of Tripoli, Reynald de Châtillon, many other nobles, and the Bishop of Acre who carried the True Cross. They all agreed to wait, believing that Saladin could not hold his huge army together in the hot and arid landscape and that it would soon break up without input from them. While they were waiting, on 2 July, a message arrived from Raymond's wife Eschiva, explaining that she was holding out against Saladin's army inside the mighty fortress of Tiberias, with a unit of loyal knights, but the situation was desperate. Frantic talks ensued in the Crusader encampment at the springs of Sepphoris, and many wanted to march to Tiberias immediately and attack the Muslim army, but despite knowing of the danger to his wife, Raymond advised the king not to. He said:

◀

Guy de Lusignan (c.1150–94) began as a knight and became king of the Crusader state of Jerusalem. He was also king of Cyprus from 1192 to 1194. His reign in Jerusalem culminated in the calamitous Battle of Hattin in July 1187, where he was captured by Saladin.

None of you is so fiercely attached, save to Christianity, as I am to the city. None of you is so desirous, as I am to succour or aid Tiberias. We and the king, however, should not move away from water, food and other necessities to lead such a multitude of men to death from solitude, hunger, thirst and scorching heat . . . Stay therefore, at this midway point, close to food and water . . . Then . . . we and our horses will be fresh; we will be aided and protected by the Lord's cross. Thus we will fight mightily against an unbelieving people who will be wearied by thirst and who will have no place to refresh themselves . . . the enemies of Christ . . . will be taken captive or else killed by sword, by lance or by thirst.

That night, several men, including Gerard de Ridefort, went to King Guy complaining that Raymond was not to be trusted as he had already sided with Saladin, and that they should not abandon Tiberias. The following day, they left their sheltered camp at Sepphoris and marched across the barren hills in the searing heat to attack the Muslims at Tiberias and rescue Eschiva and the knights with her. Tiberias was nine miles away and there was no reliable water source on the journey.

Saladin's vast army meanwhile had settled in Hattin, a well-watered village that descended towards Lake Tiberias. The entire surrounding area is called the Horns of Hattin for the two rocky peaks that rise over the brush-covered slopes behind Tiberias. By the evening of July 3, the Christian army reached a plateau above Hattin. Exhausted, they stopped there and set up camp. The place had been known to have a spring, but that had dried up and the only stream was blocked. Beneath the Christian camp, Saladin's army set fire to the brush on the hillside. Hot, thirsty, and choking from smoke that came from the burning scrub, the Christian troops spent a difficult night. Many could not sleep for need of water and some were so desperate that they left their camp and went to the nearby stream to quench their thirsts, only to be captured and beheaded by Saladin's men. By morning, Saladin's army had completely enclosed the Crusaders' camp. A chronicler of the event claimed, "not a cat could have slipped through the net." Outnumbered by ten to one as dawn approached, the parched and weak Crusaders nevertheless charged into the battle, but they were defeated within six hours.

The Crusader leaders who were still alive were rounded up and taken to Saladin's camp. This included King Guy, Gerard de Ridefort, and Reynald de Châtillon. The common soldiers were sold into slavery. Saladin demanded that all the Templars were executed without mercy except for their Grand Master, Gerard de Ridefort, who was

SHIFTING SANDS

Gerard de Ridefort

Believed to be of Flemish descent, unlike previous and later Grand Masters, Gerard de Ridefort, who headed the Order from 1185 to 1189, did not speak Arabic, nor was he a negotiator or diplomat. It is not certain when he arrived in the Holy Land, but by the late 1170s he was recorded as being in the service of King Baldwin IV. By 1179, he held the rank of Marshal of the Kingdom. It seems that Raymond III of Tripoli had promised to give him the hand of an heiress, but instead, Raymond married the lady in question to Plivain, the nephew of a wealthy merchant from Pisa who paid him 10,000 bezants for her, which was the lady's weight in gold. Furious, Ridefort's consequent hatred of Raymond of Tripoli influenced nearly all his major decisions. Once he knew he could not marry the heiress, he took vows as a Templar. By June 1183, he held the rank of Seneschal, and on the death of Arnold of Torroja in Verona, he was elected Grand Master. Opposing Raymond's claim to the throne of Jerusalem, Ridefort ended up putting the Templars in mortal danger. Arrogant, angry, impatient and impetuous, his grudge against Raymond of Tripoli had a disastrous impact on his decisions until, ultimately, the Templars suffered their most humiliating defeat at the Battle of Hattin.

to be spared. Individually the Templars and Hospitallers were forced to their knees while Muslim soldiers beheaded them. Chroniclers claim that every Templar met his death in silence and with humility. The True Cross, which was always carried by the Christians into battle, was either lost or taken by Saladin. In line with his reputation, Saladin treated King Guy mercifully, while he personally executed Reynald for his past offences. Gerard de Ridefort is believed to have traded his freedom for the Templar castle at Gaza. Once released, he joined Guy in an effort to regain the city of Acre, which had been taken by Saladin, but he was killed at the Siege of Acre in 1189. Following his victory at Hattin, Saladin had quickly captured Acre, Nablus, Jaffa, Toron, Sidon, Beirut, and Ascalon. After a short siege, by October of 1187, even Jerusalem was surrendered to him.

The news of the taking of Jerusalem spread alarm throughout western Christendom. Another Crusade was called for and on Pope Gregory VII's request, once more, thousands vowed to take the cross. Even the three greatest rulers of Europe—King Philip Augustus of France, King Richard I of England, and the Holy Roman Emperor, Frederick Barbarossa—vowed to travel to the Holy Land and re-establish Christian supremacy there. Taking charge of three large armies, the three powerful rulers set out in 1189, less than two years after the calamitous Battle of Hattin.

Richard the Lionheart

Obscured by legend as much as Saladin, Richard Coeur de Lion, or Richard the Lionheart (1157–99), was described as being tall and good-looking, with red-gold hair. His mother, the notorious Eleanor of Aquitaine, had been Queen of France when first married to Louis VII, and became Queen of England on marrying Henry II. Through his father, the King of England, Richard was a descendant of William the Conqueror and his great-grandfather was Fulk d'Anjou, later King Fulk of Jerusalem. As the third son of Eleanor and Henry, Richard did not expect to become king and spent little time in England. He never learned to speak English, although he spoke, read and wrote in French and understood Latin. But, unexpectedly, both his elder brothers died, and in July 1189, he became King of England at the age of 32.

The year before he ascended the throne, Richard had pledged to go on the Third Crusade. As soon as he was crowned, as King Richard I, he began raising money. He started by persecuting and robbing Jews, then he imposed a high tax on all his subjects, which became known as the "Saladin tithe." Next, he sold practically everything he had, including earldoms, lordships, sheriffdoms, castles, royal land, and even whole towns. When he was asked about some of his questionable money-raising methods, he declared that he "would sell the city of London if he could find a purchaser." On his way to the eastern Mediterranean, Richard decided to form an alliance with Sancho VI, the King of Navarre, and became engaged to his daughter Berengaria. This instantly angered King Philip II of France, Richard's stepbrother. Ever since they were children, Richard had been engaged to Philip's half-sister Alys and in view of this, Alys had been brought up at the English court since her childhood, but Richard refused to marry her as he said she had been the mistress of his father, Henry II. In September 1190, Richard and Philip met in Sicily and after some tense and angry negotiations, they finally reached an agreement, which included the end of Richard's betrothal to Alys. The following spring, Eleanor of Aquitaine brought Berengaria to Cyprus, where she and Richard were married. Although Richard had by then conquered Cyprus, he sold it to the Templars, who later sold it to Guy de Lusignan.

The Third Crusade

Under the Holy Roman Emperor Frederick, the German Crusaders had been the first to start off on their journey to the Holy Land. While the English and French armies traveled by sea, the German army was too large, so the entire force traveled overland. On reaching Asia Minor they were beaten back by marauding Turks as their predecessors had been on the Second Crusade. Emperor Frederick, known as Barbarossa or Kaiser Rotbart for his flame-red beard, was 67 years old and apparently still formidable, but on 10 June 1190, he drowned when crossing a swollen river. Chaos ensued and most of his demoralized army returned home. Only a small fraction of the original force, led by his son Frederick VI of Swabia, reached Acre.

Richard and Philip arrived at Acre in 1191 and added their forces to the Christian armies already there, besieging the city that Saladin had taken four years previously. After months of combat, with Richard fighting even while seriously ill, the city finally fell to the Crusaders. Richard made some bad decisions at that time which damaged his chivalrous reputation and caused him problems later. As soon as Acre fell, the Crusaders raised their standards as was the tradition at the end of a battle. Leopold V of Austria, who had been fighting for longer than either Richard or Philip, raised his standards along with the other Crusaders, but Richard immediately had them torn down. He was concerned that Leopold would take some of the booty he had agreed to share equally with Philip. Furious, Leopold returned to Austria with his troops. Philip also left the Holy Land almost immediately. His health had suffered and he had fallen out with Richard once again, this time over land in Cyprus.

After capturing Acre, Richard fought several further battles against Saladin over the next three years. The Templars' new Grand Master, Robert de Sablé, was Richard's good friend and their personalities complemented each other. Robert de Sablé was cautious and thoughtful, while Richard was intrepid and daring. In 1191, Richard and the Templars moved south, defeating Saladin's forces at the Battle of Arsuf in early September. Yet,

▶
From a woodcut by Gustave Doré in 1877, colored at a later date, this shows his dramatic vision of the 1191 Battle of Arsuf.

overleaf
Encaustic tiles from 1250–60 in Chertsey Abbey, Surrey, England, showing, on the left, Richard the Lionheart (1157–99), king of England from 1189, and on the right, Salah ad-Din Yusuf ibn Ayyub, (1137–93) known in the west as Saladin. The images imply that the two men met during the Third Crusade of 1191, but in fact they never met either on or off the battlefield.

SHIFTING SANDS

although they worked well together as a fighting force and Richard continued to display great courage, strength, and gallantry, the Crusaders failed to reclaim Jerusalem.

However, with Acre now in Christian hands, many Crusaders returned to Europe. It was not as holy as Jerusalem, but it was more important strategically and it became the political and economic center of the Christian territory in the Holy Land. Many Christians believed that with this stronghold, they would soon win Jerusalem back. Richard remained in the Holy Land as the leader of the forces there and established his headquarters at Jaffa. As the winter of 1191 approached, active campaigning was abandoned and, instead, the Crusaders occupied and refortified Ascalon. By the spring of 1192, Richard began to receive worrying news about his brother John's activities in England and the support he was receiving from Philip of France. It became evident that Richard would have to return to England soon. Realizing that he and the Crusaders could not conquer Jerusalem, he began to plan a retreat and, that summer, he traveled to the remaining Christian-ruled regions to discuss their options. Almost immediately, Saladin laid siege to Jaffa. The

▼

An illustration from an illuminated manuscript created by the 15th-century calligrapher David Aubert, showing the defeat of Saladin and his troops by the Crusaders at the Siege of Acre.

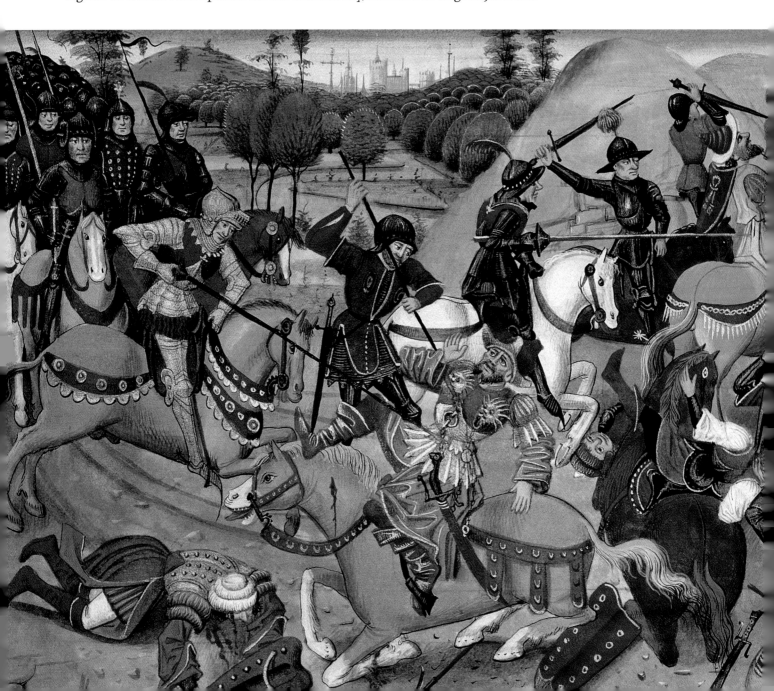

Saladin and Richard

Legend has it that when Richard's horse was felled beneath him during the Battle of Jaffa, Saladin saw him fighting on foot. Impressed by Richard's courage, Saladin ordered two stallions from his own stables to be dispatched as a replacement for his enemy. Yet although Richard requested to meet Saladin on numerous occasions, Saladin always refused, declaring: "Kings meet together only after the conclusion of an accord, for it is unthinkable for them to wage war once they know one another and have broken bread together. In any event, I do not understand your language, and you are ignorant of mine, and we therefore need a translator in whom we both have confidence. Let this man, then, act as a messenger between us. When we arrive at an understanding, we will meet, and friendship will prevail between us."

small force that had been left there fought desperately against the Muslim army, but it was huge and eventually stormed the walls of the garrison. Hearing the news, Richard hastily gathered a small army and hurried back south. Arriving by sea, he discovered that the city was almost lost, so he leapt into the water and waded ashore, leading his small force of 54 knights, a few hundred infantry, and 2,000 crossbowmen. Stunned by the sudden onslaught, Saladin's men panicked, believing them to be a just a small part of a much larger relief force, and they fled, leaving their prisoners to take up arms and chase them. As he always did, within three days, Saladin attacked again. He had reorganized his troops and mounted a fresh attack, but Richard and the Templars overpowered them. Muslim losses were even heavier than at the first encounter and, under Richard's orders, all Muslim prisoners were executed. It was the last major engagement of the Third Crusade.

The truce

Soon after the Battle of Jaffa, on September 2, 1192, Saladin and Richard negotiated a three-year truce. Richard left for England, but on his journey, he was shipwrecked and had to travel through Austria. Although he and his companions disguised themselves as pilgrims or, it is said by some, as Knights Templar, Richard was recognized and captured by Leopold's men. He spent the next 18 months in custody, first with Leopold and then with the Holy Roman Emperor, Henry VI. Although the practice was forbidden among monarchs, Henry VI demanded a vast ransom for Richard. His brother John who was ruling England had no desire for Richard's return, so despite being over 70 years old, his mother Eleanor raised the money and traveled to Germany with it to secure Richard's release.

The Third Crusade, which had lasted for three years from 1189 to 1192, became known as the Kings' Crusade. Although successful in some ways, it did not achieve its ultimate goal—the reconquest of Jerusalem. The consequence of it all was that Richard agreed to demolish Ascalon and Saladin agreed to recognize Christian territories along the coast. Christians and Muslims were to be allowed to cross each other's regions and Christian pilgrims were to be allowed to visit Jerusalem and other holy sites under Muslim rule freely and safely. Richard never returned to the Holy Land and Saladin died the following year, in March 1193.

The loss of Jerusalem

The Battle of Hattin was a devastating setback for the Templars. The huge number of losses they had sustained had not only seriously impaired their organization, but it had been highly costly as well. They had lost many valuable men, as well as expensive equipment and armor. They fought in every battle against Saladin, and although he showed clemency to many of his captives, he inflicted terrible revenge on any Templars or Hospitallers he took. Arabic sources testify to the Templars' outstanding technical skill, battle prowess and pride, as well as the fear they inspired in their opponents, and this infuriated Saladin. During every crusading expedition in the Holy Land, the Templars took the front or rear guard, they fought to the last in every battle and they covered all retreats. Years of training had made them the greatest force in the Holy Land, but with so many outstanding soldiers now killed, the entire organization was debilitated.

The continued survival of the Templar Order depended on its honor. The greater the respect it commanded, the larger the donations it received. So after Hattin, when general confidence in the Templars' invincibility was shaken, wealthy benefactors reconsidered where they would put their money and potential recruits thought hard about whether or not to join the Brotherhood. For approximately 70 years, the Templars' purpose had been the defense of the Holy Land. With the fall of Jerusalem, they had failed in that essential aim—and they had lost their headquarters on Temple Mount. Gerard de Ridefort had been the first questionable Grand Master, elected more for his combative prowess than for his honesty and integrity. His occasional underhand tactics and frequent futile decisions had led many courageous Templars to their deaths. Although he was valiant and decisive, contrary to all previous Grand Masters with their transparent reputations, he was also

The seal of Richard I of England resembles the seal of the Knights Templar, as they were in close affinity, only the king's seal shows him jousting while the Templars' seal shows their poverty in the sharing of a horse.

The Templar seal was an image of two knights on one horse to illustrate the monks' personal poverty. The Greek and Latin characters, *Sigillum Militum Xpisti*, followed by a cross means "the Seal of the Soldiers of Christ."

arrogant and reckless—more like a secular knight than a religious one. Reynald de Châtillon was another character who had created extra problems with his vengeful pride that should have had no part in a Christian struggle. And conflicts between factions over who should rule Jerusalem had also contributed to the difficulties and disharmony that ultimately resulted in the Christian losses. But no one person was ultimately to blame. Circumstances, timing, and personalities all played their part and the result was that less than a century after its conquest by the Christians, Jerusalem was back under Muslim rule. The relic of the True Cross, the most sacred Christian object that had been held aloft before every Crusader battle, was lost forever, and the Knights of the Temple of Solomon had to leave their headquarters on the most holy of sites, Temple Mount. They moved their headquarters to Acre, along with the seat of the Kingdom of Jerusalem.

> Less than a century after its conquest by the Christians, Jerusalem was back under Muslim rule.

However, all was not entirely lost. Richard the Lionheart's courage and Saladin and Robert de Sablé's wisdom and diplomacy had enabled the honor of the Templars to be rebuilt. Following Sablé's prudence, for nearly 14 years after his death in 1193, the Templars avoided further conflict with the Muslims. Instead, trade began flourishing between the Christians and the Muslims and new recruits began enlisting to be Knights Templar once more. In the reduced Christian states of Outremer, the Templars and the Hospitallers began buying property cheaply that had been left by Europeans who, in the aftermath of the Third Crusade, had returned to the West. So by the turn of the 13th century, the two orders had become the major landowners in the Christian regions of Palestine. They were regaining money, land, recruits, and respectability.

The Hospitallers

The Order of the Knights of Saint John the Hospitaller was founded as a charitable group to help sick pilgrims in the Holy Land. The military aspect of their organization only began later as an additional element in their service to Christianity, although they continued with their traditional objectives of hospitality, often stressing that this was their main duty. By the late 12th century, the Templars and the Hospitallers were frequently used together in battles and were sent on the same diplomatic missions. Ordinary people could not always tell the two orders apart, although in general the Templars were largely French and the Hospitallers Italian and Spanish—the Hospitallers had strong associations with merchants from Amalfi in Italy. Comprising of Benedictine monks and nuns who cared for female pilgrims, the Hospitallers' habits were also different from the Templars, being black with white crosses.

Along with infirmaries and hospices, the Hospitallers were also given castles and fortresses. In 1142, for instance, Raymond II of Tripoli gave them the Krak des Chevaliers in Syria which remained in their possession until it fell in 1271. While in their ownership, it was known as Crac de l'Ospital, and was not called the Krak des Chevaliers (Fortress of the Knights) until the 19th century, long after the knights had left. They began rebuilding the castle as soon as it was in their possession, completing it by 1170, after which an earthquake damaged it. They controlled several castles along the border of the County of Tripoli, but the Krak des Chevaliers was one of the most important as it functioned as a hospital, a center of administration, and a military base.

Although there was sometimes tension between them, generally the Templars and the Hospitallers supported each other on and off the battlefield. Benefactors often shared their donations equally between them. The main disagreements that occurred between them were to do with who should inherit the crown of Jerusalem, if there were various potential heirs. Both orders were subject to criticism from the outside world, the difference being that when things became uncomfortable, the Hospitallers would lie low in their hospices and infirmaries, while the Templars had to carry on in the outside world, visibly policing pilgrim routes and running their businesses. Although the Hospitallers, like the Templars, also built castles as well as several round churches in the image of the Church of the Holy Sepulcher, and they lent money, they never became as rich as the Templars and they did not attract such high-profile investors. In 1307, when King Philip IV of France began persecuting the Templars, he harassed the Hospitallers equally, but when they slipped out of his grasp he did not bother to pursue them further. When Jacques de Molay was originally summoned to meet with Pope Clement V and the King of France, the Hospitallers' Grand Master, Fulk de Villaret, was summoned too, but he avoided the meeting. His excuse was that "he was stopped in his way at Rhodes by the Saracens." Had King Philip determined to catch the Hospitallers, he would have done so, but they avoided

▼

Built by Arabs in the first half of the 11th century, the Krak des Chevaliers ("Fortress of the Knights") fell into Crusader hands in 1099. It became the headquarters of the Knights Hospitaller in 1144 and they expanded it into the largest Crusader fortress in the Holy Land. The castle remained in their hands until 1271. King Edward I of England based all his Welsh castles on its design.

vilification because the king did not covet what they had as much as he yearned for the Templars' possessions. The Hospitallers therefore continued as an order for centuries after the demise of the Templars, even gaining most of the Templars' property after their suppression.

Meanwhile, in the Holy Land after the Third Crusade, the situation was volatile once more. Although Richard the Lionheart had defeated Saladin at the Battle of Arsuf in 1191 and the Battle of Jaffa in 1192 and so recovered most of the coast for the Latin kingdom, he had not recovered Jerusalem or any of the other inland territories. Some historians have suggested that this was a deliberate move by Richard as he recognized that Jerusalem was a strategic liability because it was isolated from the sea. The Third Crusade had ended peacefully, however, with the Treaty of Ramla negotiated in 1192. Saladin allowed pilgrimages to be made to Jerusalem, and once the Crusaders had prayed at the holy sites, most of them returned home. Those remaining in the Holy Land set about rebuilding their kingdom from Acre.

The Fourth Crusade

With pilgrims still being allowed to visit the Holy City and the Templars rebuilding, retraining and recovering their strength, another Crusade was not seen as a priority by Europeans. In 1198, Pope Innocent III appealed for a Fourth Crusade, but there was little enthusiasm for it. Then, at the end of November in 1199, a zealous preacher, Fulk of Neuilly, arrived at the Castle of Ecry-sur-Aisne, where Count Theobald III of Champagne was hosting a jousting tournament. Launching into an impassioned speech, Fulk inspired all present with dreams of reconquering Jerusalem for Christendom.

Envoys were sent to Venice, Genoa, and other city-states to discuss a contract for transport to Egypt and, in March 1201, negotiations were opened with Venice. The Venetians agreed to transport 33,500 Crusaders, but would require a year of shipbuilding and training of their sailors to man the ships. These activities would severely restrict the city's usually brisk commercial activities, but a suitable payment was agreed so the Venetian shipbuilders began work. The Crusading army was expected to comprise 4,500 knights (with horses), 9,000 squires and 20,000 foot soldiers.

Although Richard the Lionheart had defeated Saladin at the Battle of Arsuf and the Battle of Jaffa, he had not recovered Jerusalem.

As in previous Crusades, the bulk of those who pledged to take the cross originated from France. Some came from the Holy Roman Empire, and now many also came from Venice. The Crusade was to be ready to sail in the summer of 1202 for the Ayyubid capital of Cairo. Since Saladin's death, his sons had quarreled over his territorial legacy, so his empire had fallen apart, and rival factions ruled in Cairo and Damascus. As there was no cohesive agreement that all the Crusaders would sail from Venice, many chose to sail from other ports, such as Flanders, Marseilles and Genoa, so by 1201 when the troops assembled at Venice, there were far fewer than had been anticipated. The Venetians had prepared 50 war galleys and 450 other boats as agreed—enough for three times the assembled army. The Crusaders gathered there did not have the 85,000 silver marks that had been agreed between them, so the Venetians refused to let them sail. By pooling their resources, the Crusaders managed to amass 51,000 silver marks, but this left them penniless and the strain on the Venetian economy

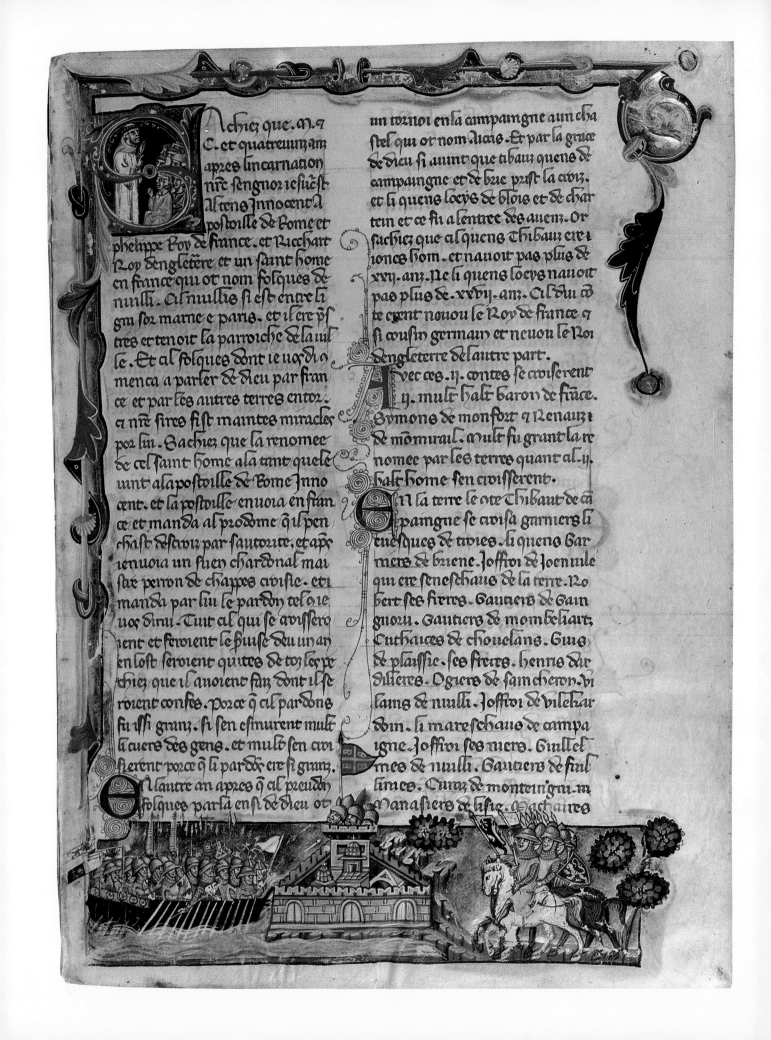

Achiez que .M. et quatrevinz anz apres lincarnation nre sengnor iesucst Al tens Innocent la postoille de Rome et phelippe Roy de france. et Ricchart Roy dengletere et un saint home en france qui ot nom folques de nuilli. Cil nuilli si est entre li gni sor marne e paris. et il ere pstres et tenoit la parroiche de la uil le. Et cil folques dont ie uos di menca a parler de dieu par fran ce et par les autres terres entoz. et nre sires fist maintes miracles por lui. Sachiez que la renomee de cel saint home ala tant quele uint ala postoille de Rome Inno cent. et la postoille enuoia en fran ce et manda al prodome quil pre chast de croiz par sauctorite. et apres enuoia un suen chardonal mai stre perron de chappes croisie. et manda par lui le pardon tel ie uos dirai. Tuit cil qui se croisseroi ent et seruient le ffuse dieu .i. an en lost seroient quites de toz les pe chiez que il auoient faiz dont il se roient confes. Por ce q cil pardons fu issi granz. si sen esmurent mult li cuers des gens. et mulz sen croi sierent por ce q li pardons ere si granz. En lautre an apres q cil pcediu folques parla en si de dieu ot

un tornoi en la campaingne a un cha stel qui ot nom aicis. Et par la grace de dieu si auint que tibauz quens de campaingne et de brie prist la croiz. et li quens loeys de blois et de char tein et ce fu a lentree des auenz. Or sachiez que cil quens Thibauz ere iones hom. et nauoit pas plus de xxii. anz. Ne li quens loeys nauoit pas plus de xxvii. anz. Cil dui co te erent neuou le Roy de france q si cousin germain et neuou le Roi dengleterre de lautre part.

Avec ces .ii. contes se croiserent .ii. mult halt baron de fiace. Symons de monfort q Renauz de momirail. mult fu grant la re nomee par les terres quant al .ii. halt home sen croisserent.

En la terre le cte Thibaut de ca paigne se croisa garniers li euesques de trioes. li quens bar niers de briene. Joffroi de ioenuile qui ere seneschaus de la terre. Ro bert ses freres. Gautiers de sain gnoru. Gautiers de mombeliart. Euthauces de chonelans. Gius de plaissie. ses freres. henris dur sistieres. Ogiers de sain cheron. vi lains de nuilli. Joffroi de vilehar doin. li mareschaus de campa igne. Joffroi ses niers. Guillel mes de nuilli. Gautiers de sint sintes. Cuns de montetigni. m Manassiers de lisle. Machaires

was enormous. Not only had they kept their side of the bargain, halting their own trading enterprise for many months, but they also had to send 30,000 men out of their population of approximately 80,000 to man the fleet, which stretched their resources even further.

The leader of Venice, the Doge, and his ministers considered what to do. The amount they had received from the Crusaders was not enough to cover their costs, but to prevent the Crusade going ahead would be counter-productive. Twenty years previously, in 1182, the Venetian merchant population had been expelled from Byzantium. So the Venetians proposed that the Crusaders could pay their debts by attacking the port of Zara on the eastern coast of the Adriatic. Zara was a Christian city, but it was also a naval and commercial rival to Venice and, although most Christians including the Pope were against this, the Crusaders went ahead and besieged and captured the unsuspecting port of Zara. Next, the Venetians persuaded them to attack Constantinople. The possession of this great capital would greatly increase Venetian trade and influence, and many Crusaders saw it as an opportunity to gain wealth and power. So against all the Crusaders stood for, in 1204, they continued in their digression from the Holy Land and attacked Constantinople, a Christian city which for centuries had formed the chief defense between Europe and the Muslims.

Contrary to all Church teachings, the Crusaders burned and slaughtered, destroying or pillaging precious artefacts, including monuments, statues, paintings, and manuscripts. They divided the lands between themselves and the Venetians and they crowned Baldwin, the Count of Flanders, Emperor of the East. But it did not last. The Byzantine inhabitants who remained there would not acknowledge the invaders and the new empire only

◄

This richly illustrated manuscript from *La Conquête de Constantinople* by Geoffrey de Villehardouin, c.1330, shows Fulk of Neuilly preaching the Fourth Crusade to some seated men in the top "s," while the lower border shows Crusaders arriving at Constantinople.

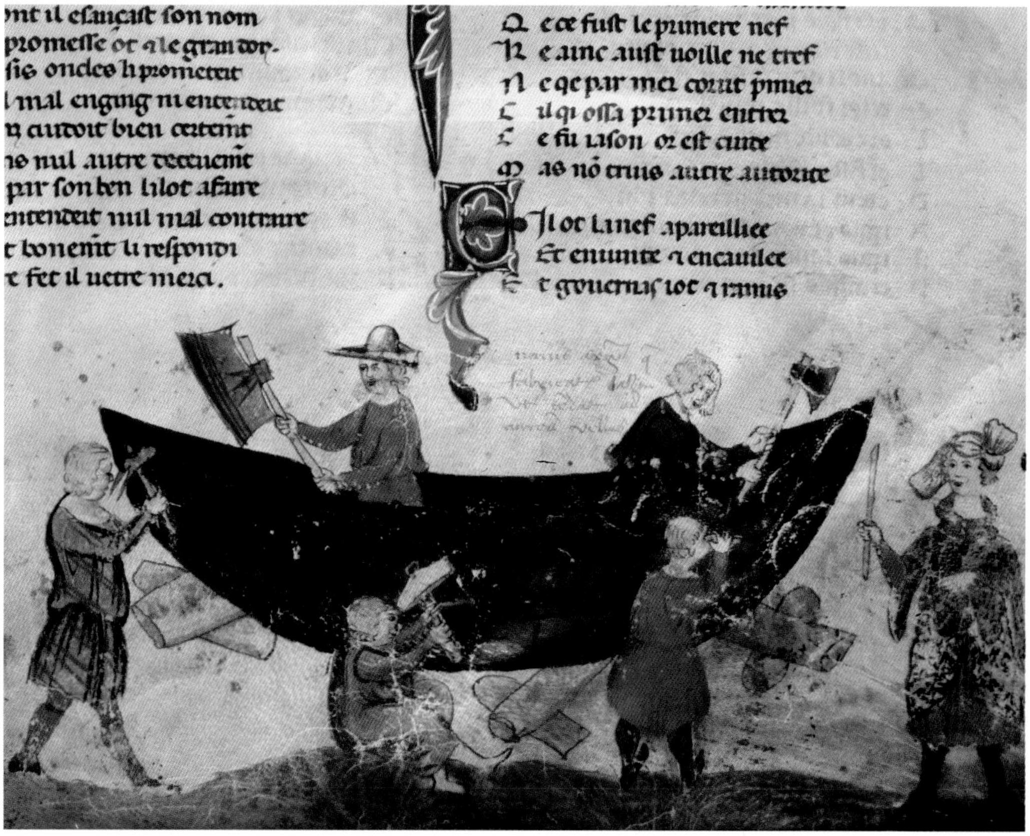

►

A 14th-century Italian miniature showing Venetian shipbuilders building a ship. During the medieval period, Venice became wealthy through its control of trade between Europe and the Levant. From the start of the Crusades, Venice was involved, as Crusaders paid for Venetian ships to assist them. In 1123, they were granted virtual autonomy in the Kingdom of Jerusalem. It is possible that Venetian shipbuilders helped the Templars build their fleet.

survived just over 50 years until 1261, when the Byzantines reconquered their own city. The consequence, however, was that Constantinople had lost its power. Two centuries later it fell to the Turks. The greed and lust for power of the Crusaders and the Venetians had given the Turks a path into Europe.

The Fifth Crusade

While many knights were conquering Constantinople, others were suppressing the Cathars in France. The Templars were not active in either of these ignominious battles, but in 1217, the Pope launched the Fifth Crusade and involved the Templars from the start. In Paris, the Templar treasurer was put in charge of donations for the cause, while various European leaders came forward to join, including King Andrew of Hungary, Leopold, Duke of Austria, and John of Brienne, the King of Jerusalem. Templars, Hospitallers, and the new German order of Teutonic Knights also gathered but, with no main leader, a papal legate was put in charge: Cardinal Pelagius, a pious man with no military experience. Nevertheless, with their prowess and courage, the Templars played a significant role. In 1219, the Crusaders besieged the port of Damietta, which controlled the eastern mouth of the River Nile. The Egyptian sultan, Saladin's nephew al-Kamil, was so distressed by the idea of losing Damietta that he offered to trade it for Jerusalem, but Cardinal Pelagius insisted that Jerusalem could not be held now without Christian control of the surrounding lands, so the Crusaders rejected the offer and continued besieging Damietta. In 1221, before they had completely secured Damietta, Pelagius ordered them to march on to Egypt, but as they approached, al-Kamil's forces opened the gates of the irrigation canals, causing the Nile to flood and trapping the Crusaders. Although the Templars valiantly covered the Crusaders' retreat, Pelagius had no alternative but to give up Damietta after all, not in return for Jerusalem, but to save the Crusaders' lives. The Fifth Crusade was abandoned and the military orders returned to Acre.

> Although the Templars valiantly covered the Crusaders' retreat, Pelagius had no alternative but to give up Damietta after all, to save the Crusaders' lives.

The Sixth Crusade

Seven years after the Fifth Crusade, a Sixth Crusade was launched. Frederick II, the Holy Roman Emperor, had sent German troops to the Fifth Crusade, but had not accompanied them himself. Feeling guilty that he had not been there, Frederick declared he would lead a new Crusade to win back Jerusalem, paid entirely with Holy Roman Empire funds. His links with the Holy Land arose from his marriage in 1225 to Yolande of Jerusalem (also known as Isabella), daughter of John of Brienne and Maria of Montferrat. Two years later, after Gregory IX became Pope, Frederick and his army set sail from Brindisi in Italy, for Acre. On the journey, the entire army suffered a severe epidemic and Frederick was compelled to return to Italy. The Pope, who feared Frederick's power and saw this as another ploy to avoid direct confrontation, excommunicated him for breaking his Crusader vow. After unsuccessfully trying to negotiate with the Pope, in 1228, in spite of his excommunication, Frederick amassed another army and set sail for the Holy Land once more. But as soon as he arrived, he realized that his small army would be no match for the powerful Ayyubid force. With the hope of regaining Jerusalem through diplomacy,

This is a detail from a 15th-century copy of a 13th-century manuscript, *Le Miroir Historial* by Vincent de Beauvais. Crusaders are disembarking at Damietta, while more ships follow and other knights march on towards the fortress ahead. There are several amusing details, including some of the knights stumbling under helmets that cover their eyes, one knight attempting to pick up something he has dropped from his horse, and a serious-looking churchman.

he communicated with the sultan al-Kamil and pretended to have a far larger army. His strategy worked. Busy crushing a rebellion in Syria, al-Kamil surrendered Jerusalem, Nazareth and other smaller towns in exchange for a ten-year truce. In March 1229, Frederick entered Jerusalem.

Although intending to join Frederick and his troops, the Templars had remained a day's march behind the German army so they would not have to fraternize with an excommunicant. The Templars, Hospitallers, and the Patriarch of Jerusalem were not as pleased about regaining Jerusalem as those in Europe were. The issue raised at the Fifth Crusade ten years earlier still stood: that Jerusalem was indefensible without Christian control of the surrounding lands. The city's formidable walls had been torn down during the Fifth Crusade and part of the agreement with al-Kamil was that neither the Templars nor the Hospitallers could rebuild or refortify their castles in any surrounding areas. Another stipulation was that Temple Mount was to remain Muslim. The Templars would be forbidden to return to their former headquarters. It was a hollow victory and the Pope condemned the treaty, saying this was not what the Christians wanted. Frederick had recovered Jerusalem without the Pope's, the nobles', or the military orders' recommendations or advice. The Patriarch of Jerusalem placed an interdict on the city, forbidding church ceremonies while Frederick was there, and the Templars and the Hospitallers kept away. So Frederick crowned himself, naming himself the King of Jerusalem and "God's Vicar on Earth." He spoke to those Christians living in the Holy Land, complaining about the Patriarch and the Templars and Hospitallers, but no one was impressed. In the end, Frederick's men were ordered to close the gates of Jerusalem, shutting out those he considered to be his enemies, which included the Templars. He also plotted to have the Templar Grand Master, Pedro de Montaigu, captured, but he was too well protected by the Order. Within two days, Frederick left Jerusalem, allegedly fearing that the Templars were plotting to murder him.

Pilgrims' Castle

In 1217, during the Fifth Crusade, the Templars began building Atlit Castle (see page 110) on a promontory on the Palestinian coast, south of Haifa. As well as Atlit, the castle became known variously as Athlit Castle, Château Pèlerin, the Castle of Jesus or Pilgrims' Castle. The Templars built it with the help of the Hospitallers, Teutonic Knights, and many pilgrims, to replace their small watchtower called Le Destroit, "the Pass." During its construction, they discovered three fresh water wells and a stash of ancient coins, which they put towards the cost of the building. In 1219, Duke Leopold VI of Austria and Earl Ranulf of Chester made further generous donations of money towards it. It became one of the major Crusader fortresses and could support up to 4,000 troops in siege conditions. With its own port, polygonal church, and defensive walls that were protected by a moat, the castle was a marvel of its time and impossible to be mined or sapped by enemies. In a gesture of his hatred of the Templars, before he left the Holy Land Frederick II tried to besiege them in Pilgrims' Castle, but failed.

Somehow, the Templars had become involved in a personal conflict between the Holy Roman Emperor and the Pope. The hostilities that continued between Frederick and Gregory overflowed into the military order that was duty-bound to the Pope. On his return to Europe, as soon as Frederick reached Sicily, he seized property belonging to the Templars, released their Muslim slaves and imprisoned the Templars living there instead.

The seal of Frederick II (1194–1250), Holy Roman Emperor 1215–50. The inscription in the center of the seal refers to his campaign of 1228 when he won back the Holy Land and crowned himself King of Jerusalem.

Muslim dissonance

Meanwhile, Jerusalem remained exposed and vulnerable, and by the time the ten-year truce expired in 1239, al-Kamil was dead and his younger son, as-Salih Ayyub, was in power. As-Salih, also known as al-Malik al-Salih, ruled the Ayyubids of Egypt from 1240 to 1249. In 1221, he had been taken hostage by Frederick's army in retaliation for the capture of John of Brienne by al-Kamil, as a pawn for the return of Damietta. In 1234, al-Kamil had sent as-Salih to Damascus, removing him from the succession in Egypt after suspecting him of conspiracy with the Mamluks, but as-Salih immediately allied with the Khwarezmian Turks against his uncle as-Salih Ismail, ruler of Damascus. The Khwarezmians began as vassals of the Seljuk Turks at the end of the 11th century and later became rulers themselves. In 1238, al-Kamil died and was succeeded by al-Salih's elder brother, but within two years, al-Salih had taken control of Egypt. In 1244, the Khwarezmians sacked Jerusalem, and later that year al-Salih and the Khwarezmians defeated another of al-Salih's uncles in Syria, who had allied with the Crusader Kingdom of Jerusalem at the Battle of La Forbie. In 1245, al-Salih captured Damascus, and was awarded the title of Sultan by the Caliph in Baghdad. The next year the forces of the Ayyubids defeated the Khwarezmians, who no longer recognized al-Salih as their lord.

The Seventh Crusade

In 1249, while al-Salih was away fighting his uncle in Syria, Louis IX of France invaded Egypt on what became known as the Seventh Crusade, and occupied Damietta. Al-Salih quickly returned, but died after his leg was amputated. While his heir, al-Muazzam Turanshah, was far away, the Mamluks gained power in Egypt. The Mamluk dynasty became known as the Bahriyya or the Salihiyya.

The appointment of the new Templar Grand Master, Armand de Périgord (1178–c.1247) in about 1231, was believed by many to have been maneuvered by Frederick II as a way of weakening the Templars. In 1232, Armand de Périgord organized various attacks on Muslim-ruled regions in Outremer, but each failed and therefore diminished the Templars' effectiveness. In one expedition in 1236, the Templars were massacred and, in 1244, when al-Salih and the Khwarezmians captured Jerusalem, the Templars, Hospitallers, and Teutonic Knights allied with the Sultan of Damascus and his army. They confronted al-Salih and his Khwarezmian allies at the Battle of La Forbie, a small village northeast of Gaza. Initially successful, the Crusaders gradually lost momentum as the Khwarezmians attacked their rear and flanks. Although the Templars fought as tenaciously as ever, the allied forces were routed. Over 5,000 Crusaders died and 800 were taken prisoner. From the military orders, only 33 Templars, 27 Hospitallers, and three Teutonic Knights survived. It is not clear whether Armand de Périgord was killed during the battle or whether he was captured and survived until 1247. The Battle of La Forbie marked a

The Thousand Man

In the 1240s, al-Salih had bought a slave, a Turk called Qalawun, for 1,000 dinars. Qalawun later rose to the position of Sultan and was always known as al-Alfi, or "the Thousand Man," reflecting his purchase price. Although he barely spoke Arabic, he rose in power and influence as a Mamluk and became an emir under Sultan Baibars, whose son was married to Qalawun's daughter. In power, Qalawun founded a dynasty that lasted a hundred years.

woute le feu dont dieu
le gart a petit pont.
Or disons dont q̃
grant grace nous
fist dieu le tout puissac
quant il nous deffen
Ci deuise comment da
miete fu prinse.

di de mort et de peril a la
riuer la ou nous arriua
mes a pie et courumes
sus a nos ennemis q
qui estoient a cheual.

rant grace
nous fist
nostre seig
neur de da

miete que il nous de
liura. la quele nous
ne deussions pas auoir
prise sanz affamer. Et

decisive end to Christian power in the Holy Land, even though the Khwarezmians were defeated just two years later in 1246. Never again were Christians a strong presence in Outremer, and Crusades and crusading lost all popularity and force.

In achieving success in the Holy Land without papal involvement, Frederick II had set a precedent and marked a decline in papal authority across Europe and Outremer. Although they never regained their momentum, further crusades were launched by

> Never again were Christians a strong presence in Outremer, and crusades and crusading lost all popularity and force.

kings rather than popes. The fall of Jerusalem once again, this time to al-Salih and the Khwarezmians, was no longer considered a crucial event to European Christians, and despite several calls to arms from the Pope, there was little enthusiasm for another Crusade. Most European rulers had their own local struggles and turmoils to contend with and the only sovereign interested in beginning another Crusade was Louis IX of France. In 1245, he declared his intent to take the cross. In the aftermath of the Albigensian Crusade, France was in a stronger position, with Provence now under Parisian control and Poitou ruled by Louis IX's brother, Alphonse de Poitiers. Alphonse and another brother, Charles I of Anjou, joined Louis on the Crusade. In 1248, Louis sailed from France with his large army of 36 ships, first to Cyprus, where they spent the winter, and then to Damietta, which they took easily from the Egyptians. Not realizing that the Nile flooded each year, however, the Crusading force found itself trapped at Damietta for six months. That was the first of many setbacks and over the next year, following a succession of mistakes, Louis was taken captive at the Battle of Fariskur, where his army was vanquished by the Egyptians. During his captivity, Louis fell ill with dysentery but was cured by an Arab physician. He was then ransomed for 800,000 bezants and the surrender of Damietta. After this humiliating and expensive defeat, Louis was set free and traveled to Acre, one of few remaining Crusader possessions in Syria. Louis made an alliance with the Mamluks, who at the time were rivals of the Sultan of Damascus, and from his new base in Acre he organized the rebuilding of the other Crusader cities, particularly Jaffa and Saida. In 1254, his money ran out, and at the same time he was recalled to France where his mother and regent, Blanche of Castile, had recently died. Before leaving, at the expense of the French crown, he established a standing French garrison at Acre. His Crusade was a failure, but he was lauded in Europe. In 1270, Louis attempted another Crusade, though that too ended in failure.

Later Crusades

The Eighth Crusade was also launched by Louis IX and is sometimes counted as part of the Seventh. The Ninth Crusade is also sometimes counted as part of the Eighth. Disturbed by events in Syria where the Mamluk Sultan Baibars of Egypt had captured Nazareth, Haifa, Toron, and Arsuf, by 1265 Hugh III of Cyprus, the nominal King of Jerusalem, landed in Acre and two years later, even though he had little support, Louis called for a new Crusade. His brother, Charles of Anjou, convinced him to attack Tunis first, to give them a strong base from which to attack Egypt. As King of Sicily, Charles had his own interests in this part of the Mediterranean. In 1270, Louis landed on the African coast in the sweltering summer heat. Poor drinking water infected much of the army with dysentery, and Louis too contracted it and died. Charles proclaimed

An elaborate 14th-century illuminated manuscript from *The History of St. Louis* (St. Louis was the name many called Louis IX after his death), showing the Capture of Damietta.

Louis' 25-year-old son, Philip III, the new king, but because of his lack of experience, Charles became the actual leader of the Crusade. Through further illness among the Crusaders, the siege of Tunis was abandoned and, on hearing of the death of Louis, Sultan Baibars canceled his plan to send Egyptian troops to Tunis to fight him. Charles meanwhile allied himself with Prince Edward of England, who had arrived in Acre.

All this time, the Templars and Hospitallers maintained their headquarters in Acre. Relations with some Muslim factions were cautiously cordial, while others were not. By 1276, the situation had become so perilous that the King of Jerusalem, Henry II, moved away from Palestine altogether and settled on the island of Cyprus. The situation worsened. In 1278, the Syrian port of Latakia fell. In 1289, Tripoli was lost. It was a desperate state of affairs, but the West had lost interest. In the end, 25 Venetian galleys and 5 galleys from King James II of Aragon arrived in Acre, carrying the new Crusader army: a crowd of ill-disciplined men with no regular pay. On arrival, they began fighting the locals and indiscriminately pillaging from both Muslims and Christians. In 1290, the Mamluks led by Sultan Qalawun marched on Acre, but he died in November before launching the attack. He was succeeded by his son, al-Ashraf Khalil, who sent a message to William de Beaujeu, the Grand Master of the Templars, telling of his intentions to attack Acre and urging him not to send messengers or gifts. Ignoring the request, a delegation from Acre led by Sir Philip Mainebeuf arrived in Cairo with gifts trying to appeal to Khalil and convince him not to attack Acre. The sultan did not agree to the request, but assembled the Islamic forces of Egypt and Syria. Four armies from Damascus, Hama, Tripoli, and Al-Kark marched to Acre to join him.

The Siege of Acre

From Acre, the various Christian forces asked for help from Europe, but nothing significant was forthcoming. A small group of knights were sent by Edward I of England, and Henry II of Cyprus also paid for the fortification of Acre's walls and sent a force led by his brother Amalric. In April 1291, Khalil's forces surrounded Acre as far as they could, and besieged the city. Despite the continual arrival of reinforcements from Cyprus to Acre by sea, the Christians lost confidence in the face of Khalil's massive army. On April 15, under moonlight, the Templars launched a sudden attack against the military unit from Hama, but their horses' legs became entangled in the ropes of the Muslims' tents and were caught. Many were killed. Another attack under cover of darkness by the Hospitallers also ended badly. On May 5, Henry II of Cyprus arrived with further forces but still the Muslim armies out-maneuvered them. Eventually, the Christians sent messengers to Khalil, who asked them if they were surrendering Acre to him, but they replied that the city could not be relinquished so easily and that they only came to supplicate for mercy for the innocent inhabitants and to make a truce. Khalil promised the messengers that he would spare the life of everyone if they peacefully gave him Acre, but the messengers rejected the offer. Some days later, Khalil gave his order to launch a full-scale attack on Acre, accompanied by the sound of trumpets and drums. That night, Henry of Cyprus escaped with his knights and 3,000 soldiers. By morning

Louis landed on the African coast in the sweltering summer heat. Poor drinking water infected much of the army with dysentery, and Louis too contracted it and died.

▶

An illustration from a 15th-century French manuscript, *The Book of St. Louis*, showing King Louis IX of France and Marguerite of Provence leaving for the Eighth Crusade on August 12, 1248. The baptism is of a Jew in the presence of Louis, demonstrating what a marvelous king he was to turn infidels into Christians. The image at bottom left shows them arriving at Carthage and the one on the right shows the death of Louis at Tunis in 1270 from dysentery.

SHIFTING SANDS

Comment mons[eigneu]r saint loys p[re]nt la seconde fois la croix pour
aler oultremer : & de son testam[ent]. xl.e chap[itre].

L'annee dessus   este curieux et ententif de
dit mil. cc. lxx.   cueur & de pensee de suiur
Le bon roy s[aint]   a dieu. Advint que la tir[es]
loys qui toute sa vie auoit   sainte auoit besoing de

the attack resumed. Against such vast numbers, all valiant efforts made by the Hospitallers and the Templars to defend the city were futile. William de Beaujeu and the Hospitaller marshal, Matthew de Clermont, were killed.

By nightfall on Friday, May 18, 1291, after a six-week siege, Acre was taken by al-Ashraf Khalil and his army. Only the huge headquarters of the Templars which stood on the west side of the city remained under Templar control. The following week, Khalil negotiated with Peter de Severy, the Marshal of the Templars, responsible for the military side of the Order's activities. They agreed that the Templars and anyone else taking refuge inside the fortress would be granted a free passage to Cyprus. But when Khalil's men went to the castle to supervise the evacuation, the Templars attacked and massacred them. Under

cover of darkness, Theobald Gaudin, at that time the Templar Grand Commander or Grand Preceptor, took a few of the knights and the Templar fortune, sneaked out of the castle and sailed to Sidon in Lebanon, where a Templar fortress still stood. Within two months, Theobald had continued on to the relative safety of Cyprus. Meanwhile, Peter de Severy went to Khalil to negotiate anew, but in retaliation for the massacre of his men by the Templars, he and his entourage were arrested and executed. From their fortress, the Templars continued to hold firm until Khalil's men mined the castle and within ten days it collapsed, killing nearly everyone inside, including all the Templars and about half of Khalil's men. That was the final breakthrough for the Muslims. Chaining his Crusader captives by their feet, Khalil traveled to Damascus and paraded through the streets in celebration. The Crusader standards were carried upside-down as a sign of their defeat. Khalil continued the same victory parade through Cairo.

The fall of Acre in 1291 definitively ended the Crusades and any form of Christian power in the Holy Land. In Europe, many questioned why they had lost so much to the Muslims. Few blamed any laxity within the Church, and Pope Nicholas IV, keen to deflect any criticism, announced in various synods that discord between the Templars and the Hospitallers had been a main contributing factor to the disaster. He proposed therefore that the two orders should be merged. The idea of converging the two orders had been discussed at the Council of Lyon nearly 20 years previously in 1274, but nothing had been done and the proposal was now endorsed at the Church Council. In addition, it was proposed that a new Crusade should be organized and paid for out of Templar and Hospitaller contributions, but when Pope Nicholas died in 1292, the idea was forgotten.

The fight for Acre was protracted and merciless. When the Christians finally lost it to the Muslims in 1291, they lost their last vestige of authority and control in the Holy Land.

The Templars and the Hospitallers had vehemently disagreed with the proposed amalgamation of their two orders. The Hospitallers had never abandoned their original function of caring for the sick and the Templars' primary role was to protect pilgrims and fight against the infidel. Although their reputations had declined over the losses in the Holy Land, they were still powerful individually and vital to any future Crusade.

The Latin kingdom moved to the island of Cyprus, with the Templars and the Hospitallers both setting up new headquarters there. In 1192, they had bought Cyprus from Richard the Lionheart. He charged them 100,000 Saracen bezants for it and they made an initial payment of 40,000 bezants, aiming to raise the rest of the money by taxing the Cypriot people. This was so unpopular with the inhabitants that a plot was hatched to murder the small force of Templars stationed there. On hearing of this, the Order gave the island to Guy de Lusignan (who had lost his right to be King of Jerusalem on the death of his wife Queen Sibylla in 1190). While Guy's descendants ruled Cyprus, the Templars and the Hospitallers built castles there and a small group of each Order maintained a presence to protect the de Lusignan kings. So when the Christians were banished from the Holy Land, the Templars were not as badly off as those civilians who had escaped with their lives but little else. Most ordinary Christians fled with only what they were wearing and had to fall upon the charity of their fellow Christians in Europe. The Templars simply joined their brothers in Cyprus and made plans for rebuilding their future.

However, this was not as straightforward as might be supposed. Although they had castles on Cyprus, the entire rationale of the Order had changed. They had been formed in the East with the singular purpose of protecting pilgrims as they traveled to the holy shrines and of defending the holy sites against the infidel. Though there were also important sites of Christian pilgrimage in the West, none were as significant as those in the Holy Land and the Templars found themselves being needed, not to fight and defend, but to farm and make money to sustain the Order. With few battles to be fought, they used Cyprus mainly as a base for their financial and commercial endeavors and, in July 1296, Pope Boniface VIII issued a papal bull, granting them a tax-free status on exports and imports to and from Cyprus. They held this privilege virtually everywhere else, but this affirmed their continued standing in the eyes of the Church.

The Fall of Ruad

In 1293, Jacques de Molay was elected Grand Master of the Knights Templar. Having spent 30 years serving the Order as a knight in Outremer, his ambition was to lead a new Crusade and win back the Holy Land for Christendom. One of the first things he did was to travel across Europe to raise support for the Templars and for another Crusade. Along with the Pope, Charles II of Naples, and Edward I of England also pledged their support and helped the Order to rebuild their forces after their terrible recent losses. De Molay had reasons to believe that his plan would be successful. In the Holy Land there were already several uprisings against the brutal and oppressive Mamluk rule and a Christian Crusade would benefit from such disunity. Food and ships were amassed, and a surge of fresh hope swept across Europe in 1300 in anticipation of the forthcoming campaign. As the year was also the 1,300th anniversary of the birth of Christ, Pope Boniface announced it to be a jubilee year, promising salvation and redemption to all who visited St Peter's Basilica in Rome.

To continue the celebration of the Christian faith, that summer the Templars, Hospitallers, Teutonic Knights, and Henry, the King of Cyprus, sailed to the small island of Ruad (also known as Arwad) in Syria, and launched a series of attacks on it. In 1291, the Templars had lost Atlit Castle, and since then, the Mamluks had been consistently destroying any remaining Crusader ports and fortresses. The Crusaders decided that the Syrian port of Tortosa was the best location to establish another stronghold, with a view to attacking the Mamluks and recapturing territory in the Holy Land. They planned to coordinate an offensive with the Mongols, with whom they had been negotiating and who fiercely hated the Mamluks. By landing on Ruad, they were just two miles (three kilometers) from Tortosa, but although the Crusaders reached there at the appointed time and began their raid on Tortosa, the Mongols did not arrive, and the Crusaders were forced to retreat back to Cyprus. They left a small garrison on Ruad and, from the end of 1301, under the command of the Templar marshal Barthélemy de Quincy, 120 Templar knights, 500 archers, and 400 servants were established in the newly strengthened fortress.

In 1302, the Mamluks sent a fleet of 16 ships from Egypt to Tripoli from where they besieged Ruad. After weeks of hardship and near-starvation, the Templars were forced to emerge and fight. Barthélemy de Quincy was killed, all the bowmen and Syrian Christians were executed, and the surviving Templars were taken as prisoners to Cairo, where they died of starvation anyway. Ruad had been the last Crusader foothold in the Holy Land. Though they had their headquarters in Cyprus and maintained various enterprises, the Templar Order now had no clear purpose or influence, although it still had enormous financial power.

▶

This is a colored engraving of 1805, showing the castle of Ruad or Arwad, off the coast of Tortosa.

SHIFTING SANDS

CHAPTER 6

The Descent

Founded to defend the Holy Land and protect pilgrims there, after the final, crushing loss of Ruad, the Knights Templar were left without a purpose. Yet Pope Boniface appeared undaunted, and continued his assertion of Papal dominance as if nothing had happened to challenge the authority of the Catholic Church.

More than any other pope, Boniface VIII made lofty claims about papal supremacy. In his Bull of 1302 he pushed the concept of papal power to an unparalleled extreme in proclaiming that "it is absolutely necessary for salvation that every human creature be subject to the Roman pontiff." This belief and his constant intervention in worldly matters led to many bitter quarrels between himself and various European powers, including the Holy Roman Emperor Albert I of Habsburg, the Roman Colonna family, King Philip IV of France, and even the writer Dante Alighieri, who wrote his essay *De Monarchia* to challenge Boniface's claims of papal domination. His disagreements with Philip IV of France arose out of their common, incompatible ambitions about increasing their individual power.

During his reign, Philip hired lawyers instead of the clergy for all his legal administration. Since the Fall of Rome, legal issues had been dealt with by the clergy, but the legal profession was redeveloping by the mid-13th century and Philip was one of the first monarchs to depend on secular lawyers rather than having the monastic orders deal with his legal matters. He also taxed the French clergy to finance ongoing wars against the English. To counteract this, in a bull of February 1296, *Clericis laicos*, Boniface forbade secular taxation of the clergy without prior papal approval. Philip retaliated by stopping the export of gold, silver, precious stones, and even food from France to the Papal States, effectively obstructing an important source of Church income. Philip also banished papal agents from France. Angrily, Boniface declared that "God has set popes over kings and kingdoms." But although the resentment continued, in September 1296, Boniface almost capitulated, by sanctioning voluntary contributions from the clergy for the defense of the state, and he gave the king the right to determine when that would be necessary. So Philip revoked his ruling about exports and accepted Boniface as mediator in one of his many disputes with Edward I of England. In his negotiations, Boniface settled most of the issues in Philip's favor.

However, in 1301, the feud between the Pope and the French king escalated once more, and Boniface sent Bishop Bernard Saisset to protest against Philip's opposition to Church influence in political affairs. Instead of tactfully easing the situation, however,

King Edward I of England (1239–1307) with priests and members of his court. In 1263, Edward ransacked the treasury of the London Temple to aid his fight against the Barons's Revolt. Eight years later, in an unrelated event, his life was saved by Thomas Bérard, the master of the Knights Templar. Edward had been attacked by an assassin with a poisoned knife and Bérard sent drugs to cure him.

Bernard Saisset's outspoken comments against the king resulted in Philip arresting him and charging him with high treason. Boniface ordered the king to free his bishop and, in February 1302, he issued a new bull, *Ausculta fili*, that pointed out the king's offences against the Church and State and invited him to do penance and change his behavior. In response, King Philip had the bull ceremoniously burned in Paris before himself and a large crowd. That November, Boniface issued another bull, *Unam Sanctam*, that claimed papal supremacy and stated that kings were subordinate to the Pope. In response, William de Nogaret (1260–1313), Philip's chief minister, publicly denounced Boniface as a heretical criminal. While Boniface prepared to excommunicate both the king and Nogaret, on March 12, 1303, a royal assembly was held in the Louvre at which Nogaret read a long series of accusations against the Pope, and demanded that a general Council be called to try him. By September of that year, Nogaret had gathered a large force of men and marched to Anagni in Italy, Boniface's birthplace, where he demanded the Pope's resignation. Boniface declared that he would "sooner die" than resign from the papacy. Although he was protected by a few Templars and Hospitallers, Nogaret's large band of men overpowered and captured him. Some of the band called for his murder, but instead they beat him up and then released him. The shock and humiliation left him a broken man, and the following month in Rome, he died.

Philip IV of France

Philip IV (1268–1314) was nicknamed "Le Bel" or the Fair because he was tall, blond, and handsome. At the age of 16, he had married his childhood sweetheart, Joan I of Navarre, and the following year, 1285, when he was just 17 years old, he became King of France. Through his marriage, he had the additional titles of Philip I, King of Navarre and Count of Champagne. From the start of his reign, however, his arrogance and inflexibility gained him several other nicknames and enemies. Bernard Saisset, who described him as "more handsome than any man in the world," also said of him: "He is neither man nor beast. He is a statue." As a sign of his extreme piety, Philip wore a hair shirt beneath his finery and his piousness earned him the description from Giles of Rome as "more than man, wholly divine."

As a consequence of the wars his predecessors had fought against the English and the Albigensians, the land he ruled was larger than it had been for previous French monarchs. His ambition was to lead a Crusade, to gain glory and to found a French empire in the eastern Mediterranean, while he aimed to establish his brother Charles as ruler of the Byzantine Empire. Yet this determination to follow his father and grandfather's examples and strengthen the power and standing of the French monarchy resulted in many unpopular policies. Given his intention to lead a Crusade and continual conflicts with the English and their allies in Flanders, as well as financial problems inherited from his father's war against Aragon and his own personal extravagances, he was constantly desperate for money. One of his most unpopular methods of raising money was to devalue the French currency, and by 1306 it was reduced to a third of the value it had been when he came to the throne in 1285. In consequence, rioting broke out in Paris, forcing Philip to briefly seek refuge in the headquarters of the Knights Templar: the Paris Temple that was

William de Nogaret, Philip's chief minister, publicly denounced Pope Boniface as a heretical criminal.

also their center of finance. In another of his efforts to acquire revenue, Philip imposed taxes on the French clergy of one half of their annual income. The ensuing disquiet among the clergy prompted Pope Boniface to issue his bull forbidding the transference of any church property to the French Crown without his permission. It provoked the prolonged quarrel between the king and the Pope and led to Philip sending William de Nogaret to put Boniface under house arrest, which ultimately resulted in the Pope's death. Clearly a man who bore a grudge, for years afterwards, Philip pursued legal action to have Boniface posthumously condemned.

Pope Clement V

The new Pope immediately following Boniface, Benedict XI, died within a year. After pressure from Philip IV, the next Pope was a Frenchman. Raymond Bertrand de Got (c.1264–1314) came to the papal throne as Clement V in 1305 and never set foot in Rome or even Italy. For the first four years of his pontificate, he moved between Lyons and Poitiers and, in 1309, he set up court in Avignon in Provence. Early in 1306, he annulled Boniface's *Unam Sanctam* bull that had threatened Philip's political plans. Clement's great ambition was a new Crusade, but for this to work, he required the collaboration and leadership of the French king. He succeeded in persuading Philip to take the cross in December 1305; he negotiated peace between Philip and Edward I, and he gave 10 per cent of the Church's income in France to Philip's exchequer to help fund the Crusade. In his plans for this Crusade, Philip was determined to merge the Templars and the Hospitallers to create a larger, more unified force.

In view of this plan, in May 1307, Clement met with the Templar and Hospitaller Grand Masters at his court in France. The Grand Master of the Hospitallers, Fulk de Villaret, favored the idea of the two orders remaining separate but thought that first they should send a modest expedition containing members of both orders to the East to conquer small areas, preparing the ground for a large Crusade to follow. After the loss of Ruad, Jacques de Molay opposed the idea of small-scale attacks, so he disagreed with Villaret's plan. He wanted to call upon the European rulers to unite and raise a vast army

Pope Boniface VIII, proclaiming the jubilee in 1300; a fragment from a fresco painted in 1300 by Giotto di Bondone (1266–1337).

Clement's great ambition was a new Crusade, but for this to work, he required the collaboration and leadership of the French king.

between them who could then be transported on ships from Venice and Genoa to Cyprus and from there on to Palestine. His argument against the unification of the two orders was that the competition between them was stimulating; when one followed one tactic, the other tried something else. Any successes within one order were swiftly challenged by the other. But partly because Philip and the Pope were considering a Mongol alliance for the proposed Crusade and neither Grand Master had suggested this, both men's ideas were ignored by the Pope and his ministers.

Jacques de Molay's suggestions were dismissed as being particularly unrealistic in the circumstances. The time of European monarchs leading large allied armies to the Holy Land had passed and the Templar Order was not big enough to do it alone. It is ironic that the Templars were one of the few groups who throughout the decades had retained the original focus of the Crusades, but they had simply not been large enough on their own to win. Now, once again, they were left without a direct function.

The arrests

After the meeting, Jacques de Molay traveled to Paris where, on Thursday, October 12, 1307, he was one of the main mourners in the funeral cortège of Philip IV's sister, Catherine de Courtenay. The following morning, on Friday, October 13, 1307, a group of the king's men led by William de Nogaret marched to the Paris Temple and arrested him. Across France, it is believed that approximately 15,000 Templars were arrested simultaneously. The order for the arrests had been circulated secretly a month before, and there is much debate as to whether or not the Templars were taken completely by surprise or whether they had known about what was coming and had taken measures to protect themselves. Whatever had been happening, among the arrests were many middle-aged and elderly men who worked for the Order as farmers, servants, artisans, ploughmen, or sergeants. Unarmed, confused, and living in unfortified properties, they put up little resistance. Made in the name of the Inquisition, the arrests followed the pattern established by Philip in 1291 when he attacked the Lombards, Italian bankers who were living in France, and again in 1306, when he arrested Jewish merchants also resident in France. The pattern was arrest, expulsion from the country, and then seizure of the exiles' possessions.

Although the news of the Templar arrests was greeted with shock by the public, through their banking provision many had borrowed from them and were in debt to the Order, so few men of influence hastened to their defense. Because it was so unpleasant and instigated by the king, many simply ignored what was happening. Certain nobles were already aggravated by the Templars. Their ancestors had given away land to the Order, but it was seen to have failed by not maintaining a Christian presence in the Holy Land, and so many of these nobles felt that the donations had been accepted under false pretences and many believed that, with the Templars out of the way, they could reclaim their property. The clergy, meanwhile, had long resented the special privileges enjoyed by the Templar Order, so little sympathy was elicited from that quarter. In any case, nobody took it too seriously. The Templars were under papal protection and they belonged to a holy and religious confraternity that had been established for nearly two centuries.

A 14th-century illuminated manuscript showing Philip "the Fair" of France. This is a Council meeting held by the king in Paris concerning his conflict with Pope Boniface VIII over the taxing of the clergy and on the besieging of Lille in 1297.

Reprisals

The year before the arrests, when Philip's currency devaluation had triggered riots and he had sought safety in the Paris Temple, he was made aware of the vast amount of wealth the Templar Order had amassed and was guarding for others. As soon as he left the Temple, he showed no restraint. As with Pope Boniface, William de Nogaret took charge of the attack on the Templars. Unscrupulous and merciless, little is known of Nogaret's background, but it is said that his grandparents and parents, citizens of Toulouse, had been condemned as heretics during the Albigensian Crusade. He had studied law, gaining a doctorate and a professorship, and he prospered under Philip IV's patronage. In 1299, he was made a knight and, in September 1307, the king made him Keeper of the Seal. From his study of Roman law, he adhered to the belief of the absolute supremacy of the monarch, and as a zealous royal supporter, he seemed to thrive on cruelty and the persecution of others. He was the first to bring up the notion of a link between the Templars and the Cathars, just as he was the first to proclaim that Pope Boniface was a heretic. His excommunication by Boniface in 1303 was not revoked until 1311 by Clement V. Yet he continued to act in the name of the king, and he found many enemies of the Templars to testify against them, including men who had been expelled from the Order who were prepared to give evidence against their former fellows, and he drew up the full list of accusations against the Templars a short time later. As with the Lombards and the Jews, all Templar property was confiscated on arrest. But unlike the Lombards and the Jews, the Templars were neither foreigners nor infidels: they were members of a Holy Order and subject to the Pope. Philip declared that the warrants for the arrests were recommended by the Pope, but that was not true. Clement had not been consulted and he wrote angrily to the king in October 1307:

> You, our dear son . . . have in our absence, violated every rule and laid hands on the persons and properties of the Templars. You have also imprisoned them and what pains us even more, you have not treated them with due leniency . . . and have added to the discomfort of imprisonment yet another affliction. You have laid hands on persons and property that are under the direct protection of the Roman Church . . . Your actions and rightly so are seen as an act of contempt against us and the Roman Church.

Without stating whether or not he believed the knights were guilty of the charges, Clement was merely complaining at the king's wrongful conduct and appropriation of papal powers. He asked Philip to hand over the Templars, together with all their possessions, for questioning to two of his cardinals, Bérenger Frédol and Etienne de Suisy,

▲

An 18th-century engraving of King Philip IV of France, who ascended the throne at the age of 17. Called the Fair (Philippe le Bel), through his marriage to Joan I of Navarre, he was also Philip I, King of Navarre and Count of Champagne, from 1284 to 1305.

but Philip ignored him. In his letter to the king, the words "yet another affliction" allude to the torture that was imposed on many of the Templars as soon as they were arrested. Torture had been authorized approximately 50 years previously by Pope Innocent IV, to be used in the name of the Inquisition.

Torture

In 1252, Pope Innocent IV issued a papal bull, *Ad exstirpanda*, that permitted torture as a method of extracting confessions. Torture was meant to be performed only once on any suspect, but it was commonly repeated and simply classed as a continuation of the first session. Torturers were not supposed to spill blood or to break bones, but because of the brutality of the methods, they nearly always did. Forms of torture included sleep deprivation, the rack and water-boarding, as well as hanging by the wrists with weights suspended from the ankles (the strappado), being chained to a wall for days, or bent backwards over a wooden beam with the arms bound beneath it, or even having fat rubbed on the soles of the feet before a flame was put to them. It is known that at least the rack, the strappado and the burning of the soles of the feet were used on many of the arrested Templars. One, Bernard de Vado, was tortured so badly with the burning feet method that his blackened bones fell out of his heels. He later showed these bones to the authorities when he revoked his confession.

The harshness of the Templars' treatment was a deliberate attempt to break them as quickly as possible. The Grand Inquisitor of France was also Philip's own confessor, William Imbert de Paris. His task, set by the king, was to suppress the Templars completely and, at the same time, to lessen the Pope's standing. Despite Inquisition "rules," it is said that at least 36 Templars died under William Imbert's investigation. The Templars who had

The Inquisition

The medieval Inquisition was a series of interrogations led by the Catholic Church to suppress heresy. It was started by Pope Gregory IX in southern France and northern Italy in 1231 with campaigns to overthrow the Cathars and Waldensians, although Pope Gregory did not approve the use of torture as a tool of investigation or for penance. Earlier, in 1184, Pope Lucius III had issued the papal bull *Ad abolendam*, which has been called the "founding charter of the Inquisition," as it commanded bishops to take an active role in identifying and prosecuting heresy in their own districts, but torture was not part of the procedure. Members of the Inquisition were employed from some members of the clergy, but predominantly from different religious brotherhoods and primarily from the Dominican and Franciscan orders who had a history of fighting heresy. Trained specifically for the job, Inquisitors kept detailed records of their Inquisitions. "Confessing fully" was one of the expressions they used that they said gave an individual the best chance of being dealt a lesser punishment. But full confessions always implicated others, including the accused's close relatives and friends. Inquisitors amassed evidence from anyone they could, even criminals, excommunicants, and convicted heretics, and a suspect could be left in prison for years before trial while new information was sought. If it was believed that the prisoner had not confessed sufficiently, he or she could be returned to prison as often as the Inquisitors deemed necessary. Punishments could be as ordinary as a penance, such as prayer or pilgrimage, or it could be the confiscation of property, exile, or long-term imprisonment. The ultimate punishment could be burning at the stake. As holy men, Inquisitors were forbidden to put their prisoners to death, so secular executioners were hired to conduct the task, although—contrary to popular belief—Inquisitors preferred to save souls rather than to admit defeat and have a person put to death.

been arrested in France were mainly simple men, not tough, experienced knights, and with no battle or endurance training, they quickly buckled under torture and harsh treatment. Aside from torture, while imprisoned, they were fed on bread and water, kept in dark, cold and damp conditions and, to unnerve them even more, Inquisitors often burst in during the night and beat them, or moved them roughly to different cells.

The charges

Since the Albigensian Crusade nearly 80 years before, a charge of heresy meant that even protected orders such as the Templars could be charged by the Inquisitor in France. The king's lawyers gathered information about the ways in which the Templars lived, read their Rule closely and questioned ex-Templars or those who had worked with them, and then they selected and adapted elements so they could be seen as transgressions against the Church. In October 1307, before a large crowd in Paris, William de Nogaret declared the Templars' guilt. Across France, Franciscan monks, under the aegis of the Inquisition, spread the information through sermons in churches. The declarations presented the king as a defender of the faith and a protector of his people over the enemies of the Church. Encouraging a sense of unity, the scandalous allegations helped citizens forget the king's unpopular policies, such as the debasing of their money and the crippling taxes he imposed on the wealthy.

▲

A torture scene, created around 1475; the prisoner is being stretched and water poured on his face. The medieval Inquisition began as a means to eliminate heresy and had no one authority, so "rules" were never implemented and after 1252, torture became a widespread method of extracting confessions.

Beyond France, however, many were convinced that Philip's motives were primarily to seize the Templars' wealth for himself. In the wake of the Templar arrests, in Italy, the poet Dante Aligheri (c.1265–1321) wrote *Purgatorio*, the second book of *The Divine Comedy*, attacking the king's actions by calling him a second Pilate (as in Pontius Pilate, the Roman ruler who condemned Jesus to death). The charges made against the Templars at the time of their arrests shocked almost everyone who heard about them. They included:

- During the reception ceremony, new brothers were required to deny Christ, God, the Virgin, or the Saints on the command of those receiving them.
- The brothers committed various sacrilegious acts, either on the Cross or on an image of Christ.
- The receptors practiced obscene kisses on new entrants: on the mouth, navel, or buttocks.
- Priests of the Order did not consecrate the host and the brothers did not believe in the sacraments.

- The brothers practiced idol worship of a head or a cat.
- The brothers encouraged and permitted the practice of sodomy.
- The Grand Master or other officials absolved fellow Templars of their sins.
- The Templars held their reception ceremonies and chapter meetings in secret and at night.
- The Templars abused their duties of charity and hospitality and used illegal means to acquire property and increase their wealth.

The trials

On 19 October 1307, the trials of the Templars began in Paris. On 25 and 26 October, Jacques de Molay was called to testify and, like most of the other accused Templars, he confessed quite quickly. Immediately, the king sent transcripts of the confessions to the Pope as evidence of their guilt. Suspecting foul play and still cross at the king's actions, Clement sent two cardinals to Paris to take the Templars and their possessions into papal custody. But Philip and his ministers refused to see the cardinals and they were refused access to the Templars, so they returned to Poitiers empty-handed. Caught between the king and the Templars (and those of the papal court who were outraged at the king's conduct), on 22 November 1307, Clement issued the bull *Pastoralis praeeminentiae*. It told all European rulers to imprison any members of the Knights Templar in their countries and to hold their possessions for the Church. Clement was showing the king that every other European power was acting on behalf of the Church and so Philip should do likewise. Next, ignoring the previous incident with his two cardinals, Clement sent them once again to Paris. This time, Philip was aware that if he continued to avoid the Pope's wishes, he might instantly be excommunicated and the whole of France could be put under an interdict. So, at the end of December 1307, the Pope's two cardinals were allowed to meet with Jacques de Molay and other high-ranking Templars. In the cardinals' presence, all the Templars gathered denied their confessions and showed their wounds from torture. Clement suspended the Inquisition and in reaction, the king's men tried to muster public support for the reopening of the investigations by distributing pamphlets to the public describing Templar depravity. William de Nogaret began attacking the Pope with an onslaught of libel, slander, physical intimidation, and threats against his family.

At length, in the early summer of 1308, Philip went to Poitiers to meet the Pope. Neither men were in comfortable positions. The king was going against the Church, but as the Templars had confessed, the Pope had to tread carefully. The Third Lateran Council of 1179 had stated that "Heretics and all who defend and receive them shall be excommunicated." The king and his lawyers pointed out that if the Pope tried to defend those who had declared themselves to be guilty, his position and possibly even his life would be at risk, as few would tolerate a heretical Pope.

Templar interrogation

Eventually it was agreed that Philip would release more Templars to be investigated by the Church. At the end of June 1308, 72 members of the Order selected by the king were brought from the prisons in Paris to the Pope's cardinals in Poitiers. Chained together and under military escort, the Templars were interrogated for five days by the Pope's cardinals. The Pope had wanted to know, in particular, details of their Rule that had been written originally by Bernard of Clairvaux and added to over the years. The Templars as an order had continued to adhere rigidly to their Rule;

it was necessarily extremely strict and demanding, but not every ritual or formality that they observed was written into it. Over the years it seemed, extra procedures had been developed verbally. For instance, to ascertain whether or not a new recruit would be sufficiently loyal, a test to challenge his courage and commitment was set. This test and the initiation rite were open to interpretation, so misunderstandings and confusion often occurred. It was established, however, that even though they were not authorized parts of the Rule, they had been performed for years.

It was known that if they were captured in battle by Muslims, Christians were often forced to spit on the Cross, to deny Christ and to do various other things that violated their beliefs and humiliated them. The Templars' initiation test focused on this possibility: if caught by Muslim soldiers, could they endure such atrocities and still remain true to the Order and to Christianity? The tests and rite had probably developed after stories were related by Templars who had managed to escape from Muslim prisons and had become a means of challenging the potential of a future Templar's character and determination.

▲

Pope Clement V, born Raymond Bertrand de Got, was Pope for nine years from 1305 to his death in 1314. He is remembered for his involvement in the suppression of the Knights Templar, and for moving the Curia from Rome to Avignon; the period became known as the Avignon Papacy.

Replicas of the three
seals used by the Templars'
inquisitors, lying on the
official transcript of their
trial that describes their
offences, including heresy,
idolatry, homosexuality,
secret initiation rituals,
corruption, and fraud.

The result of the investigation at Poitiers was that the Templars asked for forgiveness and the Pope granted them absolution. This is one of the many grey areas of their trials. Had they been completely innocent, they would not have asked for forgiveness and Clement would have acquitted them completely. Had they been guilty, even had they asked for his forgiveness, the Pope would not have granted it. The Pope decided that they were not heretics, but in denying Christ, albeit to strengthen their Christian resolve, they needed to repent. Sparse notes of the Poitiers questioning have been discovered relatively recently, along with the Chinon Parchment.

The Chinon Parchment

In September 2001, an Italian paleographer, Dr Barbara Frale, discovered a document that had been lost in the Vatican Secret Archives. It constitutes evidence that, in August 1308, Pope Clement V secretly absolved Jacques de Molay and the entire Templar Order from all charges brought against them by the Medieval Inquisition. The document is dated August 17–20, 1308 and was written in the castle of Chinon in France by three of the Pope's cardinals who questioned five senior Templars there. The cardinals included two

who had been involved already—Bérenger Frédol, cardinal of St Nerus and Archelius, and Etienne de Suisy, cardinal of St Cyriac in Therminis—as well as another, Landolfo Brancacci, cardinal of St. Angel. According to the documents written at Chinon, the Pope instructed the cardinals to conduct the investigation of the accused Knights Templar away from royal officials, in order to ascertain the truth. The cardinals interviewed the Templars individually. First they questioned Raimbaud de Caron, the Master of Cyprus, then Geoffrey de Charney, the Master of Normandy, then Geoffrey de Gonneville, the Master of Aquitaine and Poitou, then Hugh de Pairaud, who was the second highest-ranking Templar as the Visitor of the Temple in France and Poitou, and the Deputy Grand Master. Finally, the cardinals interviewed Jacques de Molay, the Grand Master himself. The Chinon Parchment begins:

> We . . . declare through this official statement . . . that since our most holy father and lord Clement . . . after receiving . . . clamorous reports from the illustrious king of France and prelates, dukes, counts, barons and other subjects of the said kingdom . . . had initiated an inquiry into matters concerning the brothers and the Rule of the said Order, because of which it suffered public infamy, the very same lord Pope wishing and intending to know the pure, complete and uncompromised truth from the leaders of the said Order . . . that we might . . . examine the truth by questioning the grandmaster and the . . . preceptors— one by one and individually, having summoned . . . trustworthy witnesses.

According to the document, all the cardinals' questioning was held in the presence of at least eight other churchmen who acted as official witnesses. The parchment details the appearances of the accused, the charges made against them and some of the interrogations and torture they endured through the Inquisition. The report repeats similar findings to those previously mentioned by the 72 Templars at Poitiers. When the cardinals reported back to the Pope, he accepted the Templars' testimonies: that the accusations of blasphemy and sodomy were misinterpretations of the rituals they had developed to help prepare them for some of the difficulties they might face in the Holy Land. The denial of Christ, spitting on the Cross and even kissing other men's backsides were all probable attempts to become resistant to humiliations and to learn to face any difficulties that they might be subjected to. In asking the Pope's pardon, the Chinon Parchment states:

> . . . the mercy of pardons for these acts to Brother Jacques de Molay, the Grandmaster of the said Order, who in the form and manner described above had denounced in our presence the described and any other heresy, and swore in person on the Lord's Holy Gospel, and humbly asked for the mercy of pardon, restoring him to unity with the Church and reinstating him to communion of the faithful and sacraments of the Church.

Three copies of the Chinon Parchment were made, all sealed and signed by the interrogators, the accused and the witnesses. The document is proof that in 1308, the Pope determined to save the Templars from the king's threats. However, as he did not make the details of his absolution public, the king continued to persecute the Templars and to appropriate their belongings.

Templar relics

It was said that Jacques de Molay and Geoffrey de Charney were so calm when they went to their deaths that they "brought from all who saw them much admiration and surprise for the constancy of their death and final denial." Later, under cover of darkness, friars of the Augustinian monastery nearby and other people collected the charred bones of the dead Templars as relics of saints.

▶

Illuminated manuscript of c.1410, representing the execution of Jacques de Molay. The king is looking down from above, but this was artistic licence as it is doubtful whether he was present when Jacques de Molay and Geoffrey de Charney were burned at the stake.

Suppression

The Chinon Parchment was never made public. By May 1310, nearly 600 accused Templars decided to try to save themselves and denied their earlier confessions. The king immediately put his lawyers to work and 54 Templars were suddenly found guilty of being relapsed heretics. "Relapsed heretics" were those who had been previously accused of unorthodox opinions or actions who returned to their previous beliefs after recanting. According to Inquisition rules, relapsed heretics might return to their previous unorthodox ideas and corrupt others, so they were to be burnt at the stake. Philip's lawyers argued that by confessing and then denying those confessions, the Templars were relapsed heretics. Yet even after the 54 men had been put to their deaths, the Templars who remained in French prisons continued to proclaim their innocence. By that time, with the Pope's absolution still not made public, general opinion of the Templars had plummeted. Many church officials, nobles, lawyers and other members of the public believed that there must be some truth in the accusations or they would have been released by now, so it was time the Pope used his powers and either saved them or abolished the Order entirely.

Still the Pope did not speak out. Then, bowing to pressure from the king, in October 1311, he called the 15th Ecumenical Council of the Roman Catholic Church in Vienne, chiefly to discuss the withdrawal of papal support for the Knights Templar. The majority of the 300 members of the commission, which included cardinals, bishops,

and archbishops, were opposed to the abolition of the Order, believing that there was insufficient evidence to condemn them under the order of heresy, but the king was pressing. On the second day of the Council, he appeared in person and finally imposed his will on Clement. In the presence of Philip and his three sons, the Pope's bull, *Vox in Excelso*, dated March 22, 1312, was read. It said that, although he had no sufficient reasons for a formal condemnation of the Order, because of the King of France's hatred of them, the scandalous nature of their trial, and the probable dilapidation of their property in every Christian land, he suppressed it by virtue of his sovereign power, but not by any definitive sentence. In another bull of May 2, 1312, he granted all the Templars' property to the Hospitallers. However, Philip managed to become the chief legatee of its great wealth in France. Straight after the Council meeting, he wrote to the Pope stating that he reserved the rights of the monarch to share in the Templars' property, and he made the Hospitallers pay him so much, in theory to cover his costs in bringing the Templars to trial, that they were left worse off than before.

> The king was furious. That evening, the two old men were taken to a small island on the River Seine, where they were tied to a stake and burned to death.

Nearly two years later, on March 18, 1314, the most important Templars in custody, Jacques de Molay, Hugh de Pairaud, Geoffrey de Gonneville, and Geoffrey de Charney, were served their sentences. (Raimbaud de Caron had died earlier in prison.) As self-confessed heretics they were to be condemned to imprisonment for the rest of their lives. Hugh de Pairaud and Geoffrey de Gonneville did not speak, but after all the torture, trials and tribulations they had suffered, Jacques de Molay and Geoffrey de Charney loudly protested. They proclaimed the falsity of the accusations and confessions, the honesty and piety of every man in the Order and the wrongs that had been heaped upon them. When he heard of this, the king was furious. That same evening, the two old men were taken to a small island on the River Seine, the Île de la Cité (then called Île des Javiaux or Île aux Juifs), where they were tied to a stake and burned to death in front of Notre Dame.

The Templar curse

From the moment of their deaths, rumors of a Templar curse began to circulate. Although not verified, it was said that from his execution pyre, Jacques de Molay cursed King Philip IV of France and his descendants, declaring also that he would meet the king and Pope Clement in front of God before the year was out. A little over a month later, on April 20, 1314, Clement died of the long, painful, but unidentified illness he had suffered from for some time, and on 29 November 29, that same year, King Philip died when he fell from a horse while hunting. The large sums of money he had taken from the Templars were swallowed up in the French exchequer, and within 14 years, the 300-year-old Capetian dynasty, the oldest European royal house, from which he had descended, died out.

It is not known how much Templar treasure Philip took while the brothers were imprisoned, but that and the amount he took after their suppression resolved his bankruptcy problems. Beyond France across Christendom, opinion held that the King of France had simply been after the Order's wealth and that they were not guilty. Philip was the instigator and driving force behind their downfall, but there

An illumination of the burial of Philip "Le Bel" who died suddenly after falling from his horse, just months after Jacques de Molay purportedly declared his curse.

had been additional factors. Many were jealous of the Templars' power, success and solidarity. Others had much to gain from the Order's termination. At least one person is documented as having deliberately spread malicious stories about them before they were arrested. In 1305, Esquin de Floyran had been expelled from the Order, and soon after he went to King James of Aragon to impart some shocking information about the Templars' secret, heretical activities, which James dismissed as nonsense. So Floyran took his tales to King Philip in France, where he met with a far more receptive audience. Philip sent spies to watch the Templars and they reported back that Floyran's stories were true. It is still not clear who these spies were and how they infiltrated such a close brotherhood. Most of the stories seem implausible and it appears that Floyran bore the Order a grudge, but some activities can be explained, such as the Templars' alleged initiation rites. Nearly all the Templars denied practicing sodomy or ever witnessing it. Hugh de Pairaud was the only Templar mentioned in the Chinon Parchment who said that he had seen the head of an idol and that during his initiation, he had been told "to abstain from partnership with women and, if he was unable to restrain his lust, to join himself with brothers of the Order."

From a 19th-century painting of Edward II (1284–1327), who was also called Edward of Caernarfon, and was King of England from 1307 until he was deposed by his wife Isabella (daughter of Philip IV of France) in January 1327.

THE DESCENT

Beyond France

While torture and suppression were occurring inside France, elsewhere the Templars were treated with far more respect. Initially, news of the arrests was received with disbelief, chiefly thought to be ill-founded rumors. Then rulers began receiving letters from Philip or his lawyers, telling of the accusations and asking that any Templars living in those countries be arrested at once. Still reluctant to act, however, when the Pope issued his bull in November 1307, *Pastoralis praeeminentiae*, avoidance of the issue was no longer possible. Monarchs across Europe ordered Templars living in their lands to be taken into custody. In many cases this simply meant that they were put under house arrest in their own preceptories, and as no Templar outside France was tortured, no confessions of heresy emerged. The King of France sent Inquisitors to some countries but they were largely ineffectual. In England, for instance, the Inquisitors asked the Archbishop of Canterbury if they could take the Templars to Ponthieu which was one of King Edward II's French assets, but as it was essentially part of France, it was also a place where torture could be used. Edward II refused and subsequently no confessions of the worship of false idols or strange heads were forthcoming. Kissing was admitted to, but that was only at the initiation ceremony, which was customary with several orders. When a new knight was accepted as a Templar, the Master placed the white mantle with its red cross over the shoulders of the candidate and, after reciting psalms and prayers, the Master and the Chaplain kissed the new entrant on the mouth. The Templars explained that the kissing was a sign of their total obedience to the Order and it was not the only order to do this.

In all, the dissolution of the Knights Templar was achieved with little bloodshed outside of France. In some places there had been no arrests. In others, Templars' lands were taken into royal custody. In Cyprus, owing to the Templars' support of Amaury de Lusignan over King Henry II, the king destroyed their headquarters in 1310. As well as the 56 Templars who were burned at the stake, many died in prison. Many survivors joined other religious institutions, but even more were unaccounted for. Contemporary opinions of the Order varied; but whether the view was for or against them, feelings remained strong. Over the following centuries, opinions softened and stories, poems, and operas romanticized their memory (see pages 178–211). Speculation as to where they went, what they did and whether or not any of the accusations were true have continued, escalating, changing or diminishing in the public's consciousness. Some ideas have gained greater popularity than others, such as the Holy Grail, the Ark of the Covenant, the True Cross, and the Shroud of Turin. Others that emerged later, experienced a surge of popularity, such as the 19th-century story about a mysterious event during the Battle of Bannockburn.

> When a new knight was accepted as a Templar, the Master placed the white mantle with its red cross over the shoulders of the candidate and, after reciting psalms and prayers, the Master and the Chaplain kissed the new entrant on the mouth.

CHAPTER 7

The Myths

Beliefs that they were involved in everything from the Cathar heresy to Masonic conspiracies, mysteries connected with the Bible, including the Shroud of Christ and Mary Magdalene, and other notions including hidden treasure and arcane knowledge, have continued to evolve about the Knights Templar since their demise.

Perhaps because they lasted for many more years, or perhaps because they did not have such a chivalrous reputation, the Hospitallers never acquired the same mysterious and romantic aura as the Knights Templar. Legends that began while they existed and continue to this day surrounded a number of astonishing beliefs and secret rituals that the Templars were supposed to have lived by, and various extraordinary objects that they were supposed to have owned. When they fought back against accusations in the early 14th-century, instead of the stories diminishing, they kept being added to and, in the end, the Order faced 127 allegations: accusations of heretical behavior and strange possessions. These charges were almost identical to those that had been made previously by King Philip IV of France against Jews, Pope Boniface, and the Italian bankers known collectively as the Lombards.

Mary Magdalene

One of the tentative charges the Templars faced was that they worshipped Mary Magdalene. As this was a weak accusation, it did not last long and soon disappeared off their list of complaints. That they venerated Mary Magdalene was well known, and usual among devout Christians—particularly among religious confraternities. Mary Magdalene was a female follower of Jesus and one of his close friends; some say she was his wife, although the Church does not. She was present at Christ's crucifixion, helped to prepare his body for burial and it was she who discovered his empty tomb two days after they had buried him. As with many biblical stories, parts of her story are ambiguous, or they are interpreted differently by different denominations. Nonetheless, she remains honored as one of the most important Christian saints, and most Catholics, including the Templars, revered her as a sinner whom Jesus redeemed, as a fundamental aspect of Christianity. The Templar Rule stated that Mary Magdalene should be venerated as well as other saints, but particularly on her feast day. This was July 22 and the Templars openly and legitimately recognized that day in their calendar, as did many other Catholics by saying special prayers to her,

◀

Altarpiece of the Dominicans: Noli Me Tangere, c.1470–80, tempera on panel, from the workshop of Martin Schongauer (c.1440–91), Musée d'Unterlinden, Colmar, France. This illustrates the account in the Gospel of St. John when Mary Magdalene encounters the risen Christ after his Crucifixion and he says to her: "Don't touch me!"

while across Europe, fairs were held in her honor. The fact that many chapels, churches and colleges were named after her proves her significance across Christendom. The Second Crusade was deliberately launched from Vézelay, as the great abbey church there was believed to contain Mary Magdalene's bones, which would supposedly bring good fortune to the Crusaders. The relics had been verified as belonging to Mary Magdalene in a papal document of 1058, but after some years, interest in them waned. How the bones reached France was explained in a myth contained in Jacobus de Voragine's *Golden Legend*. According to the myth, after the death of Jesus, Mary Magdalene was exiled and sailed to Provence to preach and pray. She then lived out her life as a hermit, clothed only in her long hair and eating manna from heaven.

Initially, when veneration of Mary Magdalene was brought up as a possible accusation against the Templars, it was probable that King Philip believed he could trick the Templars into admitting they worshipped goddesses. But, either when this was vehemently denied, or when more shocking charges were thought up, the notion of worshipping Mary Magdalene in the wrong way was abandoned. It was not until the 20th century that Mary Magdalene was brought up in connection with the Templars in a sensational story. It took two bestselling books to rekindle the interest in an area that had been forgotten about over 600 years before.

The idea of Mary Magdalene being the wife of Jesus was suggested from one main consideration. In traditional Jewish life, women's freedom was severely limited, so it seems highly unlikely that Mary Magdalene could associate freely with Jesus and his male apostles without a chaperone, unless she was married to one of them. Most women were restricted to the home under their father or husband's authority. They could not go out in public alone, nor could they speak to strangers or even to a man they knew without having a chaperone. Outside the home, all women had to be veiled. But Jesus is known to have questioned many of the old Jewish customs, and he overturned many of them. Openly refusing to follow conventions established by the three main Jewish religious groups of the day—the Essenes, the Pharisees, and the Sadducees—he made a point of treating women and men as equals. There are many examples of his innovative approach in the New Testament, including his teaching of women, his discussions with them, his curing of one woman's menstrual

A 14th-century illumination of Chrétien de Troyes' story that first mentioned the "Grail," which was a golden dish. This shows, left: Perceval receiving a sword from the king; right: The Procession of the Grail.

problems and his remedy for a Jewish woman with a "Satanic spirit," whom he called "daughter of Abraham," implying that she was equal to male Jews whom he called "sons of Abraham." He accepted women in his closest circle of friends, including Mary Magdalene, "the other Mary," Joanna, Susanna, and "many others," and more women than men were present at his crucifixion. He also had particular concerns for widows and he challenged the established Jewish laws of divorce, from being heavily in favor of men, to being more equal for all.

Another reason it has been suggested that Jesus was married is because he was a rabbi and rabbis are expected to marry. But there were groups of celibate Jews and movements within the religion (including the Essenes) where marriage was not compulsory or even expected. However, as Jesus did not say anything about either celibacy or marriage, the notion remains open to speculation and cannot be proved. Even in the apocryphal gospel of Philip, where Jesus refers to Mary Magdalene as his "companion," that may just be what he means. The word "koinonos" is Coptic, and translates as friend or comrade, nothing more. Contrary to claims, it does not mean spouse (although there is no reason why a spouse cannot also be a companion). This is a topic that will continue to intrigue and fascinate until it can be substantiated one way or another.

The True Cross and the Holy Grail

The secrecy that surrounded the Knights Templar and the speed with which they were disbanded has given rise to many of the legends about them. The conjecture that they

found something under Temple Mount lies at the center of most of these legends and theories, even though—or perhaps especially because—there is no physical or documentary evidence. The piece of the True Cross that the Templars carried into every battle and lost at the Battle of Hattin was almost certainly a piece of wood discovered in the fourth century by Helena, the mother of Emperor Constantine, later revered as St. Helena. Across the world, numerous pieces of timber have been claimed to be further pieces of the True Cross, but nothing has been established and the piece that was lost by the Crusaders in 1187 was never recovered. With its assumed holy connections, it was believed to have mystical powers and, like no other relic, it raised the morale of the Crusaders. Its loss caused Christians across Europe the utmost grief.

Other legends associated with the Templars include mysteries about the Holy Grail, which has also been linked with the legends of King Arthur. First appearing in *Perceval, le Conte du Graal* (Perceval, the Story of the Grail), a work of fiction written between 1181 and 1190 by the poet-composer Chrétien de Troyes (d. 1190), the "golden grail" or golden serving dish was nothing to do with either Jesus or with the Templars. But as Chrétien's story gained in popularity, the idea of the Grail captured the collective imagination and it soon became affiliated with such things as the chalice from which Jesus drank at the Last Supper and then later "Sangreal" or a holy bloodline. Chrétien wrote the story for his patron, Philip the Count of Flanders, at the end of the 12th century. Believed by most to be unfinished, the story tells of the golden dish being carried by a beautiful damsel called Blanchefleur. Perceval, a young knight, watches the procession with the damsel and the shining dish enter a ghostly castle, owned by an injured king, but the next morning everyone, including the castle, has vanished. Perceval cannot believe it until he meets an old woman, who tells him that the castle is magic but suggests that if he had asked the meaning of the Grail and who it serves, he would have healed the king and his afflicted castle and it would not have disappeared. The old woman then sets King Arthur's knights on a quest to find out what the Grail means. The story digresses to the adventures of Sir Gawain, another knight, before returning to Perceval, and there it breaks off, as Chrétien died before finishing it.

The Grail legends

At the beginning of the 13th century, Wolfram von Eschenbach (c.1170–c.1220), a German knight and poet, wrote the epic poem *Parzival*, based on Chrétien's story. *Parzival* continues the romance of King Arthur and the search for the Grail, and Eschenbach hints at a knightly brotherhood, the *Tempeleisen*, as being the guardians of the Grail. This was the point at which the Knights Templar became linked with the story of the Grail. In Eschenbach's version, the Grail was a stone, which gave rise to some theories that it was the philosopher's stone: a legendary substance said to be capable of turning base metals into gold or silver. Soon, it was conjectured that King Solomon had something to do with this stone and then later the Templars were described as being linked to it. The idea that they could have found the stone where King Solomon left it under Temple Mount for 2,000 years became popular and it was conjectured by some that this was how they attained their vast wealth. The Grail was also sometimes described as an elixir of life, used for rejuvenation and possibly even for achieving immortality.

Another poet, Robert de Boron (late 12th–early 13th centuries), first wrote about the Grail as being a sacred vessel. He was also the first to call it "Holy." His poem, *Le Romain de l'Histoire dou Graal, ou Joseph d'Arimathe*, described Perceval and Arthur once again, but it also included Joseph of Arimathea in connection with the Grail. De Boron described the vessel as a chalice that Joseph of Arimathea took from the Last Supper and used to catch the last drops of blood from Jesus as he died on the cross. Robert de Boron claimed that Joseph of Arimathea's descendants took the Grail to the vaus d'Avaron, or the valley of Avaron, which later poets called Avalon and later still was identified as Glastonbury in the south-west of England, where it was given to King Arthur. In later medieval French stories, the idea became linked with the act of transubstantiation in the Mass—in Holy Communion, the wafer and the wine are served in chalices. Further confusion arose much later over a pun on a word. Sangréal is an alternative name for the "Holy Grail." In old French, *san graal* or

Rosslyn Chapel

The story attached to the Apprentice Pillar in the Rosslyn Chapel is that it was carved by a gifted apprentice while his master had gone to Rome for inspiration. When the master returned and found the pillar magnificently carved and completed, he flew into a fit of jealous rage and killed the apprentice by hitting him on the head with a mallet. There is a cleft on the pillar that is linked to the story as it is said that this was where the master mason's mallet struck after hitting his apprentice. The story is a Masonic legend. Before 1700 and the development of Freemasonry, the pillar was called the Prince's Pillar and there were no stories of apprentices or murders in the chapel. No one knows for sure whether the pillar is hollow or solid and no one knows whether or not the Knights Templar had anything to do with the Rosslyn Chapel. As it was founded over 130 years after the Order's demise, it seems unlikely, but outside there is a grave slab carved with the name "William de St. Cler," which has a symbol next to it of a splayed cross, the design used by the Templars. In 1546, Mary of Guise, the mother of Mary, Queen of Scots, wrote to Lord William Sinclair of Rosslyn, referring to "a great secret within Rosslyn." The "great secret" has never been discovered and there is no particular reason why this should be a secret connected to the Knights Templar. However, among the many symbols carved in the chapel, some say that one appears to be the Templar seal. But the carving does not show two men on a horse as in the Templar seal. Instead, one man is clearly walking behind the horse. Additionally, there are over 100 "green men" in the Chapel: carved faces with foliage growing from them. They are said to represent fertility, growth and the months of the year, and to depict the abundance of nature. They resemble several similar carvings in a number of 11th-century churches built by the Templars in Jerusalem, but they also resemble many more similar, carved faces in Christian churches built across Europe by numerous other parties and not just the Templars. None of these notions were mentioned before the formation of Freemasonry in the early 18th century. Some still suggest that the Holy Grail is buried somewhere in the Rosslyn Chapel, but the Rosslyn Chapel Trust forbids any disruptive searching in a sanctified place where so many are buried. As the Holy Grail is one of the most sought-after relics in the world, the Rosslyn Chapel Trust would gain a fortune if it was found there, so if there was the slightest chance that it was there, it is likely that the Trust would have looked for it.

▶

The Apprentice Pillar in Rosslyn Chapel in Midlothian, Scotland. Designed by William Sinclair, a descendant of Norman knights, the chapel's construction took 40 years and contains many symbols that seem to link with the Templars.

san gréal means "Holy Grail," while *sang réal* means "royal blood." This seems likely to be merely a pun that has been exploited in conspiracy theories.

Many of the stories about the Grail contradicted each other; although most of them focused on King Arthur rather than the Templars, over the centuries theories about what the Grail is, who it belongs to and where it might be hidden have been rife. One theory is that it is hidden inside a pillar in the Rosslyn Chapel in Scotland.

Like the True Cross, there are various ancient chalices kept in sacred places that at different times have been claimed to be the Holy Grail. One, in the St. Mary of Valencia Cathedral in Spain, is said to have been left there by St. Lawrence in the third century. Other stories claim that the Grail is buried deep in the spring at Glastonbury Tor in England; that it was buried beneath Montségur Castle by the Cathars before their final demise in the Albigensian Crusade; that it was hidden by the Templars in Oak Island in Nova Scotia's "Money Pit" (see page 195), or that they hid it somewhere in northern Spain. This last theory has been given further credence by the fact that several 12th-century church paintings in the area feature the Virgin Mary holding a dish from which rays of light radiate.

The popularity of the concept of the Holy Grail that had emerged with Eschenbach's *Parzival* in the 13th century waned during the 16th century and was not revived until the 19th century, when writers including Sir Walter Scott and Alfred Lord Tennyson and artists such as Dante Gabriel Rossetti began featuring it in their work. In 1882, Richard Wagner's opera *Parsifal* gave a new impetus to the story. Yet despite such fascination by so many over the centuries about the Holy Grail and the different guises it has assumed, there has never been any solid evidence that it ever existed or that the Templars had it in their possession. Chrétien's story appeared at a time when religious relics were particularly venerated, when chivalry and romance were fashionable and when the Knights Templar were at their peak, renowned for their valor, energy, strength, and trustworthiness. There is no physical evidence to support the claim that the Holy Grail was part of secret treasure excavated by the Templars under Temple Mount. The Holy Grail was not mentioned for 11 centuries after Christ's death, then it appeared in a work of fiction. It rose in popularity at a time when holy relics were of great importance, and by the 14th century there were about 20 Holy Grails in different locations around Europe. Not one has ever been substantiated and links with the Templars remain as elusive and ambiguous as the story did when it was first mentioned by a 12th-century troubadour.

The Shroud of Turin

In the Cathedral of St. John the Baptist in Turin in Italy is an old linen cloth known as the Shroud of Turin. The cloth measures 14⅓ × 3½ feet (4.4 × 1.1 meters) and imprinted on it is the faint image of a man with a beard who appears to have been traumatized, possibly crucified. The mysterious fabric has long been venerated as the burial shroud of Christ, but despite chemical analysis and carbon-dating, no one can verify its exalted claims. The most common consensus after carbon-dating is that it was made between the 11th and 14th centuries, although other claims suggest that it possibly dates from an earlier time. At one point, it was thought that brownish-red marks on the cloth were paint, and the image was possibly even created by Leonardo da Vinci (1452–1519). Then it was thought that the image was produced by a medieval chemical process. Both those ideas have now been discarded and the origins of the shroud and its image continue to

▶

The Shroud of Turin. For many years, this linen cloth that appears to bear the image of a man who had suffered physical trauma has been studied and debated by experts. Commonly claimed to be the shroud that covered Christ's crucified body, experiments have so far been inconclusive. The shroud was initially linked with the Knights Templar after their demise in 1357.

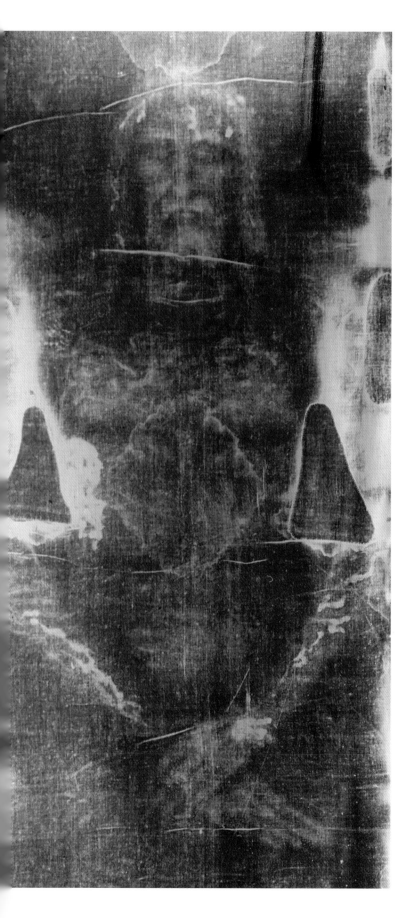

be the subject of debate. The cloth is the property of the Vatican, which refuses to declare it to be the burial shroud of Christ.

The fabric's links with the Knights Templar came with its first known public appearance in 1357, when it was apparently produced by the widow of the Templar knight Geoffrey de Charney, who had been burned at the stake with Jacques de Molay in 1314. It has been suggested that the Templars were given the cloth as a gift or simply for safekeeping in 1204 after the sack of Constantinople, which makes the 1988 carbon-dating of 1260 to 1390 incorrect. If the Templars were holding the cloth for someone else, that would explain why they did not display it or make it known that they had it. However, they kept detailed records of all their transactions and donations—and there is no written record of the shroud being in their keeping at any point. A letter was written, however, by Theodore Ducas Angelus, the ruler of the kingdom of Salonika from 1223/4 to 1230, to Pope Innocent III after the Fourth Crusade. The letter stated that part of the Crusaders' loot was the linen in which Jesus was wrapped after his death and before his resurrection and it had been taken to Athens. Another theory has been purported: that the cloth was not used by Jesus, but by either Jacques de Molay or Geoffrey de Charney after they had been tortured but before they were burned at the stake.

There might also be a visual connection. In 1185, a large tract of land was donated to the Templars in Somerset, England. They built a village there called Templecombe. It became a popular village and a number of Templars were living there during the 14th century when the Order was suppressed. In 1951, during the demolition of an outhouse in the village, a curious panel painting was discovered hidden in the roof of the building. Carbon-dated to the year 1280, the painting is of the head of a bearded man. The image has been variously described as representing Jesus or the head of St. John the Baptist, or a copy of the Shroud of Turin. There are several assumptions to be made here. If it was an image of Jesus, it is curious that it was hidden. Images of Jesus are frequently found in Roman Catholic establishments and it is usual among the religious to use these images as a prompt or focus when praying. Even if the painting was commissioned by the Templars, the mystery remains, why did they then hide it? If it represents the Turin Shroud, is this evidence that the shroud was in their possession as has been claimed? So far, no questions can be answered satisfactorily. The Shroud of Turin remains a mystery and so does the Templecombe painting. It is possible that the Templars believed the painting had magical or mystical powers. Perhaps the painting itself was the head they were accused of worshipping.

Another element to the mystery is the story of the "Mandylion." In the Eastern Orthodox Church, an image known as the Mandylion is a holy relic consisting of a rectangle of cloth imprinted with the face of Jesus.

According to the legend, during Christ's lifetime, King Abgar of Edessa wrote to Jesus, asking him if he would cure him of an illness. Jesus replied declining the invitation, but promising a future visit by one of his apostles. According to accounts from centuries later, the apostle Thaddeus is said to have been sent to Edessa by Jesus and he duly cured the king. Some time after, it was said that Thaddeus carried with him the image of Jesus on a cloth and left it in Edessa, and it was reported that a portrait of Christ had a miraculous effect during the fight of Edessa against the Persians in 544 CE. In the tenth century the image was moved to Constantinople, but it was taken during the Sack of Constantinople in 1204. The object claimed to be the Mandylion is now kept in the Pope's private chapel in the Vatican and is rarely seen by the public.

The origins of the Mandylion are obscure. Some say it was painted, others say that the image formed when Jesus dried his wet head on a piece of cloth. There is scholarly disagreement about whether the cloth is the original or a copy—as well as what exactly it is. Some believe that the painting found in Templecombe is a copy of the Mandylion and that it may have been left in the Order's possession for a while. The head they were accused of worshipping was described in some accounts as a "plaque" and in others as an "idol." The word plaque suggests a flat, rather than a three-dimensional object, so perhaps it was simply the Templecombe painting.

The head

Possibly one of the strangest accusations leveled at the Knights Templar in 1307 was that they worshipped a head. Some—but not all—were accused of owning a head that they worshipped in place of God. Like so many Templar mysteries, where the idea originated and whose head it was has become obscure and confused. In different reports, the head was described variously as the embalmed head of Jesus, of St. John the Baptist, or of Hugh de Payns; some said it had magical powers and that it could answer questions,

▲

The painting of a man's head, found in a building in Templecombe, Somerset, England, in 1951, has been carbon-dated to the year 1280. Hidden in an old Templar building, the mystery about the work has grown as much for whom it represents as why it was hidden.

Possibly one of the strangest accusations leveled at the Knights Templar in 1307 was that they worshipped a head.

provide the Templars with wealth and destroy their enemies. It was also occasionally described as the head of a cat and it was sometimes linked with the idea of a pagan deity with the name Baphomet, but even this is ambiguous. In some accounts, Baphomet was made of gold and silver, in others it was a real embalmed head with long hair and a beard. Some described it as having three faces, four legs, horns, or even that it was the Devil's head. It has since been suggested that the name developed from the Arabic word "Muhammad," which also appeared as Mahomet and Mahmoud in c.1205. Others believe that Baphomet is a corruption of Mahomet (the medieval European pronunciation of Muhammad).

Both of these notions were used in the accusations to imply that the Templars were secretly Muslims, even though Muslims do not worship idols. Raymond d'Aguilers, the chronicler of the First Crusade who followed Count Raymond IV of Toulouse to Jerusalem, calls mosques "Bafumarias," which could be connected. Around 1265, a poem written by a French troubadour widely believed to have been a Templar, who lived in the Holy Land, mentioned the name "Bafometz":

> Then it is really foolish to fight the Turks, not that Jesus Christ no longer opposes them. They have vanquished the Franks and Tartars and Armenians and Persians, and they continue to do so. And daily they impose new defeats on us, for God, who used to watch on our behalf, is now asleep, and Bafometz puts forth his power to support the Sultan.
> RICAUT BONOMEL, C.1265

Still, there has never been a conclusive definition of the word, and even under torture most Templars denied any knowledge of owning or worshipping any head at all. In total, only nine Templars did admit to owning some form of head, but this was under torture and none of their stories correspond to each other. Beyond France, where Templars were not tortured, no one even mentioned a head. In 1307, under torture, Guillaume de Arbley, who was the preceptor of the Templar house at Soissy in the diocese of Meaux, testified that he had seen the "bearded head" twice, which he claimed was gilded and made of silver and wood. Three years later, he claimed that the gilded head placed on Templar altars was a representation of 11,000 virgins.

Etienne de Troyes is described as having been a serving brother from the diocese of Meaux who left the Order because he was molested by another Templar. Before he could leave, his mother had to pay for his release. He is said to have testified that the Templars were told to worship and do homage to a head. Raoul de Gizy, a serving brother who was preceptor of the houses of Lagny-le-Sec and Sommereux, claimed to have seen a mysterious head in seven Templar houses, where it was held aloft by Hugh de Pairaud, the Templar Visitor; Raoul de Gizy described the head as being "demonic" and that the Templars had to prostrate themselves before it. Pierre d'Arbley attested to an object with two faces and four legs. Another Templar mentioned a skull, but religious buildings of the period frequently had skulls in them and this would not have been unusual, as skulls were used as symbols of mortality. The Templars did own several silver-gilt heads as reliquaries, but so did other orders and churches. The trials in Paris produced little evidence of this idol worship and nothing consistent. The name Baphomet was not mentioned in the trials, did not appear in the official list of accusations against them, and there is no mention of Baphomet either in the Templar Rule or in any other Templar document. It seems likely that their interrogators simply wanted to land a charge of idolatry and so heresy on the Templars and to imply that they were colluding with the Muslims in the Holy Land, or that they were Devil-worshippers, but nothing was ever substantiated, especially outside France where the Templars were not tortured.

Scottish legends

During the late 13th and early 14th centuries, England under Edward I was at war with Scotland. In June 1314 his son, Edward II, engaged the Scots at the Battle of Bannockburn. According to the legend that was written in 1843, the Scots were losing until a group of reinforcements appeared and changed the direction of the battle in favor of the Scottish king, Robert the Bruce. It was said that these reinforcements were the Knights Templar, emerging after their suppression, to support King Robert. Yet no contemporary or near contemporary accounts of the battle mention the Knights Templar. The vanquished English did not mention them, which they would probably have done had they seen members of a recently deposed order fighting as one force. The excommunicated King Robert the Bruce was desperate to please the Pope and the King of France, so would not have wanted to associate with the Templars. In addition, two members of the Knights Templar had fought for Edward I at the Battle of Falkirk in 1297 and Edward II had protected them against the French Inquisitors, so it is unlikely that in such a short time they would take up arms against him. In any case, it is often said that the story of the Templars at Bannockburn was never meant to be taken as factual history, but was written for Freemasons' ceremonies in the 18th century along with several others. But there had been a Templar presence in Scotland since King David I granted them lands at Ballantrodoch in 1128. It is possible that a few Templars managed to escape arrest in France and fled to Scotland, or that after their suppression, Templars in Scotland were released from imprisonment and established themselves there, but how they could earn a living when existing as a brotherhood but not sanctioned as a religious fraternity would have been a major problem and any gold that they may have secreted from their preceptories would have aroused suspicion.

> According to the legend, the Scots were losing until a group of reinforcements appeared and changed the direction of the battle. It was said that they were the Knights Templar.

The Templars in Spain and Portugal

King James II of Aragon always believed in the Templars, but when the Pope suppressed them, he had to act. Having no intention of giving their property away to others, however, he simply renamed the Brotherhood the Order of Montesa, honoring them with a duty to defend the country. The Order of Montesa remained an essential part of Spain for 175 years until Ferdinand of Aragon and Isabella of Castile drove the last Muslims from the country. Similarly in Portugal, support of the Templars remained unimpaired. In 1319, King Diniz asked Pope John XXII's permission to reform the Templars as the Order of Christ, or the Knights of Christ. The Pope approved. It is unclear, however, whether many original Templars continued in the new order, or

▶

The Battle of Bannockburn, in Stirling County, Scotland, on 24 June 1314, when King Robert the Bruce defeated the English king Edward II. This illustration is taken from the 14th-century Holkham Picture Bible.

THE MYTHS

Comēt le grant pouple bataulheront acōtre le iour de iugemēt par orguil ꞇ par enuie ꞇ par couestise.

Coment le cōmoune gent cheron leua acōtre eulx ꞇ uou ... da autre octire p̄ le auer pr̄ met aproche. sen crise. E cco est dirnt nous esperoms bien q̄ le iour de dreit iugemēt tor

Tomar Castle

The castle at Tomar was renamed the Convento de Cristo (Convent of the Order of Christ) once it was given to the Knights of Christ. It was originally built in 1160 by Gualdim Pais, the provincial Grand Master of the Templars, with round corner turrets, which were more difficult to build but easier to defend in battle. It contains a large round church, which from the outside is a 16-sided polygonal structure with buttresses, round windows and a bell-tower. Inside, the round church has a central, octagonal structure that echoes both the Church of the Holy Sepulcher and the Dome of the Rock in Jerusalem.

▶

The ribbed vaulting and sanctuary of The Convent of the Order of Christ, in Tomar, Portugal, originally a Templar stronghold, built in 1160. After the Templar Order was dissolved, the Portuguese branch was turned into the Knights of the Order of Christ, supporting Portugal's maritime discoveries of the 15th century.

◀

A Spanish painting of the 15th century, depicting Our Lady of Grace and the Masters of the Order of Montesa. The Masters' white mantles with the red cross is the same habit as worn by the Templars.

whether it was a completely new formation that simply followed much of the Templars' Rule. After a further four years, King Diniz was sanctioned by the Pope to give the new order Templar possessions, including their former headquarters at Tomar.

Grand Masters of the Order of Christ included various important individuals including Prince Henry the Navigator, the third son of King João of Portugal. Under Prince Henry's direction, the Order became involved in voyages of discovery around the coast of Africa. Henry's main aim was to explore beyond Cape Bojador, south of the Canary Islands, and to this end, he and the Knights of Christ went on many productive expeditions. The Order of Christ established and defended numerous trading posts with the Templars' splayed red cross emblazoned on their fleet's sails. It is alleged that, in 1492, the Order of Christ also provided the navigators for the voyage of Christopher Columbus. They almost definitely accompanied Vasco da Gama on his discovery of the sea route around Africa to India in 1497, as he was a member of the Order. Ships and shipping were an important element in a rather extended "modern" conspiracy theory involving the Templars.

Discoverers of the New World

The Knights Templar had a large fleet of ships which they used for combat, for trading, and for transporting pilgrims and goods. The ships were based in various ports around Europe, including La Rochelle, Bristol, Marseilles and, before their loss, in Acre in the Holy Land. After the Templar arrests in 1307 there is no further mention of these ships.

Nonetheless, stories that Templar survivors may have sailed to the New World were circulated at the same time as the Bannockburn story. It was claimed that just before the Templars were arrested in France, news slipped out about what was happening, and some brothers hastily gathered their most valuable treasures that were kept in the Paris Temple and secretly loaded them on to wagon trains which they carried overland to the port of La Rochelle. There, the hoard was loaded on to Templar ships, which sailed away and were never seen again. One theory is that they traveled to Scotland. Another theory adds that, although the Templars stayed in Scotland with their treasure, decades later their descendants sailed to Canada and America. A third theory claims that they sailed straight to Canada and America from France, even though Christopher Columbus is usually considered to be the first European to discover "the New World" in 1492. However, the Templar ships that supposedly sailed away from La Rochelle laden with treasure were never made for long ocean voyages; they were not robust enough and could not carry enough water to have journeyed across the Atlantic Ocean.

Painted in 1460 purportedly by the Portuguese court painter, Nuno Gonçalves, this is a detail from an altar thought to be showing Henry the Navigator who was responsible for the Order of Christ's voyages of discovery toward the end of the 15th century.

The second theory about the Templars' descendants voyaging to the New World suggests that the Templars sailed with Henry Sinclair, the first Earl of Orkney (c.1345–c.1400), a descendant of a Templar called Henri de Saint-Clair who allegedly fought with Godfrey de Bouillon in the First Crusade. These Templar ships were apparently captained by the Venetian brothers Nicolò and Antonio Zeno, and it is claimed that they reached Nova Scotia in 1389. Over 160 years later, the Zenos' maps and letters were published. Although these seem to show that they did reach the coast of America and Canada, in the documents no mention is made of anyone called Sinclair. It was not until 1780 that another writer identified "Zichmni" from the Zeno documents, who was described as being in charge of the voyage, as Henry Sinclair. The entire story is now generally considered by most specialists on the subject to be a fabrication, based on misinterpreted facts and false claims. The published Zeno documents are regarded as a hoax, as they have been proved to have been copied from the descriptions made by Columbus about his observations, with a few slight adjustments. The accompanying map has been shown to have been copied from a chart made in 1539. Most contradictory of all, it has been proved that Nicolò Zeno was in prison in Italy from 1396 to 1401: the time he was said to have been sailing across the Atlantic. Furthermore, no contemporary source mentions Henry Sinclair's voyages. Another reason—not verified—why the Templars may not have joined forces with the Sinclair family is that, allegedly, Henry Sinclair and his brother William testified against the Order in 1309. If this is true, then it is highly unlikely that the Sinclairs had any amicable connections with the Templars after this date.

All three theories have been linked to the Rosslyn Chapel in Scotland. As well as containing the Apprentice Pillar (see page 183), where the treasure may have been hidden, the Rosslyn Chapel is richly decorated with carvings. In the late 20th century, two of the carvings were identified by Christopher Knight and Robert Lomas in their book *The Hiram Key* as ears of corn or maize and an aloe: plants that the authors explained were native to parts of America and which, by 1446 or 1456, the time of Rosslyn's construction, had never been seen by a European. Three facts dispel this myth. One, the carvings were made some time after the Rosslyn Chapel was built; it is not clear when exactly, but they are not part of the fabric of the building. Two, the carvings do not definitively represent maize or an aloe. They could be any one of several other plant species. Three, the succulent aloe is native to Africa and not to the east coast of North America where it is claimed the Templars traveled to, and there are no cornfields in the areas they were said to have visited.

Among other historians on the subject, Dr. Louise Yeoman, who specializes in Scottish history, dismisses the Sinclair–Knights Templar connection, saying that it was invented by 18th-century fiction writers, and also dismisses any Templar connection with Rosslyn Chapel, saying that it was built by William Sinclair (grandson of Henry Sinclair) so that Mass could be said for the souls of his family. Also, the carvings in the Rosslyn Chapel that appear to resemble Templar icons, (even though they are clearly different), were made at an unknown date, almost certainly later than the date of its construction in the mid-15th century (see page 183). The claim that the layout of the chapel replicates Solomon's Temple has been analyzed by Mark Oxbrow and Ian Robertson in their book, *Rosslyn and the Grail*, and concludes that it "bears no more resemblance to Solomon's or Herod's Temple than a house brick does to a paperback book." Instead, Oxbrow and Robertson reflect that the Chapel closely resembles the East Quire of Glasgow Cathedral, which was added to the 12th-century stone church in the 13th century, and state that this resemblance was first mentioned as early as 1877 in the *Proceedings of the Society of Antiquaries* written by Andrew Kemp.

The disappearing fleet

The port of La Rochelle on the Atlantic coast in France is approximately 300 miles (483 kilometers) from Paris. The harbor lies in a natural bay, is relatively easy to defend and was said to have been developed by the Templars early in their history. Although it was not the most straightforward port from which to sail to either Outremer or England, it nonetheless became a bustling center for the Templar fleet and the town became an important Templar Province with a rapidly increasing population.

There has been a great deal of deliberation over Templar treasure: what it was, whether it existed and, if it did exist, where it ended up. Although King Philip IV took a lot of the Templars' money during their persecution, many have wondered if he took all their treasure and, if not, what happened to it? The contents of the treasure is a mystery, thought by some to be large hoards of gold and jewels, and by others as comprising more esoteric objects, such as the Holy Grail, Ark of the Covenant, or other venerated items, such as the head of Christ or St. John the Baptist, or even important religious documents, such as gospels that were omitted from the Bible or mystical knowledge about life, the universe or detailed explanations of sacred geometry, but as nothing has been found, nothing can be proved.

> The image could be a 12th-century prediction of the Order's later persecution and capture, created as a warning.

During the Templar trials, Jean de Chalon, a member of the Order from Nemours, testified that Gerard de Villiers, the Preceptor of the Paris Temple, had fled the country with 50 horses and 18 ships from the port of La Rochelle. However, there is no record of such a large number of ships—or indeed any Templar ship—leaving from La Rochelle or any other French port at that time. At the time of their arrests, the king's men would have been especially vigilant in watching the ports. Chalon did not specify when Villiers left, however, so the fleet could have left some time before the arrests. To remain inconspicuous, the ships would have had to have sailed separately as a large fleet would have alerted the king's officials. If the ships did leave like this, that is earlier and separately, then it indicates that the Templars knew in advance about their forthcoming arrests, which were meant to have been a secret. This is all undocumented so it remains speculative, but the Templar ships did disappear mysteriously. There is no record of them being taken by anyone; not the Hospitallers, nor King Philip. They had ships before they were suppressed in 1307, but none after their dissolution in 1312. Adding to the confusion, they only ever had a small number of large ships and not the 18 galleys that Chalon described. They had numerous small ships, that they used to take goods, money and pilgrims back and forth across the Mediterranean, but fewer than five galleys that would have been able to carry hoards of treasure.

One suggestion that the Templars possessed something of value and took it away to a secret hiding place before their suppression was made by the French author, journalist and editor, Louis Charpentier (b. 1905) in a book published in France in 1966 called *Les Mystères de la Cathédrale de Chartres* (The Mysteries of Chartres Cathedral). Charpentier drew attention to the carved image on the pillar in the north porch of Chartres (see page 59) that illustrates the Ark of the Covenant in transit on a wheeled cart. Charpentier reintroduced and popularized the theory that the Templars found something under Temple Mount and that this was possibly the Ark of the Covenant, but there is still no physical or documentary evidence to support the supposition. The carving might be an interpretation by a freemason working on Chartres Cathedral of what he perceived to be the method used by Moses to transport the Ark of the Covenant, but it could also represent several other things. In reality, the Ark would have been carried on poles on men's shoulders, but as Charpentier implies, it might be a depiction of either the Templars finding the Ark and moving it from Jerusalem to France when Chartres was built, or it could be showing them moving it from France to Scotland at another time. Another possible interpretation of the image could be a 12th-century prediction of the Order's later persecution and capture, created as a warning and to show what to do in such a situation. Beneath the carving is a Latin inscription that states *Hic Amititur Archa Cederis*, which means "Through the Ark thou shall work." This has had various interpretations, from a suggestion that it is a direct message from the Knights

Templar, to a simple call to all worshippers to adhere to the Ten Commandments.

As the town of Chartres was in the domain of the Counts of Champagne for a time and also probably the birthplace of the 13th-century Templar Grand Master William de Chartres, it is often claimed that the Templars helped to build Chartres Cathedral. But again, there is no authoritative evidence of this and most of the theories of their involvement appear to be inspired more by the hope of a mystery than by any substantial proof. Most historians believe that the carving illustrates the Ark being smuggled into Egypt during the reign of King Manasseh in approximately 687 to 642 BCE, as described in the Second Book of Chronicles.

The Money Pit

Another legend about the Templars reaching the New World that may or may not be linked with those stories mentioned above, is the notion that they landed at Nova Scotia at the end of the 14th century. Associated with the question over what happened to their treasure, this legend begins at the end of the 18th century. With no records about it, Templar treasure has persistently been contemplated and many suppositions and theories have been proposed. It is reputed to have contained massive amounts of gold and silver bullion, the crown jewels of European royal families, sacred artefacts, and priceless documents, but none of this has ever been verified.

In 1795, three young men were on the shores of the tree-covered Oak Island in Nova Scotia, Canada. After noticing some ship's tackle hanging from a tree and, below it, a large depression in the soil, the three began digging at the spot. They soon reached a layer of flagstones about ten feet (three meters) below and as they dug further, they discovered layers of oak logs at about every ten feet. At approximately thirty feet (nine meters) down, without special equipment, they could dig no further, so they abandoned the excavation, but public interest was aroused. Several years later, a company was formed to investigate the site. Successive oak platforms continued as they dug, until at 90 feet (27 meters), a stone inscribed with a simple code explained that treasure would be found just "forty feet below". However, the deep hole that had been dug suddenly filled with sea water, preventing any further excavation. Currently, after over two centuries, a huge amount of money has been spent on the pit as treasure hunters desperately try to get to the bottom of it. First, a series of flood tunnels were dug, then pumps, drills, dams and various kinds of machinery were all used to try to uncover the mystery and reach what many believe could be Templar treasure. This so-called "Money Pit" became associated with the Templars because not far away several old gravestones were found marked with Templar crosses. The Money Pit has so far cost treasure hunters millions of dollars and five lives, but it has still not given up its secrets. Practically nothing—and nothing of value—has ever been found there. Various other theories have been suggested as to what might be buried there—if anything, as it could be an elaborate trick—but the debate continues. The flooding of the site with sea water has been proved to be a natural phenomenon and not a clever man-made prank, but even this could have been planned on purpose, since the flooding happens when the pit reaches a certain depth. Whether it is a complicated hoax or whether something of substance is actually buried there, whoever placed the cut logs had substantial knowledge of engineering and went to a great amount of trouble.

A Renaissance relief by Nanni di Bando showing stonemasons, architects and carpenters, c.1414/17.

Freemasonry

After the Order's downfall, it is believed that many ex-Templars joined other orders and groups, not simply those in Spain and Portugal that were reformed after their demise. But with no consistent records, the issue became confused when some associations such as the Freemasons adopted Templar symbols and traditions.

Many Freemasons have alleged that they descend directly from the Knights Templar, often relaying the legend that after their suppression, some Templars fled to Scotland and found refuge with a lodge of Scottish stonemasons. In the story, the ex-Templars taught the stonemasons the virtues of chivalry and obedience, using the builders' tools as metaphors, and eventually they began rebuilding a new version of the original order, including members from the stonemasons they had been teaching. This order allegedly existed in secret from around 1550 until the formation of the United Grand Lodge of England in 1717.

Another story that relates to Freemasonry begins in the late medieval period, when there were two kinds of masons: stonemasons who built walls and foundations of buildings with rough, hard stone, and masons who created fine carved façades on softer stone. These latter masons were known as freestone masons, which became abbreviated to freemasons. As freelance workers, the freemasons traveled around Europe and stayed in lodges when working away from home. It is said that, as both Christians and masons, they were particularly interested in the Old Testament's Second Book of Chronicles that gave details about King Solomon, his worker Hiram, and the building of the Temple, particularly its detailed proportions and the huge bronze pillars known as Jachin and Boaz and the "sea of bronze" (see page 45). Information in the Bible about Hiram is sparse, but it is made clear that he was extremely skilled and, as such, he fascinated the freemasons. Gradually over many years, legends formed around Hiram Abiff as the freemasons called him. From these legends, freemasons acquired certain rituals and traditions, and individual groups began forming to support each other, rather like guilds. Aware that they needed to raise their standing in

society to gain greater respect, the freemasons began inviting influential people to serve as their patrons, and by the turn of the 18th century, these prestigious patrons known as "speculative masons" outnumbered the "operative masons" or freemasons themselves.

In 1717, four London "Lodges"—the name the freemasons gave their individual groups—merged to create the United Grand Lodge of England, with a gentleman—not a mason—elected to serve as their Grand Master. The idea spread across Europe and within 15 years, Masonic Lodges had been established in the Netherlands, France, and Germany. A culture of secrecy developed around them, giving rise to many stories and mysteries about them. One of the first stories came in 1760 from a Freemason in Germany called George Frederick Johnson, who was possibly French, but who claimed to be Scottish. Declaring that he knew the secrets of the Knights Templar, Johnson insisted that in the 12th century while living on Temple Mount, the Templars had acquired treasure that had belonged to the Jewish Essenes. This treasure was handed down to each Templar Grand Master until Jacques de Molay, who in Johnson's story is called Hiram. On the night before he was burned at the stake, Jacques de Molay (or Hiram) ordered a group of Templars to enter the Paris Temple to take the Templar treasure and escape with it. According to Johnson, this was the point at which 18 Templar galleys were filled with their treasure and sailed from La Rochelle to Scotland, where the Templars renamed themselves Freemasons.

Several facts make this story improbable. On the evening before his death, neither Jacques de Molay nor the authorities knew that he was going to be burned at the stake the following day. At that time in 1314, it was possible but not likely that there were some free Templars in France, but by then the Order had been dissolved for two years, and most French

The idea spread across Europe and within 15 years, Masonic Lodges had been established in the Netherlands, France, and Germany.

ex-Templars were probably either still lingering in prisons or had escaped abroad. It was too dangerous to remain in France. There may have been a few who were waiting to help Jacques de Molay to escape, however. The main difficulty would have been that from the moment of the arrests in 1307, the Paris Temple was heavily guarded by the king's men, and so it would have been virtually impossible to enter.

With no record of any groups called Freemasons until the 18th century and the notion of the Templars changing from a holy order of knights to a non-religious organization, Johnson's story seems improbable, but he initiated an idea that Freemasonry descended directly from the Knights Templar. Freemasonry was never a religious order and, contrary to the Knights Templar, it originally had an anti-Catholic bias, prompting Pope Clement XII to condemn it in a papal bull of 1738. With its many rituals, secret passwords and signs, however, it was always going to be the subject of a wide variety of criticism and conspiracy theories. As well as connections with the Templars, Freemasonry has been linked to Jack the Ripper, Zionism, witchcraft, and Devil worship, but there is no evidence about any of it. Most Masonic legends were openly made up as allegories. Robert L. D. Cooper, Freemason and curator at the Grand Lodge of Scotland Museum and Library in Edinburgh, wrote in 2006:

> None of the traditional histories of any of the branches of Freemasonry are, or were, intended to be taken literally. Our forebears in all the Masonic Orders manufactured suitable "pasts" for allegorical purposes. They did so with romantic notions at heart but understood that these histories manufactured by, and for, themselves were not literal truths.
> ROBERT L. D. COOPER, THE ROSSLYN HOAX?

Switzerland

That some Templars escaped to Switzerland is another theory that has been purported by a number of scholars. In their book of 1998, *The Warriors and Bankers, a History of the Knights Templar, 1307 to the Present*, Alan Butler and Stephen Dafoe conclude that the Templars helped to form Switzerland at the beginning of the 14th century, when they were first being persecuted in France. This theory discounts the ships sailing away to Scotland or Canada and America, but explains that contrary to that notion, the Templars put on ordinary clothes, shaved off their beards and separated their treasure into small, manageable amounts, then escaped overland to the mountains of Switzerland. Not widely accepted by academics, the theory is nonetheless worthy of consideration.

Many have commented on the similarity between the Templar flag of the splayed red cross on a white background and the Swiss national flag of a plain white cross on a red ground. They have common roots, but it is unlikely that the Swiss flag developed from the Templars'. The design of a white cross on a red field is believed to have originated in the war banners of Emperor Constantine after 312 CE when he converted to Christianity. It was used to symbolize the Emperor's role as protector of Christianity. In the 14th century, a loose confederation of the small cantons or states was formed, and in 1339, in the Battle of Laupen the confederacy fought against the Austrian Habsburgs. To contrast with the red St. George's cross of the Habsburgs, every Swiss fighter wore a white linen cross stitched on to his chest, sleeve and thigh. Meanwhile, in Portugal, the Order of Christ, which derived from the Templars, began using a splayed white cross on a red background as their banner as soon as they formed in 1319. The white cross on red was not introduced as an actual flag in Switzerland until the Napoleonic period at the turn of the 19th century and not introduced as an official national flag until 1889.

The hypothesis that many Templars escaped to Switzerland arose mainly because the Swiss, like the Templars, became renowned for their astute banking practices, their prowess on the battlefield, and their religious tolerance. As Switzerland is adjacent to France, it would have been relatively easy for fleeing Templars to reach from various regions across France. Additionally, the mountains had many potential hiding places for individuals or small groups of men. The theory that the Templars were forewarned of their arrests in France in 1307 makes sense of the conjecture that they sent several of their brethren over the mountains with their treasure in advance, rather than to ports and ships where they would have been seen and reported or caught by officials. No such reports or arrests were made. Although early Swiss history is extremely indistinct, the founding of the first largely independent and democratic Swiss states—or cantons—at the end of the 13th and beginning

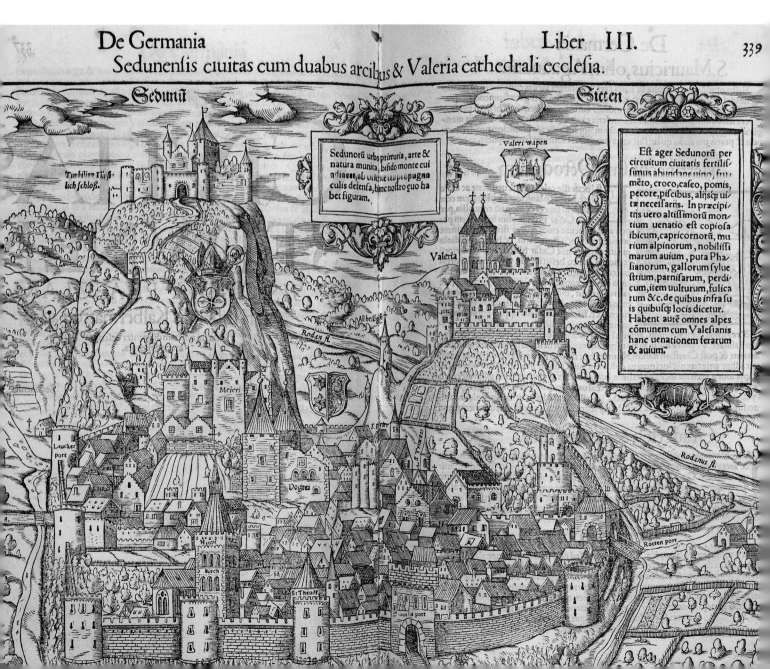

Alongside the domestic buildings were two large castles that closely resemble Templar fortresses in Outremer. Concurrently, Swiss banking began, with many of the methods invented by the Templars.

of the 14th centuries, roughly corresponds with the beginnings of the Templars' persecution in France. Some unsubstantiated tales of knights dressed in white appearing and helping the locals to gain their independence against foreign domination are legendary, but none of it was officially documented. During the medieval period, Switzerland as a region belonged to the Holy Roman Empire. As the Habsburg dynasty became stronger and sought to gain even greater power, the disparate mountain communities tried to defend their independence. Until then these communities had been free from any authority other than the Emperor. Battles ensued and the earliest cantons of the 14th century were joined by forces from the city-states of Lucerne, Zürich, and Berne, as well as allegedly by the mysterious knights who helped them to defeat the Habsburg armies and retain their autonomy.

Before the cantons were formed, the area was made up of several separate fiefdoms, but once established, each canton became an independent sovereign state with its own borders, army, and currency. The individual cantons eventually allied into the country we know as Switzerland. As conflicts with the Habsburgs ended, banking and farming became the predominant industries in Switzerland, and while these industries were developing, several towns were built. One, named Sion after the French word Zion for Holy Land, was built high in the Alps. Alongside the domestic buildings were two large castles that closely resemble Templar fortresses in Outremer. Concurrently, Swiss banking began, with many of the methods invented by the Templars, such as international transfers, current accounts, safe-deposit boxes, pensions, and strict confidentiality. These similarities have led some to believe that many Templars lived in and built towns like Sion, and that banking in Switzerland was started by the Templars. Yet with the strict Swiss laws of preserving secrecy and little reliable documentation from the period, the link with the Order is another theory that remains difficult to prove either way.

Skulls and bones

A Masonic legend tells of three Templars searching the site of Jacques de Molay's death on the night of his execution in March 1314 and finding only his skull and femurs. The three Templars purportedly took the bones and created the first flag bearing the skull and crossbones symbol. This is usually accepted by many historians to be purposely fabricated to form a Masonic legend and was never meant to be taken literally. Most significantly, it is highly unlikely that there were any free Templars in Paris on the night of the deaths of Jacques de Molay and Geoffrey de Charney.

Although it is not understood exactly when the symbol first came into use, the skull and crossbones has been found on medieval tombs in various European countries, used as a sign of death, such as during one of the epidemics of the Black Death in 1348. It was also used later by pirates as a warning to others. The Templars did use the skull as a symbol on several of their later gravestones, including some in Scotland, but this was long before their persecution and the burning of Jacques de Molay so the story of the Templars finding his bones in his funeral pyre does not fit. Skulls and bones were long used as

◀

A woodcut from 1550 of the town of Sion in Switzerland, showing its many buildings, city walls and castles that resemble Templar buildings and were erected fairly rapidly, soon after the Templars' suppression.

symbols in Europe as the ultimate "memento mori" or "vanitas": reminders of death and mortality, that life is transient and that death puts an end to all worldly achievements, contrasting with the everlasting nature of faith. The symbol also links with Christianity, as the place of Christ's crucifixion was called "Golgotha," which translates as "the Place of the Skull." The "green man," an architectural decoration often found in churches and other buildings, which also appears in the Rosslyn Chapel and at Temple Church, has sometimes been described as representing a skull, with the crossed vegetation behind his head as the bones, but it is more often seen as a symbol of rebirth, representing fertility, growth, and the abundance of nature.

Cat worship

When the Templars were imprisoned from 1307, the notion of skulls was mixed up with the accusation that they worshipped a head (see also pages 185–186). Occasionally said to be a skull or a demon, the head was also sometimes said to be the head of a cat. Without any definitive evidence, several legends and tales have become intertwined and confused. The idea that the head was not human was another aspect of confusion around this issue. A cat was the most common creature mentioned in relation to the Templars. During the medieval period, many were suspicious of cats and people who owned them. Many innocent women were accused of witchcraft because their pet cats were perceived to be their "familiars": demons or spirits from European folklore needed to assist witches in performing spells and curses. Familiars were believed to appear in various forms, often as animals, such as toads, owls, or mice, for instance, but most frequently as cats. Disparately, in ancient Egyptian mythology, Sekhmet was a warrior-goddess, depicted as a cat or lioness, and Bast was another Egyptian goddess bearing the head of a cat. If it could be proved that the Templars worshipped a cat, whether this was perceived as a familiar or a pagan idol, the Pope would have instantly excommunicated the entire Order. So ultimately, it was almost irrelevant whether the cat head was a familiar or an ancient Egyptian goddess. Either way, if the confession that they worshipped a cat could be extracted from them, there would subsequently be a straightforward charge of heresy. However, this never happened. Although they may have owned cats to inhibit the numbers of mice and rats in their farms, preceptories, mills, and castles, there was not a shred of evidence of any form of cat worship. It was an elusive accusation that the Inquisitors failed to make much of. At the time, as it was not uncommon for any religious house to own relics and the Templars may have possessed the supposed bones or teeth of saints, but pagan or Satanic worship was never established at the Templar trials.

Familiars were believed to appear in various forms, often as animals, such as toads, owls, or mice, for instance, but most frequently as cats.

One thing that the Templars never worshipped was the goat-headed, winged demon that is featured on Tarot cards. This strange image was drawn in the 19th century by Eliphas Lévi (1810–75), a French magician and author on the occult, who originally studied to enter the Roman Catholic priesthood but fell in love and so was never ordained. His first treatise on magic appeared in 1855, called *Dogme et Rituel de la Haute Magie* (Dogma and Ritual of High Magic). In the work, he depicted the goat-headed demon that he called Baphomet: an imaginary pagan deity that he revived from the 11th or 12th century as a figure of occultism and Satanism. As discussed on page 187, Baphomet had first appeared,

probably as a corruption of the word "Mahomet" or "Muhammad," and was mentioned in the Templar charges, but not pursued as a serious accusation. Even though Lévi implied that the image had Templar origins, the goat image was his own invention.

A cat's head may have entered the mix of accusations against the Templars because many of their churches featured carved heads as decoration. Often appearing in the spandrels, between the arches or by the doors, the heads were created by freestone masons, sometimes for their symbolic connotations, sometimes as a signature (the heads were occasionally portraits of the masons who made them) and sometimes purely for decorative purposes. Some of these heads are grotesque, with fearsome, ugly faces (presumably a warning to those praying below of what to expect in Hell and not the masons' portraits); some represent monarchs; some are ordinary or even grimacing faces; and others represent lions or other feline-type creatures—probably there for protection as a residuary of pagan superstitions. There was nothing unusual about having heads like these in Gothic churches across Europe and Outremer, but King Philip had an ulterior motive, and anything remotely suspicious was focused upon and used against the Templars.

Bornholm Island, Denmark

One place where the Templars were not documented as being was Scandinavia. Yet there is an island in Denmark that is often discussed in conjunction with them and their possible hidden treasure. Situated approximately 25 miles (40 kilometers) southeast of the southern tip of Sweden, the Danish island of Bornholm forms an area of approximately 230 square miles (600 square kilometers). In medieval times, it was known as Burgunderland or Burgunderholm, as it is believed to have been home to the Burgundinians, who came from a previously Germanic tribe called the Burgundes that inhabited Scandinavia. After migrating south, they settled predominantly on the island of Bornholm and, between 1050 and 1150, they converted to Christianity.

▲

One of the carved "green men" on the walls of Rosslyn Chapel in Scotland. These faces are thought to represent fertility, growth, and nature— although some believe they are associated with the skull and crossbones.

Out of 15 churches on Bornholm Island, four are round. Built in the 12th century, some historians believe they were put there for both religious and defense purposes (island inhabitants were frequently attacked by pirates). Although conical now, originally the roofs of the churches were flat, possibly so that they could be defended from any angle, while the current cone-shaped roofs were added several centuries later. Yet the small scale of these churches makes it difficult to see how they were used as defense; there is not much room inside to contain a large force of fighting men. During the time they were built, there were fortresses on the island that would have been far more effective as places of refuge, although the round churches could nonetheless have been used as lookout posts.

There are no other round churches in Scandinavia and the mystery of why they were built on Bornholm Island at that time has been the subject of much speculation. At least two authors theorize that they were built by the Knights Templar. In their book of 1992, *The Templars' Secret Island*, Erling Haagensen and Henry Lincoln present evidence that connects the four round churches of Bornholm Island with the Knights Templar. These churches, of Østerlars, Nylars, Ølsker, and Nyker, according to Haagensen and Lincoln, are complex structures that incorporate the equilateral six-sided shape which forms the star of David and is based on the theories of sacred geometry that also appear in buildings constructed during earlier periods in the Holy Land.

In 2010, Haagensen carried out two investigations of the churches using electronic equipment. The investigations discovered a deep underground structure beneath the Østerlars church that mirrors a similar chasm under the church of Rennes-le-Château in France. Although this cellar had been long forgotten, nothing has been found in it, so its original function has not been ascertained. The upper windows in the Østerlars church are positioned to align with the sunrises of the winter and summer solstices, as it is claimed

THE MYTHS

also featured in the ancient Temple of Solomon. With their complex structures, the churches must have been built by knowledgeable architects, not local builders, but this still does not establish that they were built by the Templars. Even before the Order had been founded, round churches had been built on the model of the Holy Sepulcher and they became particularly common after the First Crusade. Most military orders built them. According to Haagensen and Lincoln, historical evidence reveals a plan made between the Danish Archbishop Eskil of Lund—a friend of Bernard of Clairvaux—and the Templar Grand Master Bertrand de Blanchefort. From 1161 to 1167, Eskil stayed at Bernard's monastery Clairvaux, approximately nine years after Bernard had died, and made plans with Bertrand de Blanchefort. In this plan, the Knights Templar were to be responsible for supplying the Christian fleet on the Baltic Crusades. The Baltic Crusades were a series of campaigns fought during the 13th century that aimed to conquer and convert the pagan tribes of northeastern

> There are no other round churches in Scandinavia and the mystery of why they were built on Bornholm Island at that time has been subject to much speculation.

Europe around the Baltic Sea. Bernard of Clairvaux had supported these wars, despite their lack of a pilgrimage element, and other military orders were involved, but there is no historical evidence that the Templars took part, nor of any Templar activity or settlement in Denmark at any time. Documentation exists that the Teutonic Knights took a prominent role in the Baltic Crusades, but there is nothing to indicate that the Knights Templar did. If the churches on Bornholm were built by any of the religious-military orders, it would more likely have been the Hospitallers or the Teutonic Knights than the Templars, as they had documented connections in Scandinavia.

Haagensen and Lincoln suggest that the Templars might have used the churches on Bornholm as a hiding place for the secret treasure that they had found under Temple Mount early in their existence. Bornholm Island was remote, unknown and unlikely to be disturbed, but with no apparent connection with the Order or any reliable documentation or proof to support the claims, no further investigations have been undertaken of the location or the churches.

Rennes-le-Château, France

The treasure that the Templars allegedly possessed has been debated countless times by people with varying interests in the subject. Connections and suppositions have been made with and about several locations across Europe and beyond. Without any tangible confirmation, these locations are variously described as being the hiding place for this treasure either from relatively early on in the Order's existence, or from the time of their suppression. Nearly all these claims have been made since the 20th century. One location associated with several legends concerning Templar treasure and other mysterious notions is Rennes-le-Château, a tiny village in southwestern France that was once populated by the Cathars and still bears visible scars from the Albigensian Crusade. During the 1950s and 1960s, the entire area around Rennes-le-Château became the focus of sensational claims involving Blanche of Castile, the Merovingians, the Knights Templar, the Cathars, and the treasures of the Temple of Solomon. From the 1970s, the claims extended to include the Priory of Sion, the Holy Grail, sacred geometry, Christ's remains, and notions that Mary Magdalene settled in the south of France after Jesus had been crucified.

Rennes-le-Château began as a prehistoric encampment, but by 1050, it was controlled by the Counts of Toulouse, who allowed Cathars to live peacefully in the area. Even after their persecution and annihilation, Rennes-le-Château returned to being a quiet, remote village until the middle of the 20th century. Then, in the 1950s, a local hotel owner spread a rumor that a priest, Abbé Bérenger Saunière (1852–1917), had found some valuable documents there in the 19th century—and everything changed. From 1887 to 1897, Father Saunière had renovated the local church of St. Mary Magdalene and then had further buildings constructed in the area: the Villa Bethania and the Tour Magdala. In 1946, seven years before she died, Saunière's former housekeeper and secretary, Marie Dénarnaud (1868–1953), sold Father Saunière's estate to Noël Corbu (1912–68), an entrepreneur who had recently moved to the area with his wife. Along with the buildings constructed by Saunière, Corbu obtained the priest's papers. Corbu transformed the Villa Bethania into a hotel and opened a restaurant beneath a belvedere that connects the Tour Magdala to an orangery. He told his guests that Father Saunière had discovered something extremely valuable nearby. The hotel was soon inundated with bookings.

In January 1956, the local newspaper, *La Dépêche du Midi*, featured an interview with Corbu, who said that Father Saunière had discovered 28,500,000 gold pieces that had been hidden at Rennes-le-Château by Blanche of Castile in 1250. Corbu claimed that this had been amassed by Blanche, widow of King Louis VIII of France, to pay the ransom for her son Louis IX who had been captured by Muslims while on the Seventh Crusade. Blanche, however, became ill and died before she could send the money to the Holy Land. (In the end, Louis raised his own money for his release.) According to Corbu, the stash of money had been left in its hiding place for over six centuries, until Father Saunière discovered it. Corbu also claimed that in 1892, Saunière had discovered "parchments" while renovating the local church, which were "written in a mixture of French and Latin, which at first glance could be discerned to be passages from the Gospels."

Saunière had begun renovating the church in 1887, and was still doing so in 1892, so this is not completely inconceivable, but none of these "parchments" have been seen by anyone else, so there is no proof that they ever existed. Corbu also claimed that Saunière had only found one part of Blanche's treasure, and that before she died, Marie Dénarnaud had said: "Pray do not worry yourself, Monsieur Corbu. You shall have more money than you will be able to spend!" However, even though Corbu was joined by others in the hunt for this treasure, nothing was ever found. In July 1965, the local council was compelled to introduce a by-law prohibiting further excavations in the village.

Holy blood, holy Grail

Corbu's account of Father Saunière's discovery of the documents was later quoted in Gérard de Sède's book *L'Or de Rennes* (The Gold of Rennes), or *The Strange Life of Bérenger Saunière, Priest of Rennes-le-Château*, published in 1968, but the information in the book was later discovered to be fictitious, invented by de Sède and another author Pierre Plantard. The claim in the book was that Saunière found parchments proving that the line of the Merovingian king, Dagobert II, who was assassinated in 679, did not die with him

Corbu said that Father Saunière had discovered 28,500,000 gold pieces that had been hidden at Rennes-le-Château by Blanche de Castile in 1250.

▶

A 13th-century illumination showing King Louis IX of France and his mother Blanche of Castile, whom Corbu claimed had accumulated an incredible amount of money for her son's ransom, but had left it hidden in Rennes-le-Château when she died.

as had previously been thought. Instead, Dagobert's son had escaped the family's enemies and had taken refuge at Rennes-le-Château. The genealogical documents that de Sède declared Saunière had found led to an imaginary secret organization, the Priory of Sion, and Pierre Plantard claimed to be descended from Dagobert II. The book was later proved to be a complete fabrication. Documents the authors said verified it all were proved to be hoaxes, the Priory of Sion never existed and Pierre Plantard did not descend from the Merovingian kings. Yet, after scriptwriter Henry Lincoln read the book, he used the story as the basis for three television documentaries and a bestselling book *The Holy Blood and the Holy Grail*, which he wrote in conjunction with Michael Baigent and Richard Leigh in 1982. The book was later used as source material for the bestselling 2003 novel by Dan Brown, *The Da Vinci Code*.

According to the authors of *The Holy Blood and the Holy Grail*, the documents that Saunière supposedly found in the late 19th century had been hidden by one of his predecessors, the Abbé Bigou, who had been chaplain to the Blanquefort family, descendants of one of the early Templar Grand Masters. The Blanquefort family had given Bigou a great secret to hide, a secret which had been passed down by their Templar predecessor. This was the first link of Rennes-le-Château with the Templars, but the notion was never developed and nothing pertaining to it was found. Whatever it was that the Blanquefort family were supposed to have had was never explained and although several suggestions were made, nothing was ever proved or established.

The church of St. Mary Magdalene at Rennes-le-Château has been rebuilt several times over its history. The earliest church on the site was probably built in the eighth century, and another built on the same spot in the tenth or eleventh century. When Father Saunière renovated it at the end of the 19th century, he added some unusual statuary and sculpture, including a red demon being crushed under the font and an inscription that has been pondered over extensively. Above the front doors, the Latin words read "*Terribilis est locus iste,*" which translates as "This is a place of awe." On the arches over the two front doors, the dedication continues "*hic domus Dei est et porta coeli,*" meaning "this is God's house, the gate of heaven." Many claims have been made about the phrases, suggesting that they had deeper meanings than appeared superficially, but the same inscriptions featured in other churches and they were not particularly unusual, being extracted from a range of Christian sources including medieval chants, songs, old Bible annotations and more. It is probable that Saunière selected the phrases for no greater reason than they were traditional and he liked them.

Before she died, Marie Dénarnaud had said: "Pray do not worry yourself, Monsieur Corbu. You shall have more money than you will be able to spend!"

Saunière's secret money

One of the biggest mysteries, and the main issue that has provoked such extravagant speculation about Rennes-le-Château, is that Saunière's receipts and account books, which were handed down to Corbu, reveal that the renovation to the church, the presbytery and the cemetery cost 11,605 francs. This was a huge amount of money and far more than Saunière's monthly wages. It is not clear how a local priest could have paid for it. After the church remodeling, Saunière also paid for the two other buildings to be constructed in the village: the Villa Bethania and the Tour Magdala. Resembling a small medieval tower, the Tour Magdala, named after Mary Magdalene like the church close by, overlooks

surrounding villages, and Saunière used it as his library. He said that he had the Villa Bethania built as a retirement home for priests, although it was never used as such. Between 1898 and 1905, the buildings and land cost Saunière 26,417 francs.

Visitors to his home attest that he also owned valuable books and furniture that were not documented in his accounts; neither did he include any travel or personal expenses. But, although the sensational theories claim that he had found great treasure, he died in poverty, and his housekeeper and secretary Marie Dénarnaud was also destitute, suggesting that this elusive great treasure never existed. It is far more probable that Father Saunière committed simony or Mass trafficking. This meant that he charged the faithful to say Mass for them. Father Saunière was certainly not the only priest of the time to do this. Requesting a Mass was accepted by many to be costly and they were often said by priests without anyone even being present. It is known that Saunière also spent a great deal on postage, as he wrote to his parishioners in alphabetical order, offering to say Masses for them in return for a fee. It appears he was extremely good at this form of marketing. Priests were allowed to say no more than three Masses a day, but from his records, it can be seen that Saunière was asked to say thousands of Masses, far more than he could ever actually conduct, for which he received hundreds of thousands of francs.

In January 1909, the Bishop of Carcassonne transferred Saunière to the village of Coustouge. This was usual practice within the Catholic Church—priests only stayed in one place for a short time, until the Bishop moved them elsewhere—but Saunière refused to go and continued as an unofficial priest of Rennes-le-Château. In 1910, he built a conservatory adjacent to the Villa Bethania as a private chapel, where he continued to celebrate Mass as he could no longer use the church. That same year, he was summoned to appear before an ecclesiastical trial to face charges of simony or Mass trafficking. He was found guilty and suspended from the priesthood. When asked to account for his expenditure, he reported that he had received 82,800 francs in gifts between 1885 and 1905 from several benefactors, most of whom were anonymous. Allegedly, he was also having an affair with a wealthy woman, and the seven collection boxes in his church gained a steady income, but with no records of these either, the precise amounts are unknown. As a priest, he earned 900 francs a year. As well as charging for Masses, in another enterprising move, he had postcards made of the village, which he sold to visitors. He never recorded the proceeds from these sales, and his hobby of restoring old furniture and selling it was also omitted from his records. When asked to produce his account books, he refused to attend his trial. After he had been dismissed from the Church, he died in poverty—

▲
The Tour Magdala in Rennes-le-Château, France. Built as a library c.1900 for Abbé Bérenger Saunière, it is a bold example of his eccentric and decadent tastes.

hardly the ending of a life of a man who had found secret, priceless treasure. After his death in 1917, Marie Dénarnaud remained living in the presbytery but she ran into debt and tried several times—unsuccessfully—to sell the Villa Bethania. It was not until Noël Corbu bought the property in 1946 that her debts were settled. When Corbu and his wife turned it into the Hotel de la Tour, it was the first time the Villa Bethania had been occupied.

Another suggested mystery about Rennes-le-Château and the Knights Templar is that the buildings are based on the same construction methods and ratios as numerous churches and other buildings erected by the Order. Those who claim this allege that Saunière's buildings were deliberately placed according to a geometric pattern that is echoed elsewhere, particularly in the Holy Land. These are broad claims that have not been corroborated. Additionally, similarities appear in many other buildings across Europe, constructed by various orders, both military and purely religious.

Friday the 13th

Much of the furore attached to the Templars was intended to inflame the widespread superstitious fears of the time. Not all issues relating to their trials, however, had achieved the desired effect then. Some superstitions emerged centuries later. One of these is the idea of Friday the 13th being unlucky. On Friday, October 13th, 1307, the Templars were arrested in France. King Philip had written the order for the arrests a month earlier and the operation was meant to be kept in strict secrecy. On the appointed day, it is believed that simultaneously hundreds of the king's men opened copies of his written order and then went to every Templar property in France to arrest all ordained Templars. About 15,000 Templars were arrested, with an average age of 41. As the average life expectancy for men at that time was under 50, it is not really surprising that many of them died while in prison over the next few years. But it was not until relatively recently that the date and day upon which they were arrested has been considered specifically unlucky.

Although historically the number 13 was considered by some to be ill-omened and Friday was occasionally associated with misfortune, the amalgamation of the two traditions did not occur until relatively recently. The number 13 was considered unlucky as there were allegedly 13 people at the Last Supper, with Judas, the betrayer of Jesus, supposedly being the 13th guest to sit down. There are 13 witches in a coven, and in Norse mythology a dinner party of the gods was ruined by the 13th guest called Loki, who caused the world to be plunged into darkness. Thirteen was also perceived as one too many: there were 12 apostles, there are 12 hours in a day, 12 months in a year and 12 zodiac signs.

Friday being ill-fated was more obscure. Jesus was crucified on a Friday (although that went on to be called Good Friday as he rose again two days later). The next known reference to the idea is probably a line in Chaucer's *Canterbury Tales*, written in the late 14th century: ". . . and on a Friday fell all this misfortune". The idea of the day being associated with bad luck, however, did not become established until about three centuries later, when it obscurely became accepted by some Christians that certain things should not be undertaken on a Friday—travel, marriage, or a new job for instance. One of the most enduring but enigmatic sailing superstitions is that it is unlucky to begin a voyage on a Friday, but the origins of this superstition remain obscure. However, while Friday has always been held to

Historically the number 13 was considered by some to be ill-omened and Friday was occasionally associated with misfortune.

▶

An early 19th-century painting by the French artist Fleury François Richard, depicting Jacques de Molay, the 23rd and last Grand Master of the Knights Templar. De Molay led the Order from 1292 until Pope Clement V dissolved it in 1307. Through his ignominious downfall and execution, he has become the best-known of all the Templars, and the focus of countless legends.

THE MYTHS

be unlucky by some, others—such as many who live in the Scottish Hebrides—consider it to be lucky and the day on which seeds should be sown.

The association of Friday with 13 first occurred in the late 19th century, but was virtually ignored until the early 20th century. It is believed to have first been mentioned in the 1869 biography of Gioachino Rossini by Henry Sutherland Edwards: ". . . he regarded Fridays as an unlucky day and thirteen as an unlucky number, it is remarkable that on Friday 13th of November, he died." In 1907, Thomas W. Lawson published his dark novel, *Friday the Thirteenth*, and from that point the belief was seized upon and magnified. Among certain communities, the superstition spread and gained strength and at some point during the 20th century, someone connected it with the day of the Templar arrests. This has been further exaggerated by various books, documentaries, and films about them.

The French Revolution

Often referred to, but unproven, a legend connects the French Revolution with the Knights Templar. In 1789, the French working class overthrew their autocratic monarchy. At the moment Louis XVI was guillotined, the legend claims that a French Freemason shouted from the crowd: "Jacques de Molay, thou art avenged!" This story was mentioned in *The Illuminatus Trilogy* by Robert Shea and Robert Anton Wilson, first published in 1975, but there is no documented confirmation of the occurrence and it is unlikely that many revolutionaries would have understood the implication so it seems tenuous. Ironically, within a decade of the alleged incident, Napoleon Bonaparte had replaced the revolutionary idealism of the French working class with his own imperialism and, in 1808, he ordered the demolition of the Paris Temple.

An Enigma of History

At the time of their Order's demise, scattered across Europe beyond France, tens of thousands of Templars evaded persecution. Many of them were never arrested, or if they were, were soon released. What became of them?

Speculation has filled the void that remains in the absence of solid evidence about the Templars' activities after the deaths of Jacques de Molay and Geoffrey de Charney. Suggestions that many escaped to start new lives or secretly continued the Order are appealing. It is known that some ex-Templars did join other orders, including the Knights Hospitallers and the Cistercians, and probably the Order of Montesa and the Knights of Christ, which was what King Philip and Pope Clement intended them to do. Some went out into the secular world, possibly taking employment on estates, some returned to their families, or they lived on the charity of others. As with most of the legends surrounding the Templars, some of the conjecture about the fate of individuals seems logical, while other suggestions appear to be rather implausible and fabricated for an audience hungry for mysteries and conspiracy theories.

Sent to their deaths

As soon as the Templars were arrested in France, their interrogation and torture began, while outside the prisons their lands and property were taken into royal custody. Many died in prison, and their families were never told, while those that were burned at the stake during the trials were taken quietly for fear of arousing the anger of Templar supporters or of creating martyrs. The 54 Templars who were burned at the stake on May 11, 1310 for being relapsed heretics were probably chosen out of those who had been the most vocal in retracting their earlier confessions.

A month before the Templars were despatched in this way, the king had organized a commission of lawyers to question some of them. In April 1310, three Templars had stood before the commission and professed the innocence of the entire Order. One of these was Peter of Bologna; a trained lawyer who had previously been a Templar representative to the papal court in Rome. His arguments were far more eloquent than most other Templars or even of the king's counsellors, and he declared that "the proceedings against the Order had been rapid, unlooked-for, hostile, and unjust, altogether without justice, but containing complete injury, most grave violence and intolerable error, for no attempt had been made to keep to proper procedures." Continuing his impassioned rhetoric, he concluded that all documentation that had been gathered on the case should be brought forward and that the ban on any witnesses conferring should be lifted, and he requested that all charges against the Order should be dropped. The royal counsellors could not argue with him, but the following month, Philippe de Marigny, the Archbishop of Sens, took over the trial from the

A late 14th-century illustration on vellum from the *Treatise of the Vices*, by Cocharelli of Genoa, showing the destruction of the Templars and the death of King Philip IV in 1314.

original commission, and two days later, the 54 Templars were sent to their deaths. Soon after, when the commission asked to see Peter of Bologna again, they were told that he had retracted all he had said to them, returned to his earlier confession of guilt, broken out of jail and fled. He was never seen or heard of again.

It is highly unlikely that Peter of Bologna left prison either of his own free will or alive, and although those who remained imprisoned continued to proclaim their innocence, without an articulate and informed advocate, their downfall progressed. Many died under torture or afterwards as a result of its effects; some were probably murdered by their jailers, and others were left to die of starvation while incarcerated. Stripped of their habits, cast into dank dungeons and chained to the walls, the simple and often aging men were easily broken and were no match for the formidable Inquisition. In other European countries,

however, few Templars suffered as they did in France. In England, for instance, most were never arrested. After the Order had been dissolved, the King and other English authorities perceived them to be free from guilt and so at liberty to find themselves new places in society. Evidence of their movements in England shows that a large number joined the Hospitallers, some joined the Cistercians, and a few left religious life altogether.

Monastic vows

Yet although the Order was dissolved, the Church did not release the men from their monastic vows. It was ordered that if any were caught who had gone out into the world as laymen, or if they had married, the Church had to punish them. They were expected to simply move into other monasteries and not to draw attention to themselves. They were also meant to be granted a small pension, but this rarely seems to have been paid. In England, King Edward and the Archbishop of Canterbury asked the Hospitallers if they could help the deposed Templars, "for the love of God and for charity." With money scarce for the Hospitallers too—fewer donations were forthcoming once the Holy Land was lost and given the general feeling that these military orders were not as pure as they should have been—it is not clear whether the Hospitallers did manage to help the displaced Templars much at all.

Yet this notion of adherence to their monastic orders was not enforced everywhere. Many simply wanted to forget the Templars, and after the death of Philip and Clement, it seems that many were forgotten and left to fend for themselves. A few who were embittered by their treatment and lack of support from the community turned to petty crime, while some emerged in unexpected places. One, it was recorded, became the Ambassador for the Sultan of Tunis and another became a woodcarver for another

An illumination of 1350
depicting the 54 Templars
being burned on a funeral
pyre in 1310, accused of
being relapsed heretics.

sultan after being freed from that sultan's prison. Many other Templars were left languishing in Muslim jails, while even more were completely unaccounted for, such as those in countries where the arrests, accusations, and trials were virtually ignored.

The lost parchment

Since the discovery of the Chinon Parchment, much of the conjecture about the Templar persecution and trials has been cleared up. Contemporary opinion beyond France was closer to the truth than a great deal of the speculation since. Dante and various European monarchs were clear about what was happening: that the greedy and dishonest King Philip of France, in order to gain the Templars' wealth, deliberately twisted and elaborated upon stories about the rituals and beliefs of a religious-military order that, until then, had been devoted to the defense of Christendom. Fearing his own destruction, the Pope withheld his opinion about the Order's innocence, but he died before redressing his dishonesty and cowardice. Long after his death, when the papal court was returned to Rome from Avignon in 1376, the Chinon Parchment was misplaced, and it remained lost until 2001. None of Clement's cardinals had felt powerful enough against the king's men to defend the Templars, especially as the Pope was keeping quiet about his absolution of them. If any of them had considered speaking up in defence of the Order, they only had to remember the fate of the Templars, or to think of William de Nogaret's behavior towards Pope Boniface VIII.

Witchcraft and folklore

Yet some of the theories about the Templars continue. Some authors have rewritten history to make the stories more sensational and some continue to perpetuate theories that have been disproved. A few of the ideas are more conceivable. The Knights Templar for many have become mythical, mysterious men who had secret powers, secret knowledge, and secret possessions. Although most were simple, ordinary, honest, and hard-working men, from all classes and all walks of life, something about their lives and demise appeals to the romantic notions inherent in us all, and many of the stories about them have become established almost as firmly as folklore.

Soon after their dissolution, the Templars continued to appear in works of fiction and pseudo-historical works, and as their history became forgotten and newer generations were not sure what their role had been, authors began inventing increasingly implausible tales about them. The accusation that they used magic appeared in the 16th century at a time when magic and witchcraft were particularly feared. At the end of the medieval period, in 1487, one of the first printed books was published by the papal Inquisition. *Malleus Maleficarum* (meaning "Hammer of the Witches" in Latin) was a treatise on the persecution of witches. It developed from the irrational fear of many Christians, since the failure of the Crusades, that Christendom was being overtaken by demons. Forty-four years after the publication of *Malleus Maleficarum*, in 1531, a casual comment in another book, *De Occulta Philosophia*, provoked public paranoia and linked the Knights Templar with the notion of witchcraft and magic. The author of *De Occulta* was Heinrich Cornelius Agrippa von Nettesheim (1486–1535), a German magician, theologian, astrologer, and alchemist. He said

> The Knights Templar for many have become mythical, mysterious men who had secret powers, secret knowledge, and secret possessions.

he wrote his book "to distinguish between the good and holy science of magic and the scandalous and impious practices of black magic, and to restore the former's good name." In the book, he wrote of "the detestable heresy of the Templars; and similar things are known about witches and their senile craziness." Suddenly, the Knights Templar were brought to public attention and associated with witchcraft. Once again, they were being aligned with ignoble, distasteful practices. Because *De Occulta Philosophia* became extremely widely read, the concept that the Templars were disreputable became incorporated into European legend.

The verdict

But the Templars were not magicians, alchemists, or occultists. Although they kept themselves separate from worldly life, this was not for secret, dishonorable reasons. It was normal for religious orders to remain isolated from mainstream society because of their adherence to prayer and worship, and not because they were part of a secret sect that they had built up under the protective cloak of Christianity. The Knights Templar were not superhuman; they were simply practical men living in an unforgiving world. As an organization, they understood the fundamentals of life better than most during their time. It is unlikely that they possessed secret wisdom or sacred objects, but it is more plausible that they simply worked hard, with the determination to do their best. They made the most of their qualities. They were extremely well organized and had a strong faith; they believed in their role and they aimed to fulfil their objectives in the Holy Land and for Christendom. As the Order expanded and European society's constitution and attitudes altered, so did the behavior of the Templars, but in general they remained true to their original purpose, and for the 200 years of their existence, there was rarely a criticism of their behavior or a question about their morality. They were simply courageous monk-knights, who, although fighting and killing was really opposed to the teachings of Jesus, believed in the salvation of souls. They were also human and flawed.

As the Order expanded, it naturally became more complex. The allegations that the Templars denied Christ and spat on the Cross have been claimed by historians as the way in which they prepared themselves for what they may have been made to do if captured by the Muslims in the Holy Land. Being trained to renounce their beliefs superficially is in line with several other cultures' procedures of that time, including the Assassins, with whom the Templars were in contact. While this is feasible, it remains ambiguous—possible, but not proven.

After the fall of Acre in 1291, the Church needed a scapegoat for the loss of the Holy Land and King Philip IV needed money. In light of these facts, many historians have accused Jacques de Molay of being naïve—and of course he was. But for the role he had undertaken and was committed to—of fighting the infidel in Outremer—he was perfectly suited. Originally from a background of lower nobility, he was neither a clever nor academic man and had spent 30 years defending the Holy Land, not dealing with the politics of the Church and court. Prior to his arrest, he had been trying to garner enthusiasm for a new Crusade in which he was convinced that he and the Templars would regain Jerusalem. The reason he had been in Paris and not at the Templar headquarters in Cyprus, when he was arrested in 1307, was because he had been summoned by Pope Clement and he believed it was to discuss the forthcoming Crusade.

▶

This 19th-century hand-colored reproduction of a medieval woodcut shows a knight in armor paying homage to his lord in the late 13th century. At this time, the height of the Templar powers and reputation, chivalry was of utmost importance and members of the Order followed the chivalric code.

AN ENIGMA OF HISTORY

List of Grand Masters

Theories and legends

In the absence of further evidence, we cannot prove that the Templars owned a long-lost Biblical artefact, an ancient document, or even a potentially explosive secret, although their architects had a thorough understanding of proportion and balance and some of their buildings may contain specific geometric ratios. However, the only actual relic that they are documented as having possessed was what was believed to be a piece of the True Cross which they carried into their battles, before it was lost at the Battle of Hattin. The True Cross was believed to be a portion of the piece of wood discovered by St. Helena in the fourth century. None of the other relics or items claimed to have been found by them can be substantiated. Yet the myths continue to be perpetrated.

When Jerusalem was lost, the Order became almost redundant; it was coming to the end of its use. Their image as brave and indomitable protectors of the Holy Land had become tarnished and their popularity was waning. Despite being against their wishes, they may have been forced to amalgamate with the Hospitallers, so the legendary Knights Templar would have, in effect, faded away. They had been a product of the era in which they lived, and by the time Philip the Fair ordered their arrests, society was changing. Chivalry was no longer of paramount importance and military monks were soon to be surplus to requirements as professional armies were enlisted and trained for armed combat.

Most of the theories and legends about the Templars have arisen because of their shocking, sudden, and ignominious end, ironically at the hands of fellow Christians rather than their Muslim enemies. Even at the time, most people believed that they were innocent. We know now that the Pope did, and even King Philip must have, or he surely would not have been considering uniting them with the Hospitallers. Perhaps predictably, their isolation from society contributed to their lack of worldliness, which meant they did not foresee their demise. Ultimately, Jacques de Molay, the simple, honest and brave soldier-monk who had no arguments to save himself or his Order, encapsulated the truth when he spoke to the waiting crowd just before he was burned at the stake:

> I have suffered myself through the pain of torture and the fear of death, to give utterances to falsehoods in admitting the disgusting charges laid against the Order, which has nobly served the cause of Christianity. I declare, and I must declare, that the Order is innocent. Its purity and saintliness are beyond question. I disdain to seek wretched and disgraceful existence by grafting another lie upon the original falsehood.

Timeline

DATE	EVENT
c.993 BCE	**David conquers Jerusalem** and brings the Ark of the Covenant to the city
c.958–951 BCE	Building of **Solomon's Temple** in Jerusalem
586 BCE	Destruction of **Solomon's Temple**
c.516 BCE	Building of the **Second Temple** begins
c.444 BCE	**Alexander the Great** conquers Jerusalem
20 BCE–64 CE	Construction of **Herod's Temple**
c.33 CE	**Jesus** is crucified in Jerusalem
70 CE	**The Siege of Jerusalem**: the Romans destroy the Second Temple
324–5	**Emperor Constantine** reunites the empire. Christian immigration to the city begins
326	**Constantine's mother Helena** visits Jerusalem and orders the destruction of Hadrian's temple to Venus which had been built on Calvary. She allegedly discovers the True Cross
335	**First Church of the Holy Sepulcher** built on Calvary
620	**Muhammad's Night Journey** to heaven
629	**Byzantine Emperor Heraclius** retakes Jerusalem and returns the True Cross to the city
632	**Death of Muhammad**
750	**Umayyad dynasty** overthrown by the Abbasid dynasty
813	**Caliph Al-Ma'mun** visits Jerusalem and undertakes extensive renovations to the Dome of the Rock
969	**Fatimids invade Egypt** and found Cairo
1056	**Muslims forbid Christian pilgrims** to enter Jerusalem
1064	**Hundreds of unarmed Christian pilgrims** are murdered by Muslims near Jerusalem
1071–80	**Seljuk Turks occupy Asia Minor,** Syria, and Palestine
1074	The **Byzantine Emperor** appeals to the Pope for help
1095	At the **Council of Clermont Pope Urban II** preaches the First Crusade
1099	**The first Crusaders** capture Jerusalem and slaughter most of the city's Muslim and Jewish inhabitants. The Dome of the Rock is converted into a church
1104	**The Al-Aqsa mosque** becomes the Royal Palace of the Kingdom of Jerusalem
1113	The **foundation of the Knights Hospitaller**
1119	The **founding of the Poor Knights of the Temple of Solomon** by Hugh de Payns and Godfrey de St. Omer, with quarters within the Al-Aqsa mosque
1127	**Hugh de Payns** meets Bernard of Clairvaux
1129	**Council of Troyes,** establishment of the Templars' Latin Rule
1139	The **papal bull *Omne Datum Optimum*** establishes the Templars as an independent and permanent order within the Catholic Church, answerable only to the Pope
1144	The **papal bull *Milites Templi***
1145	The **papal bull *Militia Dei***
1140s	The **Templars build the Paris Temple,** which becomes the head of their international financial empire
1148–9	**The Second Crusade**
1149–50	**Gaza** is granted to the Templars
c.1165–84	**William of Tyre** writes *History of the Kingdom of Jerusalem*, also called *History of Deeds Done Beyond the Sea* (Historia rerum in partibus transmarinis gestarum)

1169 ◆ **Saladin** becomes vizier of Egypt

1174 ◆ **Nur ad-Din dies;** Saladin takes over Damascus

1181–90 ◆ **Chrétien de Troyes** writes his romance, *Perceval, le Conte du Graal*

1185 ◆ **Temple Church** in London is consecrated by Patriarch Heraclius of Jerusalem

1187 ◆ **The Battle of Hattin;** Saladin captures Jerusalem from the Crusaders. The Dome of the Rock is converted to an Islamic center of worship again

1189–92 ◆ **Third Crusade** under Richard the Lionheart fails to recapture Jerusalem, but ends with the Treaty of Ramla in which Saladin agrees that Christian pilgrims can worship in Jerusalem

1191 ◆ The Templars establish new **headquarters at Acre**

1191–2 ◆ The Templars occupy and briefly hold **Cyprus**

1202–4 ◆ **The Fourth Crusade** is diverted to the Byzantine capital of Constantinople

1208 ◆ **The Albigensian Crusade** is launched against the Cathars

1217 ◆ **The Fifth Crusade**

1217–21 ◆ The Templars build Atlit or **Athlit Castle,** also known as the Pilgrims' Castle

1228–9 ◆ **The Sixth Crusade;** a ten-year treaty is signed between Frederick II, the Holy Roman Emperor, and the Ayyubid Sultan al-Kamil, allowing Christians freedom to live in the unfortified city of Jerusalem

1244 ◆ **Fall of the Cathars' castle** at Montségur; loss of Jerusalem; Battle of La Forbie

1249–54 ◆ **The Seventh Crusade,** led by Louis IX of France—the Templars fight with him and hundreds are killed

1285 ◆ **Philip IV** is crowned King of France

1291 ◆ **Fall of Acre** to the Mamluks; the Templars leave Tortosa and Atlit Castles

1297 ◆ **King Louis IX** is canonized by Pope Boniface VIII

1302 ◆ **Loss of Ruad** and massacre of the Templar garrison

1303 ◆ **Attack on Pope Boniface VIII** by William de Nogaret, adviser to Philip the Fair; Boniface dies

1306 ◆ **King Philip expels all Jews** from France and seizes their property

1307 ◆ **Mass arrest of the Templars** in France

1308 ◆ **Jacques de Molay** and the Templars are secretly absolved by Pope Clement V

1310 ◆ **Fifty-four Templars are burnt at the stake** as "relapsed heretics" near Paris

1312 ◆ **Clement V produces two papal bulls:** *Vox in excelsio*, which dissolves the Order of the Knights Templar, and *Ad providam*, which transfers their property to the Knights Hospitallers

1314 ◆ In March, **Jacques de Molay** and Geoffrey de Charney are burned at the stake in Paris; in April, William de Nogaret and Pope Clement V die, and in November, Philip IV dies

1319 ◆ **Establishment of the Knights of Christ** in Portugal

1418 ◆ **Prince Henry the Navigator** becomes Grand Master of the Knights of Christ

1446 or 1456 ◆ Construction of the **Rosslyn Chapel**

1571 ◆ **Destruction of the Templars' archives** by the Ottoman-Turks in Cyprus

1717 ◆ Foundation of the **Freemason's Grand Lodge** in London

1789 ◆ **The French Revolution** begins

1793 ◆ **Louis XVI is executed** in Paris

1798 ◆ **Napoleon I takes the island of Rhodes** from the Knights Hospitaller and loads Templar artefacts on to his ship, which later sinks off the coast of Egypt, fueling centuries of speculation about the cargo

2001 ◆ Discovery of the **Chinon Parchment** in the Vatican Secret Archives

Index

Page numbers in *italics* denotes
an illustration

Picture credits

Quercus
New York

Quercus Publishing Inc.
31 West 57th Street, 6th Floor
New York, NY 10019

© 2013 Quercus Editions Ltd

All rights reserved. No part of this publication may be reproduced, stored in a retrieval system, or transmitted, in any form or by any means, electronic, mechanical, recording, or otherwise, without prior written permission from the publisher.

ISBN 978-1-62365-052-0

Library of Congress Control Number: 2013937380

Distributed in the United States and Canada by Random House Publisher Services
c/o Random House, 1745 Broadway
New York, NY 10019

For information about custom editions, special sales, and premium and corporate purchases, please contact Quercus Publishing Special Sales at specialsales@quercus.com.

Manufactured in China

Designed by Austin Taylor

2 4 6 8 10 9 7 5 3 1

www.quercus.com